MILITARY TRAINING IN
THE BRITISH ARMY, 1940–1944

CASS SERIES: MILITARY HISTORY AND POLICY
Series Editors: John Gooch and Brian Holden Reid
ISSN: 1465-8488

This series will publish studies on historical and contemporary aspects of land power, spanning the period from the eighteenth century to the present day, and will include national, international and comparative studies. From time to time, the series will publish edited collections of essays and 'classics'.

MILITARY TRAINING IN THE BRITISH ARMY
1940–1944
From Dunkirk to D-Day

Timothy Harrison Place

University of Leeds

Routledge
Taylor & Francis Group

LONDON AND NEW YORK

First published in 2000 in Great Britain by
Routledge
2 Park Square, Milton Park, Abingdon, Oxon, OX14 4RN
270 Madison Ave, New York NY 10016

Transferred to Digital Printing 2008

Website: www.Routledge.com

British Library Cataloguing in Publication Data

Place, Timothy Harrison
    Military training in the British Army, 1940–1944: from Dunkirk to
    D-Day. – (Cass series. Military history and policy; no. 6)
    1. Great Britain. Army – History 2. Military education – Great Britain –
    History 3. World War, 1939–1945 – Campaigns I. Title
    355. 5' 0941 '09044

ISBN 0-7146-5037-4 (cloth)
ISBN 0-7146-8091-5 (paper)
ISSN 1465-8488

Library of Congress Cataloging-in-Publication Data

Place, Timothy Harrison, 1964–
    Military training in the British Army, 1940–1944: from Dunkirk to D-Day /
    Timothy Harrison Place.
      p. cm. – (Cass Series–military history and policy, ISSN 1465–8488; no. 6)
    Includes bibliographical references and index.
    ISBN 0-7146-5037-4 (cloth) – 0-7146-8091-5 (paper)
    1. Great Britain. Army–History–World War, 1939–1945. 2. Soldiers–Training
    of–Great Britain–History–20th century. 3. World War, 1939–1945–Great
    Britain. I. Title. II Series.

D759.53 .P53 2000
940.54'1241–dc21   00-031480

Typeset by Regent Typesetting, London

Publisher's Note
The publisher has gone to great lengths to ensure the quality
of this reprint but points out that some
imperfections in the original may be apparent.

Contents

For Christine,
Ben and Clara
with love

Series Editor's Preface

The combat performance of the British Army in North-West Europe from June 1944 until May 1945 has for some time been the subject of much analysis and no little criticism. In comparative terms, it has been measured against that of the German Army and found to be wanting in almost every respect, saved from the embarrassment of its own inadequacies chiefly by the combined weight of Allied superiority in the air and the support of high volumes of artillery fire. The search for the causes of what a goodly number of authors have seen as its relatively undistinguished performance has involved historians in analysing weapons statistics, assessing command performances and considering the cultural propensities of the society which produced the forces that landed in Normandy on D-Day – in a word, in trying to measure and to explain the military effectiveness of Montgomery's army. In these debates – just as in the debates about comparative military performance in the First World War – military doctrine has come to be recognised as a factor of central importance. As the bridge between thought and action, it is the articulating agent which ensures – or should ensure – that everyone knows the right thing to do and that they all do the same things in the same circumstances. In all armies and in every war, doctrine is the glue which holds everything together, and training is the instrument through which it is imparted. A study of these issues is therefore central to the debates about D-Day and its aftermath which still continue. Tim Harrison Place's study of the doctrine and training of the British Army between 1940 and 1944 makes an important contribution to those debates, for it now allows us – for the first time – to understand exactly how and why the invading armies were underprepared for the task which faced them on the morning of 6 June 1944.

The obstacles that faced would-be reformers of infantry training were in some cases well-founded and in others not: on the one hand, the need to ensure that exercises tested particular units in particular problems dictated a degree of control which squeezed out the unplanned and the improvised (and readers may perhaps agree that, as an illustration of this, the feat of Lance-Corporal Higgins (page 26) deserves its note in history), while, on the other hand, objections to the development of battle drill as a standardised solution which would stifle initiative are redolent of a degree of professional conservatism which seems to have characterised the higher levels of the British Army. As the author concludes, too little – not too much – battle drill deprived the infantry of initiative.

The twists and turns in armoured warfare doctrine, patiently and carefully disentangled and recounted here, resulted from a complex concatenation of factors. Prewar doctrine had to adjust to a variety of different experiences whose import was not easy to work out: desert warfare against the Germans produced different lessons from desert warfare against the Italians, fighting in Libya was different from fighting in Tunisia, and new weapons such as the 88 mm anti-tank gun, the anti-tank mine and the hand-held anti-tank Panzerfaust missile produced new problems in tank warfare which had to be accommodated in new doctrine. Working out the most effective way to use tanks against this kaleidoscopic background was difficult enough but, as the pages which follow make clear, it was made much more so by the ways in which the Army as an institution responded to the need to solve these problems. In some cases little or nothing was done, even by senior officers whose job it was to oversee matters of doctrine. In others, junior and middle-ranking officers found their own preferred solutions to the problems, which were not always in harmony with one another. In one notable case, the general picked to command British forces in Normandy intervened four months before the landing to change established doctrine, thereby throwing everything into confusion.

Whether things went wrong after D-Day as far as the British Army's performance is concerned is still an open question. Whether they might have gone better had the pre-invasion preparations been different is no longer a matter for dispute. This account of the shortcomings in both doctrine and training shows us clearly both how difficult is the task of those charged with shaping doctrine and how costly their mistakes may turn out to be. As a case study of the central task which every army must meet and overcome, it will be of as much value to those concerned with the future as it will be to those whose interest is in the past.

John Gooch
Series Co-Editor

Acknowledgements

The author wishes to acknowledge with thanks permissions received from the following: Lieutenant H. J. Belsey, for permission to quote from his wartime letters; Revd H. Temple Bone, MA, for permission to quote from his wartime journal; Mrs Elizabeth Brind and Mr Christopher Brind for permission to quote from the papers of Brigadier James L. Brind, DSO; Mr Harold Buckle, for permission to quote from his unpublished memoir 'Recollections from Yesteryear'; Mr Dennis Burton, for permission to quote from the wartime diaries of Major B.E.L. Burton; Dr Alan S. Wallace, for permission to quote from his memoir on battle school; the Lionel Wigram Memorial Trust, for access to and permission to quote from the papers of Lionel Wigram; the Montgomery Collections Committee of the Trustees of the Imperial War Museum and Viscount Montgomery of Alamein, CBE, for permission to consult the papers of Field Marshal the Viscount Montgomery of Alamein. Crown copyright material is reproduced with the permission of the Controller of Her Majesty's Stationery Office; material in the Liddell Hart Centre for Military Archives is reproduced by permission of the Trustees of the Liddell Hart Centre for Military Archives.

Every effort has been made to contact and obtain permission from other relevant copyright holders – any omissions can be rectified in later editions.

This book started life as my doctoral thesis at the University of Leeds. I owe a huge debt to my doctoral supervisor, Professor John Childs, for his unfailing support and encouragement over a number of years. I must also thank the co-editors of this series, Professor John Gooch and Dr Brian Holden Reid, for their advice in the process of transforming the thesis into a book. I am particularly grateful to John Gooch who has been generous with his time and counsel throughout the time I have known him.

I am grateful to the University of Leeds for its financial support, firstly while I was reading for my doctorate and more recently as co-sponsor of my post-doctoral research fellowship. In connection with the latter I owe grateful acknowledgement to the Leverhulme Trust, whose award of a precious Special Research Fellowship enabled me to prepare this work for publication and to start work on fresh research.

I have benefited from the interest, encouragement and assistance of numerous people both within and without the academic world in the course of my work. I must particularly thank the following: Dr Stephen Brumwell, Professor Terry Copp, Dr Craig Gibson, Professor John Ferris, Professor

David French, Dr Stephen Hart, Mr Stephen Prince, Professor Edward Spiers, Mr Mike Taylor and Mr Anthony Wigram. I am most grateful to the staffs of the various archives and libraries in which I have carried out research for this book for their assistance. Lieutenant-Colonel 'Tug' Wilson and Major John Oldfield of the Weapons Museum at Warminster deserve special thanks for their splendid hospitality and company. The three days I spent working there in August 1994 were quite the most enjoyable days I have spent in archival research.

I should like to thank the following veterans of the British Army of the Second World War who either allowed me to interview them, answered my letters or wrote memoirs for my use: Brigadier James L. Brind, DSO; Field Marshal Lord Carver, GCB, CBE, DSO, MC; Major Richard Hargreaves, MC; Major Michael Kerr; Mr Nigel Nicolson, MBE; Mr David Rooney; Major Raleigh St Lawrence; Captain Paul Stobart; Major John P. Vivian; Dr Alan S. Wallace; Mr Len Waller. I must thank Brigadier and Mrs Brind, Major Hargreaves, Major Kerr, Captain Stobart and Major and Mrs Vivian for their generous hospitality. I thank also Mrs Olga Wigram for her hospitality during my visits and for allowing me to interview her.

My parents, Pat and Dicky Harrison Place, and my parents-in-law, Joy and John Greenwood, have provided much appreciated support for my family and me in many ways while this work has been in progress. I am deeply grateful to my sister, Julia Harrison Place, for her generosity and forbearance in allowing me to stay in her flat in London for long periods while I was carrying out research at London archives.

I have dedicated this book to my wife and my children. A mere dedication at the front of a book is mean recompense for everything Christine has given. As for my children, I do not know what they have done to deserve it.

Any errors of fact or interpretation are of course mine alone.

List of Abbreviations

AFV	armoured fighting vehicle
AORG	Army Operational Research Group
AP	armour-piercing
ATI	*Army Training Instruction*
ATM	*Army Training Memorandum*
BEF	British Expeditionary Force
BGS	Brigadier General Staff
BLM	Montgomery Papers
CAB	Cabinet Office documents
C-in-C	Commander-in-Chief
CIGS	Chief of the Imperial General Staff
CO	Commanding Officer
CRAC	Commander, Royal Armoured Corps
CRO	*Current Reports from Overseas*
DCIGS	Deputy CIGS
DCLI	Duke of Cornwall's Light Infantry
DMT	Director of Military Training
ERY	East Riding Yeomanry
FFY	Fife and Forfar Yeomanry
FOO	Forward Observation Officer
GHQ	General Headquarters
GOC	General Officer Commanding
GOC-in-C	General Officer Commanding-in-Chief
HE	high explosive
HQ	Headquarters
IWM	Imperial War Museum
LAA	light anti-aircraft
LHCMA	Liddell Hart Centre for Military Archives, King's College London
LMG	light machine-gun
MG	machine-gun
MTP	*Military Training Pamphlet*
NAAFI	Navy, Army and Air Force Institutes
NCO	non-commissioned officer

NTW	*Notes from Theatres of War*
OCTU	Officer Cadet Training Unit
OR	other rank
PRO	Public Record Office
RA	Royal Regiment of Artillery
RAC	Royal Armoured Corps
RE	Royal Engineers
RHA	Royal Horse Artillery
RTR	Royal Tank Regiment
SHAEF	Supreme HQ Allied Expeditionary Force
SP	self-propelled (gun)
TEWT	Tactical Exercise Without Troops
VCIGS	Vice-CIGS
WMWTC	Weapons Museum, Warminster Training Centre
WO	War Office

1

Introduction

It is perhaps the function of historians to split hairs. The backdrop to this work is the highly successful campaign waged by British troops against Germany in North-West Europe, starting on 6 June 1944 and ending with Germany's unconditional surrender 11 months later. The success was not wholly or even mainly Britain's: American troops far outnumbered British for most of the campaign; Canada provided substantial forces, as on a lesser scale did exiled Poles, French, Belgians and Dutch; all served under American supreme command. Nor would the victory have been possible without the hard fighting of Soviet troops against the Germans on the eastern front. None the less, it is with the British contribution to the military forces that overcame Germany that this book is concerned.

For all its success, controversy has roamed the campaign's annals almost since the day it started. Most of it has centred on issues associated with high command, including the very command structure and a host of questions surrounding grand strategy and campaign strategy. None of those issues will be revisited here. Two relatively recent contributions to the campaign's literature, however, have introduced new bones for historians to pick over. The works of D'Este and Hastings, first published in 1983 and 1984 respectively, for the first time went into detail on the frequently poor tactical performance of British troops in Normandy, the three-month-long battle that arguably determined, although it did not actually seal, Germany's fate. Their findings form the point of departure for this study.

Using a variety of sources, both D'Este and Hastings highlight the poor standard of co-operation between tanks and infantry among British troops and the reluctance of the infantry to fight without high volumes of fire-power in support or to continue the struggle when their officers became casualties. D'Este argues that the lacklustre performance of the British Army in Normandy was partly the product of the cautious strategy of attrition by which Montgomery directed the operations of the British and Canadian troops in the eastern sector of the lodgement area.[1] Hastings' interpretation, contrarily, holds that Montgomery's generalship was constrained by the mediocre tactical qualities of his troops.[2] That the general standard of British troops in the Second World War was mediocre is confirmed by Professor Sir Michael

Howard, a veteran of the Italian campaign as well as a distinguished military historian.[3]

Numerous reasons have been advanced for the British Army's mediocrity. The parochialism engendered by the regimental system has been cited as a bar to effective co-operation between tanks and infantry.[4] British weapons and equipment were frequently inferior to those available to the Germans: not only were German tanks better armoured and better armed than their British counterparts, but German infantry weapons, especially anti-tank weapons, were superior.[5] In Normandy the bocage terrain supposedly favoured the defence. This factor had not been foreseen in training and the three veteran British divisions in Normandy, which had won their spurs in the desert, found the adjustment peculiarly hard.[6]

In his wide-ranging treatment of the British Army's tactical effectiveness during the Second World War, Murray cites the revelations in Hastings' work and numerous other sources of circumstantial evidence relating to other theatres in which the British Army was engaged pointing to a similar malady, before offering the following diagnosis: 'The real cause of such a state of affairs lay in the failure of the army leadership to enunciate a clearly thought-out doctrine and then to institute a thorough training program to insure its acceptance throughout the army.'[7]

The assurance of that sentence belies what is quite properly a rather tentative discussion of the subject, for the evidence that Murray adduces in its support is thin to say the least. None the less, although it offers no hint of the full complexity in which tactical doctrine and training became entangled, Murray's diagnosis is meaningful enough to serve as the text for this study.

Murray's conviction is not only that the British Army was tactically retarded but also that it need not have been. Other commentators have been far more indulgent. Howard suggests that the rather unmilitary ethos of the typical British citizen soldier caused regular officers to lower their expectations of the wartime army.[8] It is beyond the scope of this study to pursue that theory, although it doubtless has some validity. Bidwell, however, maintains that the British Army of 1939–45, a largely non-professional outfit manned mainly by temporary soldiers drawn from 'civvie street' simply did not have time to become skilled in its business. It therefore resorted extensively to the expedient of sweeping its tactical inadequacies beneath the carpets of fire-power provided by its most effective component, the Royal Regiment of Artillery (RA).[9] Let us examine that claim, for it is not devoid of truth.

Firstly, the British and Allied Armies' heavy reliance upon artillery fire-power and other forms of metalline force is not a point of historical dispute. Indeed, it has recently been comprehensively catalogued in a study aptly entitled *Brute Force*.[10] Murray agrees with Bidwell that reliance upon fire-power was the 'response to tactical weaknesses (and perhaps partially their cause)'.[11] Secondly, of course the British Army was largely a non-regular outfit. Particularly in the early years of the war the large numbers of conscripts, called-up reservists and territorials could not have received the degree of training that they might have got had strategic conditions been more accommodating of the requirements of military preparedness. Such were the pressures upon the Army at home after Dunkirk, due to the requirements of home defence, non-military commitments, overseas drafting and the shortages of equipment and facilities, that of six armoured and 19 infantry divisions surveyed in April 1942 only three were immediately fit for battle.[12] The process of raising a mass army under pressure of war was undoubtedly fraught with difficulty. Not only should it not be surprising but it should also be forgivable if troops sent into the North African fray in 1941 and 1942 lacked the full range of professional tactical skills one should expect in fully trained career soldiers.

But can one accept such an excuse for the troops sent across the English Channel in June 1944? In the first place, three of the 12 British fighting divisions involved had recent battle experience in the Mediterranean, as did two of the ten independent brigades. Citizen soldiers or no, the troops of those formations could, and undoubtedly did, consider themselves the equals of the many regular soldiers whom fate had confined to the home islands. Secondly, the British Army at home had enjoyed four years of respite since Dunkirk in which to prepare itself for the challenges of Normandy. And since the end of 1942, home defences (given the bare minimum of precautionary attention) had inflicted little diversion from training. The formation under which British troops fought the campaign, 21 Army Group, cannot be compared to Kitchener's New Armies, thrown into battle virtually untrained in 1916, whose troops – those who survived their first battle – had to learn their trade under fire. Their successors of June 1944 might have been unblooded, but there was no excuse if they were untrained.

It simply will not do to put down the lacklustre tactical performance of the British Army in North-West Europe to a lack of opportunity for training. There was no such lack. Murray's hypothesis – for that is all it is – that it was unsuitable doctrine and training that hampered the tactical performance of British arms clearly stands the test of logical reasoning. This book investigates whether it can be sustained by the evidence of what the British Army at home actually did during the four years between Dunkirk and D-Day. That is why the campaign in North-West Europe provides only the backdrop to this study. Its main focus is the hitherto neglected subject of those four tedious years of home service.

Naturally, that renders this study an incomplete test of Murray's hypothesis. Doctrine and training among formations that took part in the Mediterranean and Far East campaigns will not be covered here, although extensive reference will be made to the lessons learned from the former. Nor will there be much reference to training in the prewar or Phoney War periods. This is a Dunkirk to D-Day study. There is also an important conceptual limitation in that the analysis in this work is confined largely to the infantry and armoured arms of the British Army. It is as well to elaborate upon the reasons for this.

The combatant arms of the British Army included not only the Royal Armoured Corps and the infantry but also the Royal Regiment of Artillery, the Royal Corps of Signals, the Corps of Royal Engineers and the Reconnaissance Corps. These were in one sense or another support arms which is why they are not considered in this study. With the exception of the artillery, their primary function was not to fight but to perform some other function that served to facilitate the fighting action of the infantry and armour. That is not to say that the jobs of personnel in those arms were not dangerous – they certainly were – nor that they did not at times have to fight. They did, but only so far as it was necessary to facilitate their main job and, of course, in self defence.

The exclusion of the Royal Artillery might seem perverse. There are two reasons for it. Firstly, chiefly thanks to the labours of Bidwell and Graham,[13] British artillery doctrine and tactics during the Second World War are well understood. It is also generally accepted that the Royal Artillery was by far the most professionally skilled fighting arm of the British Army during this period.[14] Secondly, the role of the artillery was not to close with and directly effect the enemy's overthrow. On many occasions the enemy closed with the artillery: close-quarters combat was by no means foreign to gunner experience. However, always in theory and usually in practice, the artillery was an arm of remote fire-support that participated in the attack from positions often thousands of yards behind the front line. This book is concerned chiefly with the attack and the actions of the troops who carried out the attack, namely the infantry and armour. Reference will be made, where appropriate, to the function of supporting artillery fire. A minute examination of artillery doctrine and technique is not necessary because it has already been done and close attention to training in artillery units would be mainly technical rather than tactical.

That leads to another important point to be made in defining the object of this study. The chief concern will be with doctrine and training for the minor tactics of the attack. 'Minor tactics' is conventionally defined as single-arm tactics, that is the tactical methods of, for example, infantry, without reference to the input of other arms with which the infantry co-operate in battle.[15] This further explains why artillery is not a central concern of this book: infantry or tanks acting alone can attack and overthrow the enemy but artillery acting alone can only cause a nuisance to him. However, by the war's end it was widely recognised that tanks acting alone were in most circumstances incapable of attacking successfully without infantry in close attendance. Minor tactics by the conventional definition thus came to represent a purely theoretical notion that was meaningless in practice. Necessarily, therefore, this book will consider co-operation between tanks and infantry. Higher tactics, however, the business of divisions and higher formations, are of merely peripheral concern here: operations and strategy, exclusively the business of generals and their staffs, will not be broached at all.

To restrict the scope of this book to the attack only is to ignore the activity in which most fighting troops on active service spent most of their time: defence. Indeed, every successful attack must rapidly be transformed into defence so that the ground won can be held against enemy efforts to recover it. German defensive tactics made extensive use of prepared counterattack to evict successful attackers from the position they had won before they could consolidate it. Accordingly, British doctrine stressed the need to organise gains for defence without delay.[16] Important though defence was, it was not in defence that the British Army's shortcomings were most obvious, at least not in North-West Europe. Moreover, although the design of a defensive position offered plenty of scope for tactical creativity among the commanders responsible, especially in regard to the achievement of surprise against an attacking enemy, for the troops involved defence was mainly a matter of hard toil digging and concealing positions, staying awake while on guard and obeying orders, particularly in regard to the control of fire, when an attack came. Of course it was rather different when the defensive task of a unit or sub-unit was counterattack, but the minor tactics for such an operation fall into the category of attack rather than defence.

Turning to sources, readers will find in the Bibliography an account of the wide variety of official and unofficial records consulted. A brief introduction to two categories of those records is appropriate here, however. This book compares doctrine for the attack with the training actually carried out in units and formations. Doctrine, a word of which the literal meaning and etymological origin is 'teaching' (as a noun), existed on many different levels. For the purpose of this study it means the officially sanctioned doctrine of the British Army as expressed in the many manuals and pamphlets published by the War Office and other military authorities. Those publications represent a primary source of the first importance in this study. The arrangements for formulating and publicising doctrine are of such interest that Chapter 2 is made over to exploring that very subject.

The main source of evidence on training in practice is the War Diary kept by every unit and formation HQ. Because the quality of such sources is very patchy, to secure a fair picture of training in a particular division demands examination of War Diaries at unit, brigade and divisional level across the period covered by this book. This has been done in the case of three divisions: 43rd Infantry Division, 11th Armoured Division and Guards Armoured Division. Those of one independent brigade, 34th Tank Brigade, have also been covered. The War Diaries of numerous other units and formations have been examined in a more selective manner. The object has been to form a picture of the training of those troops that saw no action before OVERLORD. For that reason the three divisions and two independent armoured brigades repatriated for OVERLORD after fighting in the Mediterranean campaigns have been excluded.

The evolution of doctrine in response to the lessons of battle in the

Mediterranean theatres is an integral feature of the analysis unfolded in the following chapters, especially those concerned with armoured forces. But no work of this nature could be complete without some effort to judge doctrine and training, as informed by such lessons, against the test of battle in North-West Europe. A closer look at the backdrop is necessary. Chapters 5 and 9 answer that need. Contemporary after-action reports are the main sources used. War Diaries and secondary sources have also been used. However, the material on battle experience in North-West Europe included in this book, while allowing some firm conclusions to be drawn on the real quality of doctrine and training before D-Day, represents only a first attempt in this particular field. The recent publication of a comprehensive study of the combat experience of the US Army in North-West Europe[17] merely under-lines the need for similar work on the British Army.

Before getting started it will help the reader to know something of the higher organisation of the British Army at home during the war. The head office of the British Army was the War Office, which exercised authority over all British troops everywhere through the commanders-in-chief located in the regions where those troops served. All British troops in Great Britain came under the Commander-in-Chief (C-in-C) of Home Forces, except those detached to form expeditionary formations, such as First Army in 1942 and 21 Army Group in 1943, and those in Anti-Aircraft Command. The office of C-in-C was held firstly by General Sir Walter Kirke, who retired in May 1940. General Sir Edmund Ironside, his successor, lasted only two months and was succeeded by General Sir Alan Brooke who remained in the post until December 1941 when he became Chief of Imperial General Staff (CIGS). General Sir Bernard Paget succeeded Brooke.

The C-in-C was based with his General Headquarters at St Paul's School, Hammersmith, to where it moved from Twickenham during Ironside's tenure. In July 1943, 21 Army Group HQ was formed to control the forces slated for the invasion of Europe. Paget relinquished his Home Forces job to become C-in-C of the new formation which appropriated St Paul's School as its HQ. GHQ Home Forces moved to Hounslow with its new C-in-C, General Sir Harold Franklyn. Before July 1943 GHQ Home Forces was in effect an Army Group HQ and the C-in-C an Army Group Commander. Ranked below GHQ were the five home Commands: Southern, Western, Eastern, Northern and Scottish, joined in 1941 by the new South-Eastern Command, which took over Kent, Sussex and Surrey from Eastern Command. Headed by a GOC-in-C (usually in the rank of lieutenant-general but in some cases a full general) each of the Commands would in the event of active operations in Britain have become an operational army. Indeed GOsC-in-C were styled Army Commanders, the Commands were often referred to as Armies and in some exercises operated as such. The troops within each Command area were organised in corps, divisions and brigades as in any other operational army.[18]

With the formation of 21 Army Group in 1943, Home Forces reverted to its peacetime functions of home defence, draft-finding and administration. The task of preparing field formations for active operations overseas passed to 21 Army Group. Paget's supersession as C-in-C by General Sir Bernard Montgomery in January 1944 constituted a final destruction of the links with 21 Army Group's Home Forces past. Montgomery sacked many members of Paget's HQ team, bringing in trusted lieutenants from Eighth Army, his previous command, to replace them. He also slimmed down the HQ structure, reducing the training branch, rendering Brigadier Pyman, its head, redundant, and abolishing the infantry branch under Major-General Utterson-Kelso.[19]

In the latter case abolition probably made no difference to training. As will be shown, Utterson-Kelso's role at GHQ and 21 Army Group and the new emphasis on the infantry arm dating from Paget's appointment as C-in-C had not prevented a general failure in infantry training. Montgomery's action merely confirmed and compounded that failure. The removal of Pyman had more concrete consequences, especially when linked to the replacement of Major-General Norrie, Paget's Royal Armoured Corps adviser, with Major-General G.W. Richards who had performed the same function in Eighth Army. As will be seen, Montgomery disagreed fundamentally with War Office and Home Forces teaching on the use of tanks. While his position was defensible, indeed even sensible, the new regime at St Paul's made little attempt, and probably had too little time, to resolve the contradictions thus created. Moreover, the new brooms swept away some sound Home Forces doctrine on tank–infantry co-operation and thus laid the foundations for a number of lost battles and many broken British bodies in Normandy.

2

The Dissemination of Doctrine

All that the unblooded troops training in Britain before D-Day knew about fighting and battle was what they were taught. Having no battle experience on which to make judgements, doctrine was all. Ultimately, doctrine was disseminated by word and deed. In drill-halls, classrooms, parade grounds and training areas, officers and NCOs instructed their men by demonstration, explanation and practice. It is likely that much of what those officers and NCOs taught their men they had themselves learned in much the same way. Yet every large organisation needs some written means of recording the methods and practices by which each individual member should perform his duties. Accordingly, during the Second World War the British Army produced a great deal of printed doctrine.

Aimed at officers and NCOs, rather than private soldiers, this doctrinal literature was at once an *aide-mémoire* of long-forgotten instruction and a substitute for instruction never received. But it was undoubtedly regarded by those who wrote the pamphlets and the authorities who commissioned them primarily as the normative standard. Without it, uniformity of method throughout a three-million-strong army would have been quite impossible. This does not mean that uniformity of method was achieved. It is open to question as to how carefully much of the doctrinal literature was read. In the following chapters, the contents of the manuals and pamphlets published by the War Office and others will be explored and comparisons made with what the troops actually did in training. Indeed, contrasts between doctrine and training are as apparent as comparisons.

This chapter, however, focuses on the publication system. Doctrine did not comprise a single 'bible' of dicta and dogma cast in metaphorical stone. Instead, a great many individual publications constituted the British Army's official teaching and supersessions took place frequently, reflecting tactical and technical developments. Doctrinal publications appeared in a number of different series, each with its own function within the overall purpose of doctrinal dissemination. This chapter is both a general introduction to those publications and a general commentary on their effectiveness.

The main bulk of the British Army's official doctrine during the war appeared in the War Office's *Military Training Pamphlet* (*MTP*) series. The titles published in this series covered the vast majority of trades and specialisms practised in the British Army, everything from foot drill to motor-cycling and from minor tactics to divisional handling. Some important specialisms were, however, catered for outside the *MTP* series. So far as tactics are concerned, the most important of these were the *Infantry Training* and *Infantry Section Leading* manuals, the latest prewar editions of which were published in 1937 and 1938 respectively. Both were eventually superseded by a new edition of *Infantry Training* published in multiple volumes in 1943 and 1944.

Who formed the intended readership of these pamphlets? Most pamphlets carried an indication of their intended distribution. Although often rather vague in the first year or so of the war,[1] by 1941 formalised codes denoting scales of distribution had been introduced. Under this system, manuals on higher operations were not distributed below unit commander level, while manuals on minor tactics might be issued down to corporals. There was no provision for lower ranks to receive training literature. The scales were often qualified by the stipulation of certain types of unit where the contents of a particular pamphlet made this appropriate. For example, manuals on armoured tactics did not receive wide distribution among infantry.[2]

Before the war, training manuals were written by committee and published under the authority of the Army Council. In September 1939 the committees were disbanded and thereafter manuals were written by officers specially employed for the purpose by the Directorate of Military Training. For the duration of the war most training manuals appeared by the authority of the CIGS rather than the full Army Council.[3] The prewar system was ponderous and time-consuming, not least because Army Council publications were subject to bureaucratic editorial supervision. But, at least so far as fully official doctrinal material was concerned, the wartime system was hardly fleet. For example, a new manual on the infantry division in defence published in March 1942 had been under preparation for at least 15 months.[4] Another example was the revised *Infantry Training* manual. This was one of the few manuals published during the war to appear under Army Council (rather than CIGS) authority which affords a glimpse of the impact of that condition upon publication schedules. The officer who wrote Part VIII, *Fieldcraft, Battle Drill, Section and Platoon Tactics*, started work in April 1942. Delayed by the many amendments demanded by War Office departments, he did not complete his part of the process until October 1943 and the pamphlet did not appear until March 1944, little short of two years after work had started.[5]

The 1937 *Infantry Training* manual had been out of date in the crucial matter of platoon organisation within a year of its publication.[6] The dilatory production of its replacement reflects poorly upon the War Office. None the less, the lack of a valid War Office manual did not leave battalions without a useful pamphlet. GHQ Home Forces had in October 1942 published *The Instructors' Handbook on Fieldcraft and Battle Drill* under the authority of the Commander-in-Chief. At 190 pages, 58 pages longer than *Infantry Training* Part VIII

9

(which, repeating quite a lot of its contents, superseded it), *The Instructors' Handbook* was written by Lieutenant-Colonel Lionel Wigram and Major R.M.T. Kerr of the School of Infantry, and went from conception to publication in less than ten months. Throughout that time both authors were fully employed at the School.[7] This shows what could be achieved when writers were freed from the laborious validation processes required if a manual was to enjoy full status as official doctrine.

Recognising that troops in the field should not have to wait so long for the latest tactical advice, the War Office published two other series of pamphlets to promulgate new or revised doctrine on a provisional basis. The first was the *Army Training Memorandum (ATM)* series. *ATMs* were an interwar creation, appearing once or twice a year. In the first year of the war, however, they appeared monthly. Thereafter publication became irregular with up to seven months between issues. Twenty-nine editions appeared during the war. Wartime *ATMs*, which were issued to each officer, contained a series of usually short articles on tactical, administrative and training matters variously of interest to all ranks of officer in all arms. They were frequently used to announce changes in tactical doctrine resulting from battle experience. For example, that tank guns should generally be fired at the halt rather than on the move was first ordained in an *ATM*.[8]

Curiously, *ATMs* continued to be issued under Army Council authority until January 1944.[9] They were, none the less, capable of responding quickly to events. For example, *ATM* No. 33 of June 1940 was devoted largely to the lessons of the British Expeditionary Force's (BEF's) experience in France and Flanders. These were drawn from the report of a committee chaired by General Sir William Bartholomew which had concluded its sittings only on 21 June.[10] No time was allowed for extensive deliberation on the report, for *ATM* No. 33 was distributed just 11 days later. Among other things, it followed Bartholomew in directing that the brigade group (an infantry brigade with field artillery and other supporting arms under command) rather than the division would henceforth be the basic fighting formation of all arms. The absoluteness of this change would later be regretted.[11] At a lower level of tactics, *ATM* No. 33 followed Bartholomew in lauding the lightly armoured tracked vehicles used by the infantry known as carriers. Each battalion held ten (later 13) of these vehicles, each armed with a Bren gun, in a designated carrier platoon whose intended function was to provide the battalion with a mobile fire-power reserve. Carriers were not designed as fighting vehicles and crews were expected to fire the Bren gun dismounted except in emergency. Their armour was proof only against normal small-arms fire, not against armour-piercing projectiles. However, the BEF had used carriers for a variety of unauthorised purposes, including reconnaissance, transport of stores up to the front and to carry forward bombers to neutralise an enemy strongpoint. *ATM* No. 33 appeared to endorse this. Someone in the War Office took exception and the very next *ATM* laid down that such uses were 'exceptional and would often result in heavy losses'.[12] This was a rare and relatively minor example of the War Office embarrassing itself by uncritical regurgitation of the lessons of battle.

Another of the functions *ATMs* served was as a vehicle for the dissemination of good ideas and advice from units and formations, especially but not exclusively those serving in active theatres. For example, in 1943 and 1944 a number of letters from 'Paul', a subaltern on active service in the Mediterranean theatres to his friend 'Tom', stationed in Britain, were published under headings such as 'A Few "Tips" from the Front'. In fact, 'Paul' was no subaltern but Major Paul Bryan of 6th Royal West Kent Regiment, who acquired a fine reputation serving with his battalion in Tunisia and went on to command it in Italy.[13] *ATMs* were used also to reinforce existing doctrine. In August 1944, the War Office published a series of games suggested by members of a battle-experienced formation (presumably one of those repatriated from the Mediterranean to take part in OVERLORD) as the best means of maintaining fieldcraft skills.[14] This was by no means a new idea. The War Office had suggested games of its own in a manual on fieldcraft published in 1940.[15] With fieldcraft skills at a premium in Normandy, it was presumably felt worthwhile reminding those responsible for training replacement drafts, or for organising the training of units during rest periods out of the line in France, of suitable techniques.

ATMs were not used for the promulgation of substantial bodies of new or replacement doctrine. When the War Office wished to publish such material quickly, without going through the lengthy editorial vetting process required for *MTPs* and the like, it published an *Army Training Instruction* (*ATI*).[16] The first *ATI* appeared in January 1941 and concerned the tactical effects of recent changes in the organisation of the infantry division.[17] Most of the changes resulted from the recommendations of the Bartholomew Report, which suggests a period of about six months from conception to publication. In fact it is likely that the production of ATIs could be accomplished rather more quickly than that. *ATI* No. 3, *Handling of an Armoured Division*, appeared on 19 May 1941. Yet two cloth model exercises at which armoured formation commanders resolved upon the outline doctrine for the employment of armour took place only in January and March.[18] Indeed, a summary of doctrinal preparation work underway in the Directorate of Military Training in November 1940 included nothing recognisable as *ATI* No. 1 published two months later and envisaged only the issue of directives concerning the tactics of the armoured divisions then being raised, not the publication of a pamphlet. Nor did the list include *ATI* No. 2, which appeared in March 1941.[19]

The function of ATIs was to fill a need for printed doctrine pending the production of an *MTP*. In most cases they were later replaced by an *MTP*. An exception to this rule was *ATI* No. 2, *The Employment of Army Tanks in Co-operation with Infantry*, whose stated purpose was to complement *MTP* No. 22, published on the same subject early in the war. *ATI* No. 2 was prompted by the recognition that infantry tank brigades would sometimes have to be used for short periods in the roles normally filled by armoured brigades and that they would also have tasks to perform in an infantry advance.[20] *MTP* No. 22 had dealt only with their principal role, that of supporting infantry in setpiece attacks. At the same time, though, a much bolder use of tanks in the setpiece infantry support role was incorporated in the new doctrine. This, however, proved ruinous in battle, so in May 1943 a new version of *ATI* No. 2 appeared. Another year passed before an *MTP*, No. 63, was produced to replace *ATI* No. 2.

ATI No. 3, on armoured divisions, on the other hand, filled a need for doctrine reflecting new thinking on armoured operations engendered by the experience of the BEF against German armour and, probably to a lesser degree, that of the Western Desert Force against the Italians. The huge expansion in Britain's armoured forces in the year or so following Dunkirk created a pressing demand. It was not until 1943 that the War Office published an *MTP*, No. 41 in three volumes, to supersede *ATI* No. 3. Even then, continuing improvements in the technology and tactics of armoured forces rendered the new pamphlets out of date in important respects almost as soon as they were published, which had an unfortunate impact upon armoured forces training in Britain at that time. Because *ATIs* were provisional, their distribution was more restricted than *MTPs* dealing with similar subjects. For example, only one copy of *ATI* No. 3 was issued to each unit, whereas *MTP* No. 41 went to every officer in the armoured divisions and to every company or equivalent in the other formations.

In a young and fast-developing field like armoured operations it was clearly impossible for printed doctrine to keep pace with reality. But even in more mature tactical disciplines, such as that of the infantry, many detailed lessons were learned in battle that, while not requiring changes in printed doctrine, did deserve to be brought to the attention of those training at home. As we have seen, *ATMs* provided a vehicle for the publication of such material, but only when it could be expressed briefly. There was a need for a dedicated series of publications to address such lessons at length. The War Office began to fill that need in 1942.

Two series of battle-experience publications were launched that year, *Notes from Theatres of War* in February and *Current Reports from Overseas* in September. *Notes from Theatres of War* (*NTW*) started as a fairly up-to-date publication. The first edition, published on 19 February, dealt with the lessons of the CRUSADER offensive in Cyrenaica the previous November. *NTW* Nos 2 and 3, published in one volume on 7 March, covered operations in Cyrenaica in November and December 1941 and operations in Russia during January respectively. Later editions tended to be longer delayed and dealt with an entire strategic phase in a particular theatre. *NTW* No. 6, for example, dealt with Cyrenaica, November 1941–January 1942, and appeared in July 1942. Their purpose came to be to convey the considered lessons of the operations covered, that is once both the higher HQs responsible and the War Office had sifted the battle reports to decide what did and what did not merit official endorsement. *NTWs* thus represented the 'official' lessons of battle experience. They were generally distributed one to each company or equivalent, but some were distributed more widely and others less so where the particular contents so merited. Twenty-one editions were published, the last in June 1945. No edition on the North-West Europe campaign appeared but all other major theatres were covered to the end of 1944.

Conditions in overseas theatres varied, of course, so lessons learned in one campaign were not necessarily generally applicable. Accordingly, *NTWs* usually included a warning to exercise caution in making use of the material they contained. With that qualification, however, it was implicit that where battle lessons suggested some change to previous doctrine then that change was to be embraced in training. *Current Reports from Overseas (CRO)* provided a vehicle for the publication of battle lessons that did not (yet) have the endorsement of the relevant higher HQs and the War Office and that were not, therefore, to be treated with the same reverence as those included in *NTW*. Reflecting the greater discretion required in their use, *CROs* were not distributed as far down the chain of command as *NTWs*. Their circulation below brigade HQ level was forbidden until April 1944, when distribution was deepened to include lieutenant-colonels' commands. *CRO* No. 1 appeared in September 1942; *CRO* No. 2 not until eight months later. But thereafter *CROs* appeared weekly until June 1945. Their purpose was to give formation commanders (and the commandants of certain schools, to which they were also distributed) early information to help them develop their own ideas. In the case of any conflict, previously published doctrine was generally to prevail.[21] The final edition, *CRO* No. 96, appeared on 26 September 1945.

Notes from Theatres of War was compiled exclusively from material that had come to the War Office with the endorsement of the relevant higher HQ. For example, *NTW* No. 16 on the Tunisian campaign was based mainly upon a battle-lessons document prepared under Alexander's instructions and approved by Eisenhower.[22] The pamphlet, which appeared in October 1943, dealt with the campaign systematically under the following headings: Part I, The Theatre of War (a description of the country, climate and relative strengths of the forces engaged); Part II, Outline of Operations; Part III, General Lessons; Part IV, Lessons by Arms; Part V, Administrative Lessons; and Part VI, Enemy Methods. *NTW* No. 14, of June 1943, which covered Eighth Army's operations from August to December 1942, followed much the same pattern. They numbered 144 and 128 pages respectively.

The material for *Current Reports from Overseas* came from a wider range of sources, underwent little if any editorial tampering before publication other than the deletion of the names of units and personnel, and consequently appeared in a wide variety of forms. A number of straightforward factual accounts of operations appeared, compiled by officers involved and usually followed by some effort to draw lessons.[23] After D-Day, a number of accounts by officers recovering from wounds in Britain were published, one of which came, rather frustratingly, to an end with the officer blacking out when he was hit mid-way through the operation he was describing.[24]

Some of the most interesting and useful *CRO* articles stemmed from training instructions, lectures or other works produced by commanders in the field, often for the benefit of their troops during inactive periods. One published in 1945 comprised some notes issued by an infantry CO in North-West Europe to every officer under his command 'as a guide to their conduct in operations'. Aimed especially at officer replacements newly arrived from Britain, it included useful detail on tactics that worked in action together with reassurance on the quality of their training.[25] At least one such article, encapsulating the experience of the two tank brigades that had taken part in the Tunisian campaign, later appeared almost unchanged in the *NTW* on Tunisia.[26]

Between them, *Military Training Pamphlets*, *Army Training Memoranda*, *Army Training Instructions*, *Notes from Theatres of War*, *Current Reports from Overseas* and the separate infantry training manuals represent the main sources used in the following chapters on doctrine and its evolution up to D-Day. Battle experience reports published before D-Day are generally used to help explain changes in doctrine and identify flaws in the training of Home Forces and 21 Army Group. Those published after D-Day, particularly concerning operations in North-West Europe, are generally used to illustrate the results of that training. Despite their many useful qualities, the published reports did not always tell the whole truth. One searches in vain for a candid treatment of the shortcomings (perceived and real) of British tanks in North Africa, for example. It is likely that the War Office and higher HQs censored material that reflected badly upon equipment, reasoning that since it could not quickly be improved there was little to be gained from publicising deficiencies and much to be lost in terms of troop morale.

Montgomery certainly acted by that thinking in Normandy. On 25 June he prohibited the production of after-action reports by senior officers who had been attached to formation HQs for that sole purpose. Their efforts, Montgomery found, were likely to be unduly 'influenced by local conditions'.[27] What he meant was that the reports had deliberated honestly on the problems British troops were facing in Normandy. For example, on 19 June Lieutenant-Colonel A.H. Pepys, attached to 7th Armoured Division, reported on 'the undoubted superiority of the German Tiger and Panther over our Cromwell and Sherman . . . The position of our tanks when compared with the Germans now is similar to what it was in 1941 when the Crusader and Honey tanks were matched against Mk IIIs and Mk IVs.' Before passing the report on to the War Office and the Supreme HQ of the Allied Expeditionary Force (SHAEF),[28] 21 Army Group removed this passage.

It is unlikely that Montgomery's censorship had more than a minimal effect in bolstering morale. The day after 107th Royal Armoured Corps (RAC) arrived in Normandy in early July they were visited by troops from 11th

Armoured Division who left the new arrivals in no doubt that even in their well-armoured Churchill tanks they were 'outgunned and less well protected by tank armour than our adversaries'.[29] No general could censor the grapevine. But the War Office relied upon reports from units and formations in the field to fill the pages of *Current Reports from Overseas*, and had made extensive use of the reports before Montgomery banned them. Prompted by SHAEF, Montgomery authorised their resumption on 22 July.[30] But about the four intervening weeks of operations in Normandy very little was published in *Current Reports from Overseas*. It is probable that the dearth of material through official channels prompted a War Office circular of 30 July, written under Army Council authority, requesting the assistance of commanders-in-chief in the procurement of material for *CRO*.[31]

The training publications discussed above were all, bar one, War Office productions. Regulations forbade the publication of training manuals by subordinate commanders on the grounds that such manuals would breed confusion by diverting attention from the official manuals.[32] It was a much-flouted rule. Perhaps inevitably, given the communication difficulties, Middle East Command produced its own training manuals under the series title *Middle East Training Pamphlet*. As has already been mentioned, rather closer to Whitehall GHQ Home Forces published a manual on minor infantry tactics in 1942 which plugged an important gap in War Office provision. Home Forces published at least one other pamphlet[33] and 21 Army Group published several both before and after D-Day.[34] Rather lower down the ladder of command, the then Lieutenant-General H.R.L.G. Alexander published a slim volume on infantry minor tactics for use by his troops when he was commander of I Corps in the autumn of 1940.[35] Even further down the ranks, Lieutenant-Colonel Wigram, author of the GHQ Home Forces infantry manual, published a tract on infantry training in July 1942 at his own expense. It was distributed to students on his courses at the School of Infantry.[36] The War Office showed no sign of objection in principle to such publications, let alone proceeding against those responsible, although disagreement over the contents was not unknown.[37]

It would, of course, have been absurd for the War Office to proceed against unofficial pamphleteers. They were filling a need that the War Office could not meet at the time. Early in the war a commercial publishing firm launched a periodical magazine entitled *Battle Training in Word and Picture*. The magazine, which the War Office recommended for all ranks, included heroic stories from the Great War and descriptions of the fighting in the Spanish Civil War. Of most potential use for current training, however, was the fictional Anglian–Humbrian war that the magazines serialised. Each issue described a number of tactical problems facing junior officers and NCOs during the conflict that could have formed the basis of tactical exercises without troops. As General Gort put it in a foreword to the first issue, 'when so many young men have joined the Army, the need for some means of self-education in military training is a very real one'.[38] It could only increase with the onset of war, yet the War Office published no comparable literature of its own – a serious omission in view of the inadequacies in training in the first two years of the war. Gort's pious hope that young conscripts would buy the magazine at a cost of six pence seems not to have been realised since it folded after just three issues.

None the less, Gale & Polden, the Aldershot publisher, produced numerous titles before the war intended to help part-time Territorial Army officers master tactics and training. Revised editions of some appeared during the war.[39] That Gale & Polden could find a market for such publications testifies to a hunger for printed sources of reference on tactical matters among the junior officers at whom they were aimed. In the early years of the war, that demand was not met in official training literature.

Field force officers often criticised the War Office for failing to lead in the matter of doctrinal development. In fact, a natural and proper reluctance to rush into print before new ideas were battle-proven exacerbated editorial and production delays to ensure that the War Office could not put out new material in pace with developments.[40] The distinction of purpose between *Current Reports from Overseas* and *Notes from Theatres of War* shows that the War Office was conscious firstly that it was not the fount of all wisdom and, secondly, that troops training at home looked to it as precisely that. Yet the War Office did manage to produce a very large quantity of doctrinal literature during the war, so much that it became a problem. There were complaints that there were simply too many pamphlets for officers to keep abreast with, and too much uncertainty over which were current and which had been superseded. One general feared that, heedless of orders, few officers did more than flick through most official pamphlets.[41] An investigation in 1942 found that armoured regimental officers were supposed to read some 300 separate pamphlets, and that many were so daunted by the task that they simply read none at all. Some COs (through whom all training literature was distributed) withheld certain items, so preventing subordinates from reading them (whether out of disagreement with the contents or so as not to overload officers with paper it is not clear).[42] In the opinion of one officer who served in 1940 and 1941, training literature, much of which was 'very good indeed', tended to go unread in the avalanche of largely pointless and contemptible paperwork generated by higher HQs and the War Office.[43]

Clearly the success with which training manuals reached their target readership was at best patchy. Officer cadets, whose whole purpose was to learn and who might be expected, given the ever-present possibility of failing the course, to have applied themselves to study more assiduously than those already commissioned, certainly received plenty of manuals to read during the evenings.[44] But one such student referred to 'a whole library of military training pamphlets, which I *should* read, but somehow don't think I shall'.[45] In any case, book-learning at an individual level did not amount to tactical skill. As the War Office pointed out, the last thing an officer should do in battle was refer to the doctrine before deciding his next course of action. (It probably would be the last thing he did.) 'Doctrine must have become second nature before-hand.'[46] To achieve that required lengthy collective practice in which the potential for good in an officer who had read the latest doctrinal guidance (assuming that such guidance was good, which it was not always) could be crushed by general inertia in a unit or formation that knew some inferior method and was not inclined to change. It is, or should be, a tenet of military history that one cannot assume that what the manual said was what the soldiers did. Otherwise this book would (perhaps mercifully) be rather shorter than it is.

3

'Full-Sail' Exercises

An army marches on its stomach. During the summer exercises of 1st Highland Light Infantry in Malta in the early 1930s, midday saw the suspension of operations. While their soldiers tucked into stew and duff under the hot sun, the officers repaired to a large marquee where they consumed an enormous lunch prepared by the civilian mess staff.[1] This was real soldiering, just as in the days of Asterix the Gaul, who found that the Britons broke off their battles for tea promptly at 4 p.m. Outrageous displays of this nature did not survive in the more professional climate of the war, when regimental officers shared their men's privations during exercises. This often meant sleeping rough in freezing temperatures, marching long distances and eating nothing but chewing gum between an early breakfast and a late dinner. One of the principal functions served by major exercises during the war, so far as junior officers and their men were concerned, was to acquaint them with the administrative conditions of active service. Indeed, in some cases proper subsistence was not forthcoming at all for extended periods during exercises.[2]

But this study is not about food and drink, nor about the vagaries of military administration. What about tactics? To what extent did exercises prepare soldiers for the tasks they would have to perform in battle? In the military world an exercise generally means the practical rehearsal of an operation or series of operations by a sub-unit, unit or formation. It is an occasion for each individual to practise his role (which he has previously learned individually) in concert with his colleagues who are each practising their individual roles. In other words, an exercise (often known alternatively as a scheme) is a collective practice rather than an individual one. The larger the scale of the exercise the more it involves the collective practice of a series of component organisations, each operating by the collective performance by a number of individuals of their separate roles. Thus an exercise can be at the level of the smallest sub-unit – the infantry section, individual tank and so on – or at any higher level up to army or, conceivably, army group.

The possibilities open to the smallest sub-units operating individually are limited. They do not command the administrative resources such as food, drink, ammunition, fuel, mechanical maintenance and repair, medical treatment, and so on, needed to sustain themselves for longer than a few hours.

For such necessities, and for intelligence, planning and command, they look to parent sub-units and, principally, to the unit. Units look to brigade, brigade to division, and so on, for more powerful administrative and command resources. Because fighting troops cannot for long fight effectively without higher direction and administrative services, no programme of collective training could be regarded as complete unless it exercised those faculties in concert with the fighting elements. That is why it was so unfortunate that the British Army had carried out so few large-scale exercises in the 1930s.[3] Senior commanders and their staffs had gained little practice in managing all the components of their commands so that the troops were in the right place at the right time with the right equipment and the right consumables to enable them to do their fighting job.

The Second World War saw probably the largest military manoeuvres ever to take place on British soil. Interarmy exercise BUMPER, held in the autumn of 1941, saw 12 divisions and three independent brigades engaged, plus elements of the RAF – more than 250,000 men in total. Exercise SPARTAN, 18 months later, was slightly smaller, with ten divisions and four independent brigades, but still qualifies as an enormous military manoeuvre.[4] Such exercises were exceptional, but countless schemes at corps, divisional, brigade and battalion level took place during the war with the purpose of exercising the units and formations concerned in the arts and techniques of operating as a whole. Not all included an element of fighting. There were, for example, many exercises whose sole purpose was to test units in the business of planning and executing movement from one location to another. But many others included not only movement but also a battle at the end of it together with all the administrative ancillaries. As a corps commander in 1940 and 1941, Montgomery took his divisions out on exercise regularly for up to four days at a time, with every unit leaving nothing behind in camp and functioning as it would have to in war: 'under full sail', as he put it.[5] The purpose of this chapter is to explore the value of such 'full-sail' exercises as battle-fighting training for soldiers and their immediate commanders.

UMPIRES AND UMPIRING

If, as Clausewitz tells us, battle is the cash payment of war, then casualties represent the coin.[6] For battle training even to approach realism some means must be found to judge the effect of both sides' actions in terms of casualties inflicted and suffered without actually hurting anyone. This was one of the functions of exercise umpires whose job, as the War Office put it in the manual on umpiring, was to fill in the gaps in exercise realism that could not be filled by the use of training expedients.[7]

This demanded more than simply telling men that they were dead or wounded. In a real battle, death and injuries were (usually) administered by the enemy. In an exercise the umpires needed to know what the enemy was doing, how efficiently and where. This involved liaison with the umpires supervising the enemy side and, in the event of an engagement, the combined study of the plans and/or action of the two sides to reach an agreed decision on the outcome. It also involved the continuous feeding of information to the troops to make them aware of circumstances that in real battle would be obvious but which could not be simulated in the exercise: a task known as 'picture-painting'. Thus an umpire might have to tell the troops that the area was under shell-fire. In real battle the troops would either take cover or move elsewhere. According to the efficiency with which they did so in training, the umpire could decide how many casualties to impose. This descriptive role demanded a degree of discretion. Some battlefield sensations struck only a small number of the men and fighting efficiency depended upon the alacrity with which they acted upon what they discovered thereby. A gas attack upon resting troops might at first be detected only by the man detailed as gas sentry, and it was the umpire's duty to inform only that man of an imaginary gas attack and then observe his performance in alerting his comrades: if the umpire told the troops, the gas sentry's role would not be tested. Similarly, if an entire platoon was adjudged wiped out, it was not the umpire's duty to tell the company commander. Rather he should find out for himself by whatever means might be available in battle.[8]

In order to judge the actions of 'his' troops realistically, the umpire needed all the information available to the commander to whom he was affiliated and a great deal more that the commander would not know about in a real battle. This meant accompanying the commander at orders groups and reconnais-sances, and mutual briefings with other umpires. So the umpire's job was a highly peripatetic one, far more so than that of the commander of the troops to which he was attached. And it demanded a high degree of practical tactical judgement. The umpire needed to know when his presence with forward troops was necessary, when he needed to accompany the commander and when to seek out other umpires for briefing. The umpire's privileged information and arbitral role naturally presented temptations to partiality. The War Office cautioned against that and against umpires telling commanders and troops what to do. It was one thing to tell the gas sentry that a gas attack was in progress, quite another to order him to go and tell his comrades. If he preferred to do nothing that was up to him, although repeated picture-painting with added vividness was encouraged as a means of persuading the recalcitrant to act.[9]

The reality gap in exercises could be very wide indeed. Thunder-flashes and blank ammunition were often used to simulate the fall of shell and report of small arms, but not always. In many exercises the enemy artillery was imagi-nary, and the enemy in its entirety largely so. Troops enjoying the sound of birdsong in the trees might well be asked to believe that they were under heavy artillery attack. Enemy action was often a matter of umpire fiction-making. In those circumstances, the umpire acted not only as the arbiter of the troops' actions but also as the agent of the director of the exercise in his purpose of testing the troops in certain types of situation. A further job of the umpires was to keep a record of what happened during the exercise, ideally of a purely factual nature without the interposition of the umpire's own opinions. In theory the facts would speak for themselves, and by collating all the facts from all the umpires a comprehensive account of the exercise could be assembled.[10] In practice it is difficult to see how hard fact could be distilled from mere opinion: many of the facts, for example casualty bills, were themselves a matter of the umpire's opinion. Be that as it may, the umpire's role was crucial. The War Office characterised a good umpire as a combination of actor, sports-commentator, war-correspondent and thought-reader, with first-class tactical knowledge and in peak physical fitness.[11] Undoubtedly such men existed, although there were probably not enough of them to secure a consistently high standard of exercises. As the War Office maintained though, bad umpiring could ruin a well-conceived exercise and good umpiring improve an indifferent one.[12]

Divisions in Home Forces and 21 Army Group before June 1944 each had a designated umpire permanently attached. This appointment, which carried the rank of lieutenant-colonel or full colonel, was neither part of the normal divisional staff nor an *ad hoc* duty for one of the division's COs or senior staff officers. It lay quite outside the operational organisation of the division. Corps and many brigades also had designated umpires attached in similar rank and again outside the operational organisation. Formation umpires did not belong to any formally organised corps or pool. A number of those whose identities are known were retired, and some appear to have had less than satisfactory careers as fighting commanders.[13] It is hard to see them as in the first rank of Britain's fighting commanders, although the information available about individuals is too scanty to make any definitive general assessment. None the less, brigade and divisional umpire appointments appear to have been used as much to give employment to the otherwise redundant as to exploit their tactical skills. Meanwhile, the War Office enjoined that only the best officers should be made umpires.[14]

The permanent umpires assigned to brigades and higher formations did not represent adequate umpiring strength to cover the whole formation's training. Rather than holding a dedicated body of permanent umpires, commanders appointed officers and senior NCOs as umpires on an *ad hoc* basis. Guidance issued by GHQ Home Forces specified that on exercise each infantry battalion should have eight officer umpires (ranging down from a major or lieutenant-colonel as senior umpire) and 12 NCO umpires plus one motor-cycle orderly. Tank units and armoured units were each to have eight officer umpires and five motor-cyclists. GHQ conceded that it would not always be possible to meet these recommended scales, in which case the available umpires should be pooled and despatched by senior umpires to the scene of action as necessary.[15] Standing Orders for exercises issued by V Corps in 1941 laid down only ten umpires (of whom only three were officers) per infantry battalion – half the quota later recommended by GHQ.[16]

In the early years of the war, shortages of suitably qualified personnel for umpiring duties diminished the training value of many exercises. Senior commanders were compelled to run special courses to train new men for the task.[17] Even a theoretically sufficient umpiring contingent might through some oversight or hold-up be absent when they were needed. Touring operations in his car during an Eastern Command exercise in December 1941, the BGS came across an incipient attack for which there were almost no umpires present. He stayed and officiated himself.[18] But the existence and timely presence of suitably qualified personnel did not entirely solve the problem, for if umpires were to be truly objective in their assessment of troops' performance they needed to be from units that had no part in the exercise. If this was not possible, the War Office advised, they should not umpire troops of their own unit or formation.[19]

Neither the less nor the more onerous of those two conditions was always observed. An example is exercise CUCKOO – a battalion exercise to practise an assault river crossing set by the CO of 5th Wiltshire Regiment in August 1943. The assaulting troops were to be umpired by their own company commanders, who were to issue their orders for crossing the river and then metamorphose.[20] The 43rd Division's exercise VULCAN in December 1943, a four-day scheme involving the whole division advancing against elements of 61st Division and 31st Tank Brigade, was umpired internally throughout. Each infantry brigade detailed one senior major and three captains (one per battalion) as permanent umpires for the exercise and three junior officers and three NCOs to umpire patrolling activities. In the event of contact with the enemy or a warning order for action, all company seconds-in-command were to don white armbands (the standard 'umpirial' uniform) and supervise for the duration of the particular action. The finale of VULCAN was to be an attack on the enemy's main position by 214th Brigade. Only for that stage of the exercise were the minimum requirements of umpire disinterestedness observed, since the attack was to be umpired at the scale specified in GHQ guidance by officers from the other two brigades of the division.[21]

Exercise VULCAN neatly illustrates the problems of umpire provision. It was entirely a 43rd Division show and was umpired internally. For most of the exercise all three infantry brigades were in action or potentially so, and they thus had to find their own umpires on a scale that fell far short of that specified by GHQ. But in the final act only 214th Brigade was committed. Since for the other two the exercise was over, they were free to provide a sufficient umpiring contingent to cover 214th Brigade's attack at the approved scale. Exercise MARS, an earlier two-day scheme for 214th Brigade, was likewise umpired by personnel from the other two brigades of the division.[22] Where that exercise differed from, for example, 5th Wiltshires' exercise CUCKOO (mentioned above) was that MARS was set by division, that is at a higher level than the formation engaged in the exercise, whereas CUCKOO was a battalion exercise set by the battalion itself. Divisional HQ had the authority to require those brigades not involved in MARS to provide umpires. The 5th Wiltshires had no power to demand umpires from other battalions and so had to provide for itself, just as the brigades of 43rd Division had to do for most of VULCAN.

When engaged in exercises set by higher HQs, however, divisions could expect to be umpired externally. The 43rd Division provided umpirage for corps interdivisional exercise HAMMER I in January 1943 between 3rd and 53rd Divisions, and for corps exercises CANUTE II for 59th Division and CANUTE III for 53rd Division in November.[23] Those divisions belonged at the material times to XII Corps. One may infer that, whatever the level of command, it was unusual for those responsible for setting an exercise to contract umpires from outside their own command. If the whole of a command was engaged in the exercise this meant that umpires arbitrated in situations in which their units and formations had an interest even if, as did not happen in CUCKOO, personnel were assigned to umpire units or sub-units other than their own. This less-than-ideal situation is easily explained. Disruptions to training born of persistent extraneous demands upon manpower, postings of officers and men and heavy bureaucratic workload remained the bane of commanding officers at home for much of the war. The provision of officers and NCOs for umpire duty elsewhere was simply another drain upon scarce resources, one to be tolerated only if ordered. It is likely that commanders at all levels, knowing that each other's problems were similar to their own, observed a tacit convention not to add to them by seeking external umpirage unless expressly required to do so.

An individual's suitability for umpiring work depended upon his expertise in the particular type of operations involved. This raised peculiar problems for armoured divisions. When armoured divisions each held two armoured brigades, divisional HQ could order one to provide umpires for exercises by the other. Both Guards Armoured Division and 11th Armoured Division adopted this practice, although it was not possible when both brigades took part in the same exercise on opposite sides.[24] However, with the reorganisation of armoured divisions in mid-1942 which left each with just one armoured brigade (except Guards Armoured Division which retained both until January 1943), cross-provision of umpires was no longer possible. Thus in exercise BULL, set by XI Corps District for 11th Armoured Division in September 1942, senior unit umpires came from outside the division but squadron umpires and their assistants were provided by armoured units for themselves.[25] Guards Armoured Division umpired itself in Northern Command intercorps exercise BLACKCOCK in 1943, although divisional HQ stipulated that officer (but not NCO) umpires should not supervise their own units.[26]

The dangers of 'self-catering' umpiring are easy to perceive. Umpires were invariably junior in rank to the commander of the sub-unit, unit or formation to which they were attached. Half-colonels did not umpire companies or squadrons. Permanent umpires at divisional and brigade level were between one and three rungs lower on the promotion ladder than the associated commander. Units were usually umpired by a major. Companies and squadrons, as we have seen, were at times umpired by their own commanders. If not, the umpire would usually be a captain who, if it was a 'self-catering' exercise, would be the second-in-command. Although umpires were not supposed to issue operational orders, they did issue umpiring orders which, naturally, might be unpalatable to the recipient. The War Office advised umpires to be tactful and to avoid giving offence,[27] a sure indicator that offence was sometimes given, or at least taken. At platoon level, if umpires were provided at all they were usually sergeants – a breed one does not associate with tact and inoffensiveness. No commander would relish all his troops being made dead and it being made clear to him that his operation had been a miserable failure. In many situations such decisions were not in the hands of one umpire alone. None the less, if the umpire concerned were junior in rank to the commander and if, in a two-sided exercise, the opposing commander was also junior, the temptation existed to pull rank. If the umpire concerned usually answered to the commander whose operation he now judged a failure, that temptation was all the stronger.

In May 1942 Montgomery issued express orders that umpires' decisions in his forthcoming intercorps exercise TIGER were to be obeyed without question, even if they were unsound. Breaches of discipline on this point were to be reported to him personally.[28] Such cases undoubtedly occurred. Montgomery had perhaps learned of an incident during GHQ exercise BUMPER (for which he had been chief umpire) the previous autumn: upon receiving no response from a Canadian soldier when he told him he was killed, an umpire repeated himself in French, to which the Canadian replied with a plain English expletive and carried on fighting.[29] And it was not only private soldiers who were wont to disregard umpire instructions. On 2 October 1943 during intercorps exercise BLACKCOCK, Lieutenant R.C.G. Pember, commanding the reconnaissance troop (mounted in armoured cars) of 3rd Tank Scots Guards, managed to get across the River Derwent by bluffing an umpire.[30] That morning the engineers were constructing bridges across the river to a bridgehead gained by infantry formations overnight.[31] It is unlikely that they could have completed their work by 8.30 a.m. when Pember crossed. Almost certainly his bluff involved the use of the 'blown' regular bridge. In other words, displaying all the verve that together with his courage would later win him a Military Cross, Pember cheated. Once across the river by means of this prank, he sent back a stream of valuable information, earning personal congratulation from Brigadier G.L. Verney, commanding 6th Guards Tank Brigade.[32] Whether Verney knew of the circumstances surrounding Pember's crossing of the river is not clear. A lengthy account of the exercise compiled by brigade HQ stated that he had got across legitimately,[33] although it is unlikely that such a document would have admitted cheating even if its authors knew of it. But the Scots Guards CO must have known, for the War Diary mentions the bluffing of the umpires. If an officer of lieutenant-colonel's rank was prepared to connive at such cheating it is a safe bet that many more junior officers were too.

Cheating by troops in defiance of the umpires was one way in which an exercise could be perverted. Cheating by troops with the connivance and even active assistance of the umpires was another. During exercise EAGLE, an intercorps scheme held in February 1944 under the auspices of Northern Command, 11th Armoured Division recorded two such occurrences. On the night of 17–18 February an attack by 1st Herefordshire Regiment on an enemy strongpoint failed 'due to the fact that a formidable wire obstacle (type umpire) had been put up during the day, the chief peculiarity of which was its invisibility to a patrol which had kept the position in full view all day from a haystack only 50 yds away'.[34] Four days later, the division found that enemy tanks withdrawing after a (presumably unsuccessful) counterattack were able to retire 'through gaps in their own minefields, which were filled with a remarkable rapidity, in view of the fact that no one approached them after the enemy had passed through'.[35] It is noteworthy that owing to an acute shortage no umpires were provided for the enemy side in exercise EAGLE. Instead, all officers of the enemy side were empowered to act as umpires where necessary.[36]

REALISM AND TRAVESTY

So far we have discussed the umpire's role in the imposition of realism upon inherently unreal exercises. This function included informing the troops of circumstances and events that they were, for the purposes of the exercise, to assume (including casualties) and the arbitration of actions taking into account such factors as the troops' performance in relation to those circumstances. Some specific examples have been given in which troops undermined the realism of an exercise by direct or indirect defiance of an umpire's will. Given Montgomery's concern over failures to obey umpires' orders it is reasonable to assume that such instances were not rare. Although it cannot be proved, we have suggested that the frequency with which officers and NCOs were called upon to judge the performance of their own units or sub-units and the inferior rank umpires held in relation to the commander whose troops they were supervising tended to encourage disobedience of umpires' orders or less direct subversion of their will. However, the imposition of realism was not always the first duty of an umpire. Indeed, at times realism ran contrary to the judgements umpires handed down.

For example, during exercise BLACKCOCK 2nd Armoured Irish Guards (VIII Corps) crossed the Derwent a full two days before the illegitimate crossing by the Scots Guards reconnaissance troop (also VIII Corps) 'only to be "umpired" back'. Indeed, before crossing the river, the battalion's War Diary claimed, they had defeated the enemy's reconnaissance regiment not once but twice.[37] This was not realistic. During exercise HAMMER II, an interdivisional scheme between 53rd and 43rd Divisions in January 1943, the umpires pronounced a company of 4th Wiltshires destroyed following a night attack upon it in its defensive position by an enemy battalion. The Wiltshires felt particularly aggrieved because only one enemy section had actually made contact with their troops and then only with one platoon.[38] Clearly this too was unrealistic. During the same exercise, 153rd RAC was pronounced 'wiped out and captured before it could carry out its counter attack' (the regiment's role in the divisional plan), a decision the unit's War Diarist ascribed to bad umpiring.[39] A final example: during an exercise in Devon in June 1941, Lance-Corporal R.I. Higgins of 8th Bedfordshire and Hertfordshire Regiment took part in a night patrol that captured the opposing brigadier and his staff. For their trouble the umpires made Higgins and his comrades the victims of a retrospective artillery concentration and the brigadier carried on as if nothing had happened – as indeed did Higgins' patrol, resurrected after a short rest.[40]

Apart from these few examples, we might raise the experience of 11th Armoured Division during exercise EAGLE, described above, which we implied was the product of partial umpiring by umpires whose first loyalty was not to realism but to the interests of their own units. Yet there is another explanation for the indignities inflicted upon 11th Armoured Division and for the other cases of apparently 'bad' umpiring.

A tactical exercise could take one of several forms, each with its own particular characteristics and usefulness. Both in field formations and in schools of instruction, a frequent resort for the collective training of commanders in tactical decision-making was the tactical exercise without troops (TEWT). As the term suggests, private soldiers did not actually take part in such exercises: they were largely of a theoretical character only, although they did deal in practical problems to the extent that they were usually based upon some real piece of territory. In some cases that territory was represented on a cloth or sand-table model and the exercise was conducted indoors. In others the participants went on to the actual ground. The practice was for the director of the TEWT to select ground or construct a model suitable to test the participants in a particular situation or series of situations. Participants usually worked in syndicates. Their solutions, generally in the form of orders to imaginary troops, were then discussed collectively and appropriate lessons drawn.

TEWTs functioned as individual training for commanders, an opportunity for them to develop their personal tactical thought and benefit from the experience and ideas of others without the complicating presence of troops. Their limitations as a means of training officers in tactics will feature in Chapter 4. None of the exercises mentioned so far in this chapter were TEWTs. Indeed, in most TEWTs there was no need for umpires since the purpose of such exercises was to test command decisions rather than practical tactics. The pace of events could be adjusted to suit those taking part, and arbitration on participants' solutions could easily be undertaken by the officer conducting the exercise. Thus there is no need here to explore the subject of TEWTs in great detail. However, TEWTs were often carried out as the prelude to exercises with troops, especially one-sided exercises or exercises with a controlled enemy. The TEWT's function in such a context will be discussed shortly when we consider such exercises.

Exercises with troops could be either one-sided or two-sided, that is to say they could involve troops attacking or defending against a live enemy, or they could involve only a notional enemy. In many exercises with a live enemy, that enemy was 'controlled': the director of the exercise laid down, in advance or during the course of the exercise, the actions the enemy was to take. This enabled him to ensure that the troops for whose benefit the exercise was intended were presented with the kind of problems he wished them to face, although it could be tiresome and frustrating for the controlled enemy. In many controlled-enemy exercises the numbers actually taking part on the enemy side were lower than required for the operations the director wished to see practised, the umpires redressing the deficit. Genuine one-sided exercises likewise required the director to define the problem to be dealt with quite specifically and demanded that the umpiring fill the reality gap. Thus one-sided exercises and exercises with a controlled enemy offered much the same nature of training. They tested the troops taking part in a specific situation or series of situations, determined beforehand by the directing officer.

Because the situations in one-sided and controlled-enemy exercises were determinate, it was particularly easy to prepare the commanders involved by putting them through a TEWT. The War Office recommended this practice in sub-unit and unit training because it would help to preclude serious command errors and imbue inexperienced leaders with confidence.[41] An example at unit level occurred on 20 October 1942. In the afternoon the officers of 5th Wiltshires assembled on the Princes Firing Range near Sandwich for a TEWT, followed the next morning by a practical exercise with troops on the same ground. Both TEWT and exercise with troops involved an attack by a battalion group (that is with field guns under command). The narrative of the exercise specified that the battalion group was advancing to engage a failed German raiding party as it re-embarked on beaches north of Sandwich. As the lead company neared the beaches it was to come under heavy fire, represented by the exercise director using thunder-flashes. The lead company commander was to report back to the CO who was to carry out a reconnaissance and stage a full battalion attack with gunner support. From the fact that a TEWT was to be carried out beforehand one can assume that the problems they would face and the solutions to be applied were well known to the officers concerned well before zero hour. In this case live firing was to be practised and, apart from the exercise director and his thunder-flashes in the early stages, the enemy was to be represented by cut-out figure targets only.[42]

The 5th Wiltshires' exercise was a small-scale affair. Operations on 21 October were scheduled to last no more than three hours and the TEWT on the previous day, which did not start until 2.30 p.m., cannot have lasted much longer because of failing light. The combination of TEWT followed by practical exercise was also used at a higher level. For example, in August 1942 HQ 43rd Division hosted a series of cloth-model TEWTs for senior officers of all units, dealing with 'reorganisation', 'the break-in attack' and 'the break-out attack' in relation to the recently adopted mixed division organisation. The following month, 129th Brigade, a component of 43rd Division, repeated these TEWTs before taking part in brigade exercises with troops directed by divisional HQ.[43]

A TEWT did not precede every one-sided or controlled-enemy exercise, and an associated exercise with troops did not follow every TEWT. But such schemes were intended to exercise the participants in highly specific situations that left little room for innovation and flair outside the parameters set by the director. That was not necessarily a bad thing, for much valuable training could be achieved by educating all ranks in specific techniques suitable for particular situations. One such problem was the reverse slope defence, extensively used by the Germans in Tunisia.

This practice exploited the general tactical principle that it is always advantageous to hold the commanding (meaning high) ground, which led commanders to specify the crests of German-held hills as objectives for attacking troops. The Germans, however, placed only limited forces on the crest, whence they trained automatic fire on the forward slopes, up which the attacking troops had to assault to gain the ridge. Artillery and mortars, pre-registered on likely targets and directed from observation posts near the crest, supplemented the defensive fire. Any attack that reached the ridge would immediately come under fire from lightly held outposts a few yards down the reverse slopes. But the main German defences were held much further down the reverse slopes, ready to counterattack in strength.[44] Against a reverse slope defence, the attackers often gained their objectives with little difficulty only to find themselves under strong enemy counterattack when they were at their most vulnerable, that is as they began to organise the objective and themselves for defence and before they had brought up heavy weapons.

The reverse slope defence was simply a variation on the old German defensive theme of rapid counterattack in strength. This was well-enough known to the British General Staff for a warning of it to be included in the standard manual on operations, published in July 1941.[45] That British troops apparently were rather taken by surprise by it in Tunisia testifies to the superior tactical flair of the Germans in using the opportunities offered by the topography. The War Office's recommended solution was to pre-empt the counterattack by attacking to a depth greater than that which one actually wished to hold.[46] Other solutions included the use of tanks to bring fire to bear on the reverse slopes from the flanks and rear, and, somewhat less adventurously, simply making sure that consolidation of the ground won was effected before the counterattack came.[47]

By the summer of 1943 troops training in England were aware of the reverse slope problem, alerted by tentative battle lessons published in May.[48] In the late summer and early autumn Major-General G.I. Thomas (GOC 43rd Division) held cloth-model exercises for all officers down to company (or equivalent) commanders to discuss the reverse slope problem.[49] Although these were not followed by exercises with troops at brigade or divisional level, at least one battalion covered the reverse slope problem in exercises over the succeeding months. The codename of one of those exercises, ARSEWAZE, with its vulgar connotations, perhaps reflected the distaste with which the gentlemen of the British Army viewed this rather unsporting tactic.[50] It is surprising that there was not more emphasis on the reverse slope problem at brigade and divisional level. At least one battalion in Normandy, 6th Royal Scots Fusiliers, could have used better training on this matter before operation EPSOM, in which they suffered from a reverse slope defence, something that they had apparently never expected.[51]

In fact, at the minor tactical level there was little to distinguish an attack against a reverse slope defence from other types of attack. What the soldiers in the sections and platoons at the sharp end most needed was reasonably accurate information about the enemy's strength, position and weaponry. Had the Royal Scots Fusiliers had such information during their EPSOM attack they would probably have approached the crest with more caution than they did. Had senior officers suspected the true layout of the defence they would have arranged the operation and the supporting fire-plan to neutralise the problem accordingly. For the reverse slope defence was primarily a problem to be addressed by command and staff work. TEWTs, one-sided exercises with troops and controlled-enemy exercises with troops, were particularly suitable vehicles for the resolution of such problems in training. The TEWT demanded that a theoretical solution be decided, based upon theoretical actions and reactions by the enemy. The exercise with troops facilitated the rehearsal of that theoretical solution to see whether, against the predetermined enemy behaviour, the solution proposed was practicable, or to rehearse and test commanders and troops in the execution of an operation that was known by experience to be feasible given the specified enemy behaviour.

Regardless of the fighting qualities and abilities of the troops, the feasibility of virtually any military operation depended upon pre-zero hour activities of an administrative and planning nature, carried on by commanders and staffs. These included reconnaissance and tactical planning, arranging the movement of troops to the start line, arranging communications, the provision of sufficient fuel and ammunition, feeding the troops and setting up medical facilities to care for the wounded. Even in a company scheme many of these processes featured in the duties of the company commander and his aides. The result was that in many one-sided and controlled-enemy exercises, the tactical performance of the fighting troops became almost insignificant beside the enormous effort necessary to get them into the firing line in the first place. Let us consider in detail a specific controlled-enemy exercise.

Exercise MARS (27–29 October 1943) was set by Thomas, GOC 43rd Division, 'to practise the 214 Inf Bde in operating as a complete Bde Gp'. Also taking part in the exercise were divisional HQ (with Brigadier F.Y.C. Knox of 130th Brigade acting as commander in place of Thomas who was assumed to have been killed), HQ 129th Brigade and the divisional bridging engineers. Elements of 53rd Division and 34th Tank Brigade represented the enemy.[52] For all exercises, the director included in the exercise papers a description of the opening situation. In a two-sided exercise such as MARS this was in three parts. The first part, known as the 'General Idea', set the general picture of operations applicable to both sides. The second and third parts were known as the 'Special Idea' and each was issued only to one side in the exercise. The Special Idea described the situation and initial tasks of the troops concerned, together with such information on enemy dispositions as would be available in real battle. For MARS the General Idea postulated that England represented northern France. Second Army, having landed on the South Coast, had concentrated in the Rolvenden and Hawkhurst vicinity in Kent. Ashford had been destroyed by bombers and all roads through it cut (no doubt a convenient tale to spare the inhabitants the trouble of large-scale military movement through their town). The 43rd Division was a follow-up division whose task was to expand the initial bridgehead to the east. The Special Idea for 214th Brigade was that by 6 p.m. on 27 October, 43rd Division had relieved the assaulting troops in a series of positions on the east flank of the bridgehead and was in contact with enemy reconnaissance forces.[53] MARS represented 214th Brigade's part in the divisional drive to the east, working on the right of the divisional front with 129th Brigade (in skeleton only) working on the left.

A week before the exercise, divisional HQ issued a number of narratives of events, one of which covered 214th Brigade's activities during the exercise. This specified not only the actions of the brigade but also the actions of the enemy and the decisions of the umpires, who were to be provided by 129th Brigade on the scale laid down by GHQ. The document was issued only to the exercise directing staff, the umpires and the enemy, not to 214th Brigade. The latter's first substantial action came on the morning of 28 October. Having begun to push eastwards at 7 a.m., enemy troops were to retire before them until they reached the line of the River Stour south-east of Ashford. The enemy was to destroy two minor-road bridges over the river before the advancing troops reached them, and defend the crossings with a company at one site and a company and a half at the other. When 214th Brigade reached the river at 9 a.m. they were to come under heavy fire from across the river, demanding a battalion attack at each of the bridge sites. With unrealistic alacrity, these were to be launched at 10.30 a.m. The umpires were instructed that both battalion attacks would succeed, with 30 casualties at the southern site and 150 at the more strongly defended northern one. For every other engagement during the exercise the outcome and scale of casualties was predetermined in this way.[54]

Clearly, in exercise MARS the quality of the minor tactics used by the troops was not to affect the course of operations. The troops attacking the northern position could have conducted themselves impeccably against an incompetent enemy and still suffered heavily: the troops in the other attack could have paddled across the river as if on a picnic and still succeeded at small cost. In the case of MARS the umpires were required to act not as the imposers of tactical realism, the scourges of incompetence or the champions of excellence, but as the agents of the exercise director who wanted the schedule of events he had planned fulfilled. Thomas's chief interest was not in the tactical conduct of operations but in the 'stage management' work of the senior commanders involved. After the attack across the Stour the brigadier was to move up his reserve battalion to replace the more badly mauled of his two leading units, which could then recover in the relative calm of the reserve.[55] The arrangements for such a relief were no doubt something Thomas wished to see practised. By specifying exact numbers of casualties he could be sure of testing the casualty processing system, and the success of the two attacks across the Stour exercised the bridging engineers and the procedures for their deployment.

MARS was by no means a uniquely predetermined exercise. Thomas laid down casualty figures in advance for divisional exercise VULCAN, in December 1943.[56] In VULCAN, according to the general instructions, 'clashes with the enemy will be considered to be less important than the carrying out of the varying type of operations in the correct manner and using the proper drills'.[57] The 11th Armoured Division's exercise BRIDLINGTON in August 1943 consisted of two days of successive engagements between the armoured and infantry brigades, the outcomes of all of which were decided long before the first simulated shots were fired.[58]

Minor tactical realism was not the highest priority in one-sided and controlled-enemy exercises. The very need for the exercise director to conceive a schedule of specific operations to be practised militated against such realism. So such exercises tended to function as opportunities for the exercise of higher command, staff-work and administrative duties rather than the practice of actual front-line fighting. Yet none of the examples of unrealism and apparent bad umpiring mentioned above, from exercises BLACKCOCK, HAMMER II and Higgins' exercise in Devon, came from one-sided or controlled-enemy exercises. They were all two-sided exercises with each side allowed as much freedom of action as could be tolerated in a democratic, densely populated country. In fact, not even two-sided exercises could be completely devoted to tactical realism. The chief reason, one that applied equally to the more heavily stage-managed, one-sided and controlled-enemy exercises, was that every exercise was, and is, a work of contrivance with no operational existence outside the imagination of those running it and no existence at all outside the allotted period of time and spread of territory.

The process of contriving an exercise was not simple. Having decided the purpose of the exercise, the director needed to select and reconnoitre suitable ground. He had to brief the umpires and the commanders of any controlled troops. He had to plan the administrative arrangements. And he had to produce a great deal of paper notifying all concerned.[59] As an example, preparations for Guards Armoured Division exercise BLACKMORE of February 1943 were in hand before the end of 1942. Apart from the large preparatory investment of what would now be called 'management time', exercises also demanded the forbearance of parties other than those taking part. The Guards' commander needed clearance from neighbouring formations for incursions into their territory and asked for large vehicular movements to be kept off the roads.[60] Farmers in particular suffered the depredations of military training with damage to crops, fences and hedges not to mention the occasional loss by fire of hayricks and dry vegetation ignited by carelessly discarded cigarette ends, hot motor exhausts and stray incendiary projectiles.[61]

Having gone to great lengths to prepare an exercise, obtain the necessary clearances from other parties affected by it, and conscious of the probable costs in compensation to land-owners, exercise directors were understandably keen to ensure that their investment was not wasted by some unexpected feat of arms by one side or the other. The capture of the enemy brigadier and his staff by Lance-Corporal Higgins' patrol would in real battle have brought Higgins and his comrades high praise, perhaps even the odd decoration. In training it merely irritated the exercise director since it threatened to bring the scheme to a premature end through the decapitation of one side. In March 1941, V Corps exercise No. 5, directed by Montgomery, threatened to come to a premature conclusion as a result of an ingenious plan implemented by Major-General J.A.H. Gammell. The latter's 3rd Division with the Dorset coastal defence division under command formed one side in the exercise, 4th Division and the Hampshire coastal division the other. The exercise involved an attack by the Hampshire forces into Dorset. Gammell withdrew before the Hampshire advance, leaving behind a number of sabotage patrols. They executed a series of demolitions carefully designed to sever the Hampshire forward echelons from the reserves and supply services, rendering them vulnerable to the counterattack that Gammell planned to deliver. Gammell's plan was so successful that Montgomery ordered its premature termination. Had he not done so the Hampshire forces would have been at such a disadvantage that he would have had to call the whole exercise off early and forfeit all the valuable operational practice that the troops ultimately got.[62]

Without doubt similar reasons attended the umpires' decision in BLACK-COCK to deny the Irish Guards (VIII Corps) the fruits of their success in getting across the Derwent on 30 September 1943.[63] This threatened to prevent the enemy, who had been defeated in battle that day, withdrawing across the river destroying the bridges behind them and so presenting VIII Corps with an assault crossing and bridging problem to solve. The failure of the 1st Herefordshire Regiment (again VIII Corps) attack during exercise EAGLE, strung up on barbed wire 'installed' by the umpires,[64] was not the fault of partial umpiring but of the conception of the exercise. This was that VIII Corps had landed on the east coast and come up against strong inland defences mounted by the defending II Corps that required a setpiece attack by an infantry division, the success of which was to be followed through by the armoured divisions. They would engage the now disorganised enemy in a battle south and east of the Derwent. The enemy remnants would withdraw across that river which would serve as the basis of the next defensive line. No *coup de main* that threatened the orderly development of that conception could be permitted. Apart from anything else, the exercise was to take place mainly in the Yorkshire Wolds training area, which did not extend beyond the Derwent. It was out of the question for II Corps to be routed, flee and form a new defensive position a long way to the west.

Thus it is true to say that, to a great extent, the forces engaged in large-scale exercises simply performed to a script in the sense that a theatrical company does when it performs a play. That is not to deny the military value of such exercises. There is, after all, artistic value in producing, performing and watching Shakespeare even when the plot is well known to all. The War Diarist of 3rd Irish Guards commented upon exercise EAGLE thus:

> What further benefit there was to be derived from yet another scheme of such dimensions, after the Bn had endured two years training of a similar nature in this country, came from the experience of a prolonged period of existence 'in the field' without the usual amenities that are familiar in camp life . . . Like all large scale exercises it was of value primarily to the higher staffs and provided practice to lower formations along lines which have become conventionalised after a protracted period of home campaigning.[65]

The general opinion in 1st Oxfordshire and Buckinghamshire Light Infantry following interarmy exercise SPARTAN in March 1943 was that the exercise had 'limited tactical value' but proved valuable as a test of administration and the battalion's machinery of command. Indeed, after the earlier interarmy exercise BUMPER, the same battalion found that it 'badly needed time to rub up individual training and minor tactics which seem always to fall off during higher training'.[66] The reason for this was that individual and minor tactical skills were just not needed in large exercises.

A School of Infantry observer attached to another battalion during SPARTAN reported that 'the whole exercise was heavily umpired, and the final stages of battle [were] seldom played out'.[67] What did he mean by that? The May 1943 *Army Training Memorandum* complained that in many exercises mopping-up was given minimal attention in the attack plan. The mopping-up phase of a battle was the stage after a successful attack, when isolated enemy posts that survived the artillery bombardment and the passage of the assaulting troops needed to be eliminated. If not, they represented an enemy within and behind friendly lines, capable of causing confusion and panic, potentially disastrous to the success of operations.[68]

However, the mopping-up phase was very difficult to replicate in training. It was a type of activity for which heavy weapons were likely to be neither available nor appropriate. If the surviving enemy were determined to resist, eliminating them was most probably a job for platoon weapons in a miscellaneous collection of platoon or even section operations, many of them culminating in a hand-to-hand fight with grenade, bayonet and sub-machine-gun. Indeed, it was not just the mopping-up phase of an attack that demanded close-quarters combat, for enemy troops on an objective might well fight back against their attackers as they reached their objective. But, as the 1944 manual on umpiring recognised, hand-to-hand fighting in exercises was impossible to umpire and should therefore be avoided.[69] It requires little imagination to follow the War Office's reasoning here. Accurate snap-shooting and adroit bayonet work, the stuff of hand-to-hand combat, could not be practised against a live enemy. A skilled umpire might paint a realistic picture of the effects of fire delivered from a distance in accordance with a known fire-plan and impose a realistic scale of casualties. But the outcome of hand-to-hand combat was too dependent upon the skill-at-arms and reactions under stress of each individual concerned to judge with verisimilitude in a training environment where there were no bullets flying or bayonets thrusting.

At times close-quarters fighting clearly did occur during exercises. Private C.T. Framp of 70th Leicestershire Regiment recalled how his comrade in an outpost position during an aerodrome defence exercise in 1941 threw a sod (representing a Molotov cocktail) at a cyclist approaching from the enemy direction. It hit the man square on the mouth, knocking him off his mount. He turned out to be an umpire.[70] Corporal Dudley Anderson of 12th Devonshire Regiment recounted that during exercises against 'enemy' from other battalions, attacks would usually end in hand-to-hand fighting with bare fists – rifles and bayonets discarded for the duration. Moreover, the officers did not intervene 'until things showed signs of getting out of hand'.[71] Perhaps this was a peculiar feature of training in elite formations (12th Devons was an airlanding unit in 6th Airborne Division). In any case, adhering to the line clearly preferred by the more fastidious tastes in the War Office, before one exercise in May 1942 Montgomery ordered that although intercorps rivalry was generally a good thing 'there must be no hand to hand fighting, throwing of bricks or stones or anything of that sort'.[72] It is unlikely that he would have mentioned this had brawling not occurred in the past. Indeed, in one exercise in which British troops were pitched against French Canadians interallied hostility was such that lives were lost on both sides.[73] Presumably Montgomery decided that if anyone was going to get hurt on his exercises they would be hurt professionally with proper weapons. He had perhaps forgotten how useful unprofessional methods of combat had proved to him in October 1914 when, armed only with a sword that he did not know how to use, he took his first prisoner after incapacitating him with a kick to the stomach.[74] None the less, even if brawling took place during an exercise, without the use of proper weapons it could not replicate reality. So in practice the outcome of battles in training had to be assessed without reference to the potential culmination of every attack.

Not all battles culminated in hand-to-hand combat. The Germans were good at withdrawing front-line troops before fighting came to close quarters and then attempting to recover the ground lost by means of prompt counter-attack. British training literature claimed repeatedly that German troops generally fled or surrendered when faced with the bayonet.[75] None the less, close-quarters combat with the bayonet and fire-arms was not a rare occurrence during the Second World War. Brigadier G.P. Harding, commanding 138th Brigade in Italy, in an interview published by the War Office in June 1944, referred to numerous successful bayonet charges by his troops that inflicted many German casualties.[76] The then Lance-Corporal Anderson of 12th Devons, while lying wounded during an attack at Bréville in Normandy on 12 June 1944, saw one of his colleagues 'stab a German in the middle of his body, withdraw his bayonet and charge on just as if he was going round the assault course on Salisbury Plain'.[77] Yet, if close-quarters combat was ruled out of the umpires' deliberations in the arbitration of battle outcomes, what factors were they permitted to consider and what impact did this practical limitation in exercise umpiring have on tactical training?

War Office guidance to umpires stressed the balance of the weight of fire that each side could bring to bear at the decisive place and time as the crucial factor: 'to succeed against an alert and well organised defence, the attackers must be able to develop . . . fire of at least three times the intensity of that which the defenders can bring to bear against the attackers'. Unless the defenders surrendered or fled, they could be defeated only if their assailants generated enough fire to cover their movement to a position whence a close-quarters assault could be launched. As a principle of tactical doctrine this was perfectly sound. As a basis for umpiring actions during training it left much to be desired, for it allowed umpires to adjudicate by a process of arithmetical calculation rather than by tactical observation. Indeed, War Office guidance counselled opposing umpires to confer before the launch of an attack to compare the two sides' fire-plans and decide the probable outcome. This advice was tempered to some extent by a caution to avoid 'rigid prejudgement of the engagement' and to take into account the manner in which the respective plans were carried out. None the less, umpires were instructed that they 'should not allow an attack to succeed before the opposing fire plans have been weighed and the necessary three-to-one fire superiority has been established.'[78]

CONCLUSION

In large-scale exercises the outcome of the campaign or battle which the exercise was supposed to represent was usually predetermined. This was because each exercise took place within a perimeter established by timetabling, geographical and conceptual limitations. Exercise directors had good reasons for ensuring that the space defined by that perimeter was fully utilised and that none of the operations they wished to see practised were avoided. So it was not at all certain that the outcome of an engagement, as determined by the umpires, would reflect the comparative tactical performances of the two sides. Input and outcome could, and on occasion did, run quite contrary when umpires acted as executors of a directorial schedule rather than as independent arbitrators.

The assumption that sloppy performance would go unpunished and unremarked if it suited the exercise schedule to overlook it is perhaps wide of the mark. There was nothing to stop the umpires reporting accurately upon poor performance by troops under their supervision even if they could not impose the proper penalty for it actually during the exercise. An exercise whose primary purpose was not to test minor tactics could be used as an occasion for troops to practise their part in operations none the less. Unfortunately, evidence that would allow a definitive judgement as to the extent to which this opportunity was taken is not available. However, the remarks from the two infantry battalions cited above as to the tactical worthlessness of major exercises do rather suggest that it was not, and that regimental officers treated such exercises as occasions for resignedly going through the motions. Such attitudes evidently infected the other ranks: the official film of exercise SPARTAN included a number of sequences of clearly bored troops conducting themselves with minimum tactical propriety.[79] Corporal Higgins' great, if unrewarded, success in capturing the enemy brigadier during one exercise failed to give him any enthusiasm for exercises in general, which, he wrote, 'never ceased to bore and annoy us'.[80]

Even if the potential value of large-scale exercises for minor tactical training was exploited, the potential ultimate and decisive phase of the attack, the hand-to-hand struggle, could not realistically be practised in an exercise against a live enemy, and was discouraged. With hand-to-hand fighting ruled out and, if it did take place, quite unrealistic anyway, the adjudication of engagements came to rely heavily upon calculation of the balance of fire-power, with the three-to-one rule as a guide. With this rule the strands of tactical unreality that ran through wartime exercises can be twisted to form a strong twine of bogus verisimilitude. It was not that the three-to-one rule was wrong, nor the general premise that fire-power was the principal tactical key that could unlock an enemy defence and secure one's own. Far from it. 'You must win the fire fight' was the shrill cry of the training manuals.[81] Only if one could send enough bullets and bombs to the enemy to prevent him sending many back could one advance to close quarters. It is hard to disagree with that. The problem was that the crucial importance rightly accorded to fire-power acted with the predetermined time and event schedules in major exercises to produce an exclusive reliance upon the fire-power of those weapons whose action was readily amenable to centralised planning and control, the guns of the Royal Artillery. Artillery fire-plans needed to be worked out carefully in advance and were usually based upon an anticipated rate of progress by the troops leading the attack. For example, in 4th Lincolnshire Regiment exercise COUNTER in November 1943, a live-firing scheme in which a field regiment took part, a rate of 100 yards per two minutes was specified.[82] A similar rate of progress was allowed in 15th Division exercise CATTERICK, in which 6th Guards Tank Brigade co-operated with 46th Brigade.[83]

Although the Royal Artillery prided itself on seeking always to conform to the requirements of the troops whose action their guns were supporting and therefore sought to avoid imposing gunner demands upon assault arms' tactical plans, in practice the artillery fire-plan became the skeleton of the wider tactical plan. Assault arms could not depart from it without either coming under friendly fire if they advanced too quickly or losing the benefit of gunner support if they advanced too slowly. Of course every effort was made to build into artillery arrangements the facility to add bones to the tactical skeleton at short notice. Such facilities depended upon precarious communications between forward troops and the guns, generally positioned far behind the start-line, usually through the intermediary of an artillery forward observation officer either moving with the forward troops or established in an observation post that afforded a good view of their progress. Thus, if forward troops encountered unforeseen opposition they could expect additional artillery fire to help overcome it.

Exercises to practise the arrangements for this intimate form of interarm co-operation were not unusual. For example, HQ 43rd Division arranged for battalions to exercise with the divisional artillery during the latter's October 1943 practice camp. The scheme focused upon the battalion part as one of the two leading units in a brigade attack supported by the entire divisional artillery. During the action, resistance arose that the original fire-plan did not foresee. This tested first the company commanders and then the CO in improvising artillery fire with the affiliated field battery or regiment.[84]

Such practice was vitally important. It is no criticism of close attention to the finer points of interarm co-operation to point out that neither artillery covering fire nor the remote fire-support of other arms, such as medium machine-gun troops and aircraft, were battle-clinchers in themselves. Only against troops who had not dug themselves in could it be relied upon to inflict many casualties. Its main function was to neutralise rather than to kill. There came a point when the fire-support had to lift to allow the assaulting troops to close with the enemy. With artillery that point was generally one that allowed a gap of 200 yards between the shell impact area and the nearest friendly troops. This made for a close-quarters struggle over any piece of ground that the enemy chose to contest, which demanded minor tactical action by the assaulting infantry. This was well comprehended in official doctrine.[85]

As we have seen, hand-to-hand fighting was impossible to umpire and so its practice during exercises was discouraged, and mopping up (a variety of hand-to-hand combat) was generally neglected. The kind of action we are focusing upon now was not necessarily either of those things: it could be conducted at ranges far above those bridgeable by bayonet action, grenade-throwing or sub-machine-gun fire. It would start at about 200 yards range, or more if the attacking infantry had not kept as close as possible to the falling shells. It required the infantry to cross the remaining distance to the enemy positions covering their movement with fire from their own rifles and light machine-guns, until action with the really close-range weapons mentioned above was feasible.

Accounts of operations during exercises in unit War Diaries provide little evidence that this phase of the attack was actually practised. A telling admission in the War Office manual on umpiring suggests why. Advising that due credit should be given for a stubborn defence, the manual conceded that the unrealistic speed at which exercises had been expected to move had led to defensive obstinacy being disregarded.[86] An earlier admonition of umpires' tendency 'to wipe out at once a sub-unit surrounded', published by the War Office in September 1943,[87] permits one to reconstruct the pattern by which attacks were umpired. If the attacking side produced a fire-plan with the requisite fire-superiority, made the necessary administrative and technical preparations to implement that plan and made sure that the attacking troops crossed the start-line at the right moment in the right direction and at the right speed, then they would prevail. A spirited defence with small arms mounted when the covering fire lifted and the continued belligerent existence of small posts when the attackers reached their objective would be disallowed or otherwise discounted, because to permit the battle to be decided at such a level would involve a commitment of time that was not available in the exercise timetable and might also lead to an unhelpful outcome.

This does not mean that British troops were untrained in minor tactics. It does mean, however, that major exercises were not occasions on which minor tactics were practised. There is a general exception to that truth. Given that exercise attacks tended to be setpiece affairs, the acquisition and effective use of intelligence on the enemy's dispositions was given considerable attention. The processing and application of field intelligence lie outside the scope of this study, but one means of acquiring information, the small-group patrol, necessitated the utilisation of important minor-tactical skills. Extensive patrolling was a feature of most major exercises and represented perhaps the most valuable aspect of such exercises from the tactical point of view for the troops because it demanded that soldiers depend upon their fieldcraft skills to avoid detection and their own weapons to get out of trouble if the enemy did detect them. But main offensive efforts in training exercises made little call upon the ability of small units to achieve results using only their own weapons and their guile and cunning. As the War Office observed in calling for more attention to this kind of operation, the reason was that it was very difficult to umpire infiltration activity.[88] One might also observe that infiltration did not lend itself to the certainty of outcome and time-scale required if exercises were to run to schedule.

One cannot therefore look to 'full-sail' exercises for evidence that troops were well trained in the full range of their tactical duties in battle because such exercises did not provide opportunities for the application of minor tactics in large-scale operations. The reason for this lay principally in the strict limitations of time and space within which such exercises had to be conducted, supplemented by the arithmetical process by which umpires were encouraged to judge engagements.

4

Infantry and Battle Drill

As we have seen, 'full-sail' exercises did not usually rehearse the infantry in minor tactics. An infantry attack for exercise purposes generally included no replication of close-quarters fighting on and in the vicinity of the objective. Exercise directors and umpires instead simply assumed the successful prosecution of this crucial phase of the battle. That they could make such an assumption depended upon the troops having undergone a separate process of minor tactical training, which this chapter investigates.

We now know that, despite their reputation as donkeys leading lions, British general officers and their aides in the Great War learned many tactical lessons from the numerous disasters their troops suffered. During the Somme campaign the Royal Artillery began to perfect the creeping barrage technique which made a repetition of the campaign's first-day slaughter far less likely. Parallel improvements in infantry weapons, organisation and tactics allowed foot soldiers to profit once the gunners had placed them in the enemy's midst. Britain's 'citizen army' in the last year of the war was a far more effective body than it had been three years earlier.[1] The key to modern tactics was the principle of fire and movement. Where the enemy's fire made advance impossible, bringing fire to bear upon his positions forced his troops to take cover, thus neutralising them. Even if few were hit, while they sheltered they could not fire their own weapons, allowing the attacking troops to move. The creeping barrage allowed this combination of fire and movement, the fire in this case coming in great weight and at high trajectory from thousands of yards behind the front. The new infantry tactics allowed the same effect on a more local level using flat-trajectory small arms.

After the war, the new infantry methods were codified in the *Infantry Training* manual published in two volumes in 1921 and 1922. The allocation of the Lewis light machine-gun (LMG), the principal weaponry improvement of the war years, stabilised at two per platoon. The platoon comprised four sections, two of which each had one LMG. When under hostile fire, the platoon was to advance by section rushes or, if fire was particularly intense, by individual rushes. Enshrined in the doctrine was the fire-and-movement principle, whereby an element or elements of the platoon fired at the enemy in order to suppress his fire while the remainder moved. Because of their high-volume fire capability, the LMG sections counted as the chief source of covering fire within the infantry battalion.[2]

By 1939 the Lewis gun had been replaced by the lighter Bren. The platoon was now organised in three sections, each with one Bren gun. A new platoon weapon had been introduced, the two-inch mortar, which fired smoke and high explosive rounds to a range of 470 yards. Each platoon held one in platoon HQ. The latter also held one Boys 0.55-inch anti-tank rifle, introduced in 1937 and replaced from 1943 by the PIAT (acronym for Projector, Infantry, Anti-Tank), a spring-loaded, hollow-charge-bomb thrower. Platoon strength was 30 other ranks (increased to 36 in May 1940) commanded by a subaltern. Platoon HQ numbered seven, including commander and platoon sergeant. Each section numbered eight (increased to ten), including a corporal as commander and a lance-corporal as his deputy. Section commanders usually carried a sub-machine-gun. Two men per section served the Bren and the remainder carried rifles. There were three platoons per rifle company and four rifle companies per battalion. Additional weapons controlled at battalion level included two three-inch mortars and ten Bren gun carriers, increased to six and 13 respectively after Dunkirk.[3]

The new equipment boosted mobility, fire-power and sophistication in general. But it did not alter the principle of fire and movement, which remained fundamental to infantry minor tactics. Intra-infantry fire and movement ought to have put paid to the notion of a tactically helpless infantry such as met its Calvary on 1 July 1916. That it did not provides the theme for this and the following chapter. In this chapter we will first examine the rotten state of infantry training in the first two years of the war before exploring the extraordinary process by which the infantry retrieved both its tactical training and its morale from a pit of inertia and depression.

THE TRAINING PROBLEM, 1940–1942

Partly for reasons beyond the direct control of the Army, infantry tactical training in the 18 months or so following Dunkirk failed to reach uniformly satisfactory standards. The infantry bore the brunt of coastal and vulnerable-point defence duties, which made collective tactical training quite impossible for months at a time. Defence was at least a military duty. Many non-military tasks came the way of the infantry. Agricultural assistance was a particular bugbear: numerous training exercises were cancelled so that troops could help in the fields at harvest time. But the steady drip of extraneous demands on military labour for a variety of tasks was a persistent irritant to commanders.[4]

Since so much manpower had been taken out of the civilian workforce to man the armed services, demands for military assistance in civilian tasks were inevitable. Churchill promised to prevent needless disruption of training, and efforts were made to contain the problem by good organisation.[5] Despite these endeavours, however, a report on the state of training in Home Forces in the spring of 1942 counted agricultural and other civilian commitments among the reasons for backwardness in a number of formations.[6] It was not only the infantry who suffered. For example, units of 25th Tank Brigade spent their last period of home service before battle in Tunisia pulling beet in East Anglia.[7] It is a well-known trick of NCOs when calling for volunteers for some unusual chore to dress the task up with a bogus specialist interest. If the piano in the Officers' Mess needs to be moved, the call will go out for musicians. No doubt by a similar thought process, sapper units found themselves excavating road-side trenches. The Army chiefs saw this as a waste of the sappers' specialist skills in tasks best left to the unskilled rank and file of the infantry.[8] Because unskilled labour was the chief requirement in most civilian labour demands, the problem bore most heavily upon the infantry, and deliberately so.

Of course, unskilled labouring was no less a waste of specialist infantry skills. As Major-General J.E. Utterson-Kelso of 47th Division complained, the infantry was treated as 'the unskilled labour exchange for the rest of the Army [that] answers every call for temporary or permanent man power to the Army, Navy, the RAF, civilian tradesmen – even the NAAFI'. As he put it, many high-ranking officers regarded the infantry as 'the legitimate dumping ground for the lowest forms of military life'. Constant changes in personnel defeated the efforts of even the most vigorous COs to raise their troops to full fighting efficiency. The abrupt posting away of a fully trained NCO or officer could set back the training of a battalion by months simply because that individual was no longer available to spread his expertise to others. Such postings were a frequent occurrence and forced COs into what Utterson-Kelso described as a 'struggle for survival' that pushed 'the urgent need to prepare for the more altruistic object of national survival . . . into the background'.[9]

Utterson-Kelso, a highly experienced and decorated officer, held that the great reliance upon artillery fire-power in the First World War and startling successes of German airpower and armour in the first year of the Second had served to obscure the decisive importance of infantry fighting. Affecting to quote a German training manual, he asserted that 'Infantry is the principal arm. It bears the main weight of battle. It suffers the heaviest casualties. All other arms support it.'[10] His implication was that, in the autumn of 1941 when he was writing, this was not how things were seen in the British Army.

Aggravating the lowly status of the infantry in both the military and the popular consciousness was a poor sense of priorities within the arm itself. Michael Joseph, a company commander in 9th Royal West Kent Regiment, found that the Army concentrated upon producing soldiers with shiny boots and well-pressed uniforms instead of the trained fighting men that it really needed in time of war.[11] Ill-judged priorities did not go entirely unnoticed at the top, and in March 1942 the Army Council reduced the time spent on tactically unnecessary training by simplifying the specified close-order and arms drills. That this step required the consent of the king suggests that excessive devotion to ceremonial splendour was an ethological problem in the British Army.[12]

As for tactical training, the situation in the early years of the war was summarised by Brigadier H.A. Freeman-Attwood. Writing in April 1941, he maintained that since the end of the Great War the Army had practised every phase of the battle up to zero hour – that is the time the battle actually starts – but not beyond. What was now needed was to train in 'those practical details which will occur FROM ZERO ONWARDS'.[13] Of course Freeman-Attwood's experience was not necessarily general. Indeed, Major-General A.H.S. Adair included in his memoirs a self-congratulatory story of his advising a junior officer on minor tactics during an exercise by 3rd Grenadier Guards in Windsor Great Park in 1938. Clearly at least some units practised, and some officers were familiar with, minor tactics. But not all: the sting in the tail of Adair's anecdote was that his CO had not the faintest idea about tactics. He had been Equerry to the former Prince of Wales for nine years. In happier circumstances he might have expected to see out his career as a courtier. In any case, militarily he was quite out of touch.[14]

Even after the outbreak of war minor tactical training received a low priority. Gort's Chief of Staff in the BEF thought digging and wiring a better use of the soldier's time than the battle training that French generals insisted upon for their troops. The memories of those who served during this period are dominated by this back-breaking, soul-destroying physical labour, and the official records bear them out. Although some troops gained active experience patrolling in the Saar sector of the Maginot Line, the staple diet of the BEF soldier's duty hours was work on the Gort Line and most of what training there was dwelt in weapons skills rather than tactics.[15]

After Dunkirk, the British Army at home was preoccupied with defence, the deleterious impact of which on training has already been mentioned. None the less, reporting on the winter training of V Corps in February 1941, Montgomery pronounced himself satisfied that his command was ready for war in all respects.[16] His next command, XII Corps, proved less satisfactory to him. In August 1941, after four months in the job, he complained that his junior officers knew very little about minor tactics and fieldcraft: 'what little they do know is not very good'. This remark was aimed at COs. Shortly after taking over XII Corps, Montgomery demanded that unit commanders interest themselves personally in minor tactical training, which should be on up-to-date lines with all 'unimagination [sic] and soul destroying methods . . . cut out'.[17] Little had improved in the meantime.

No fewer than five official manuals offered guidance on minor tactical training. The standard infantry manual, *Infantry Training, Training and War* (published August 1937), despite its 250-page length confined itself to the exposition of broad tactical principles. In important respects it was out of date since the structure of the infantry platoon had changed soon after its publication. *Infantry Section Leading* (December 1938) likewise embraced little tactical detail. Not until *MTP* No. 33, *Training in Fieldcraft and Elementary Tactics* (March 1940) did any detailed guidance on the application of the broad tactical principles outlined in earlier publications appear in print. This imaginative and innovative manual, together with *Tactical Notes for Platoon Commanders* (published the following February) was to have far-reaching consequences in infantry minor tactical training, but it would be 1942 before they were realised. Meanwhile, *MTP* No. 37, *The Training of an Infantry Battalion* (June 1940), placed the ideas put about in *MTP* No. 33 in the context of an idealised programme for the training of infantry units.

In both a deliberate attack against strong defences and a quickly mounted attack on a weak enemy, the infantry's job was to get on to the enemy position and eliminate surviving defenders. In the deliberate attack the process of closing with the enemy can be caricatured as a gentle stroll behind the barrage. Only if the barrage failed in some way did minor tactics become necessary and in those circumstances the minor tactics to be used were no different from those applicable in an unsupported attack. *Infantry Training, Training and War* was out of date on the techniques to be used because when it was published the platoon's LMGs were concentrated in one section rather than distributed among all three. The principle, though, which survived the change in organisation, was that the platoon commander should organise one or more of his sections to neutralise the enemy with fire while the others advanced. In most types of ground this would demand a certain amount of dispersion of the platoon so that the section(s) producing the fire could acquire the target without shooting their colleagues in the back. The principle was fire and movement. Because of its rate of fire, the LMG was considered the most suitable weapon to provide covering fire, but the likely need for the LMGs themselves to move, and so require covering fire from other weapons, confounded any notion of fixed roles for the two types of weapon. But, unless fire-support from ex-platoon sources became available, the final assault of the enemy position was to be carried out by the rifle sections covered by the LMGs.[18]

The new organisation, which gave each section a Bren gun, did not alter the principle of fire and movement but made its application possible within the section. Whereas before a section could execute fire or movement (but not both simultaneously), with an organic LMG it had the fire-power to cover the movement of its riflemen. So *Infantry Section Leading* carried an emphasis, quite absent from *Infantry Training, Training and War*, on the section commander's responsibilities in organising the forward movement of his men in circumstances where extraneous fire-support was unavailable.[19] This small change in organisation thus had the highly significant effect of turning the corporal in charge of a section from a mere subordinate leader into a commander, with two tactical components to co-ordinate. What was in effect a delegation of tactical authority and responsibility to the section commander was part of a wider trend that was well understood in the War Office. In modern warfare, a short burst of machine-gun fire could wipe out ten men if they were bunched together. As *MTP* No. 33 put it, such conditions demanded the dispersion of even the smallest sub-units, and so required decision-making capacity in every individual. 'This calls for initiative, intelligence and military knowledge on the part of every private soldier.'[20] The helpless 'poor bloody infantryman' of popular perception was quite out of date, and seen to be so by those responsible for framing training policy.

MTP No. 33 outlined a number of schemes to exercise the section commander and his men in attack tactics. Although it was conceded that a section would only rarely carry out an attack on its own, the manual assumed that there would be instances in which the section commander would have to take independent decisions in order to further the objects of the platoon in a larger-scale attack. Two practice schemes for the section attack against isolated resistance were suggested. In each case the scenario was that the section was taking part in an artillery-supported attack with other troops attacking on the flanks. In the first, the section was to come under fire about 20 yards from cover. The section commander's task was to give quick orders for the occupation of available cover while ensuring that he kept his men under control, and then make a plan for further action. The scenario in the second scheme was similar except that the flanking sections were to be considered under fire while the section on exercise was, temporarily at least, free of enemy attention. The ground was to be fairly open, but isolated cover made an approach to the enemy's flank possible. It was for the section commander to organise the use of that cover by his riflemen, covered by Bren gun fire as necessary, to move to a position from which to deliver an assault. The manual also offered a suggested platoon attack scheme in which one section assaulted under cover of fire from the other two and from the two-inch mortar.[21]

These very bald summaries of parts of an infantry training manual cannot convey the full flavour of the operation of a section or platoon. They do show that the platoon was potentially a sophisticated tactical instrument. The platoon commander had to co-ordinate the actions of three types of weapon. The section commander had to organise two types of weapon, and even in the platoon attack might have to conduct a fire-and-movement operation if unexpected opposition materialised as he led his men to an assault position. No mention has been made of the fieldcraft skills required not just of the officers and NCOs but of every private soldier. *MTP* No. 33 explored a variety of techniques involving the use of ground, natural cover and camouflage and methods of teaching such techniques to the troops. The War Office recognised that most recruits were townsmen with little of the instinct in fieldcraft to be expected in men raised in the country and used to stalking wild animals.[22] In wartime, the influx of socially less well-connected officers, unversed in field sports, undoubtedly exacerbated the problem of lack of fieldcraft instinct.

In short, there was a great deal of detailed learning to be done by officers and men if they were to be proficient in minor tactics and fieldcraft. Moreover, there was no reason why the process of learning should not have been relatively interesting for all concerned. Tactical doctrine required soldiers who possessed not only the technical skills necessary to maintain and fire a rifle or execute the evolutions of close-order drill, but also the individual tactical judgement to use ground well. One of the training suggestions of *MTP* No. 33 was the individual stalk. In this exercise, the man would be set to stalk an enemy sentry group over a distance of 200–600 yards and find a position from which to get a certain shot. A critic was to tail him and an observer was to man the supposed enemy position watching for any exposures.[23] Here was an opportunity to engage each man's physical and intellectual faculties, to develop his cunning so as to make him a more useful soldier, to enable him to make an intelligent contribution to exercises at all levels. Yet by August 1941, in Montgomery's judgement, fieldcraft and minor tactical skill among junior officers in XII Corps was quite unsatisfactory. Elsewhere in the Army, Michael Joseph found training 'dull and uninspired'. Major John Vivian of the London Scottish recalled that such training as there was followed 1914–18 tactical lines, and in fact that training in tactical techniques barely touched his unit.[24]

The existence of a manual on fieldcraft and minor tactics, useful though it was, did not fully meet the Army's needs at this time. Such highly practical skills cannot readily be mastered by book-learning alone. Lieutenant H.T. Bone, who joined the Devonshire Regiment in the ranks in November 1939, mentioned no training in minor tactics or fieldcraft in his journal. Neither are such things prominent in other soldiers' accounts of their training in this early stage of the war. An exception is Harold Buckle's unpublished memoir which refers to intensive fieldcraft training at the depot of the King's Own Yorkshire Light Infantry in the summer of 1940: 'even strolling outside the barracks off duty, we automatically looked for natural cover, positions for Bren gunners and riflemen in the fields, along country lanes and in hedgerows'.[25]

Such training, which in Buckle's case enthused him to think professionally even while at leisure, was exceptional. There were simply too few officers and NCOs who really knew their business in that regard. This situation is explicable partly in the inadequacy of ex-regimental training. Apart from at the very beginning of the war, all entrants to the officer corps first went through the ranks. Potential officers were removed from their units and sent to an Officer Cadet Training Unit (OCTU) where infantry candidates remained for four months. As Lieutenant-General Sir Ronald Adam observed, the training they received there 'concentrated . . . on training the cadet to be the perfect private soldier'.[26] By this he undoubtedly meant that far too much time was devoted to drill and button-polishing, a complaint made in January 1941 by one recently commissioned officer and repeated by another in sardonic verse.[27]

Tactical matters were certainly not ignored in officer-training institutions. But, as we shall see, tactical instruction of leaders depended heavily on lectures and tactical exercises without troops (TEWTs). With no actual troops involved,

TEWTs lacked a great deal in realism. They were merely theoretical exercises in command. That is not to deny their value altogether, but a course that consisted mainly of lectures and TEWTs could not possibly produce officers with proven ability in the tactical handling of men. Nor could it produce officers fit to teach the detailed individual tactical skills their men would need if they were to perform satisfactorily in battle.[28]

Montgomery concluded that newly commissioned officers fresh from OCTU were of negligible value as trainers.[29] As an infantry brigade commander in the mid-1930s, Brooke found that subalterns newly commissioned from Sandhurst, where the course was about six times the length of a wartime OCTU course, were 'quite unfit to command a platoon'. They learned their trade 'under the very doubtful tutelage of a platoon sergeant'.[30] Which brings us to the NCOs.

It is worth relating the experience of Lieutenant Bone. He gained a stripe early in 1940. Soon afterwards he and five other lance-corporals in his company underwent a three-week cadre course. Bone found most of his colleagues on the cadre 'extremely ignorant and painfully slow of intellect'. Most of the work concerned weapon training. After the cadre Bone attended a two-week section-leading course at the Small Arms School, Hythe, which consisted of lectures and demonstrations on fieldcraft, infantry weapons, section-handling and the contents of the *Infantry Section Leading* manual.[31] He then returned to the Devonshire Regiment Infantry Training Centre in Exeter, where he acquired a second stripe and worked as:

> second instructor to a most incompetent Sgt. His speech was of the most illiterate and unilluminating, consisting mainly of a few garbled and stray facts forming the instruction and the never failing remark after every two or three sentences, that 'there was nothing in it'.[32]

As a depot instructor, Bone's work would have been confined to basic individual training, probably mainly in drill and weapons. So he did not have the opportunity to put into practice the passive and theoretical tactical training he had received at Hythe until he joined a battalion later in the year. But Bone was lucky to have attended the Hythe course. Plainly his somewhat uninspiring platoon sergeant had not been so privileged, and no evidence of section leaders attending a section-leading course at Hythe appears in other sources. The course probably fell victim to rationalisation brought on by shortage of instructors and perhaps the relocation of the School to Bisley in November 1940. Certainly by the spring of 1942, when the War Office undertook a major review of the activities of military schools of instruction, the Small Arms School ran no tactical courses.[33]

The lack of designated War Office institutions left the task of providing tactical instruction for junior officers and NCOs to the field army. Home Forces formations sponsored numerous schools. Montgomery, as GOC XII Corps, maintained that not until a platoon commander had attended the corps school would he be fit to train his men.[34] Most corps operated a school of one sort or another running a variety of courses covering many different activities and disciplines. For our purpose the most relevant was the Junior Leaders' Course. In V Corps in the spring of 1942 this was a four-week course for 50 training platoon commanders and their counterparts in the other arms in all their responsibilities.[35] This of course included much more than minor tactics and fieldcraft. A platoon commander also bore responsibility for the physical and moral well-being of his troops, and one can take it that the syllabus included substantial attention to administration, discipline and man-mastership. The XII Corps School in the same period ran a purely tactical course lasting two weeks and covering map-reading, patrolling, observation, verbal orders, preparation of exercises, field firing and tactics. This was quite an unusual course in that each intake included both subalterns and NCOs in equal measure. This feature was a recent innovation in XII Corps and seems to have been singular.[36] Quite what form the tactical instruction at the V and XII Corps Schools took is uncertain, but in IX Corps early in 1941 such training followed the familiar pattern of lectures and TEWTs.[37]

Individual battalions, brigades and divisions could supplement the corps schools by organising their own institutions. For example, 129th Brigade ran a platoon commanders' school which held two 14-day courses during July 1941.[38] Many divisions operated divisional tactical schools. Other than that they existed, little information is available on such institutions. One can only speculate, but it seems likely that, in most cases, the methods of instruction departed little from the theoretical lectures and TEWTs evident in tactical instruction organised at higher levels.

The skills that comprised minor tactics and fieldcraft are and were highly practical skills. Yet most of the instruction received by junior officers and NCOs in these disciplines was theoretical. Such a training was insufficient preparation for junior leaders whose task, after all, was to prepare their men for, and then lead them in, battle. They did not always treat such training as serious preparation for what they might actually do in action. Norman Craig, a subaltern in 2nd/5th Welch Regiment attended a junior leaders' course in April 1942, during which he took part in numerous outdoor TEWTs. Recollecting this, he wrote:

> Since there were no actual troops and – more important still – no live enemy, one always chose a dynamic solution to show the required spirit of well-bred aggressiveness. The secret was to make one's answer bristle with a fair sprinkling of popular military clichés such as 'have a look see', 'pooping orf' and 'sorting out the hun'.[39]

The captain of a cricket team has usually demonstrated competence in one or more specialisms of the game and also a certain leadership quality and tactical judgement. These qualify him to choose and prepare his team, helping individual players over any particular technical difficulties they may have. By contrast, a platoon commander fresh from OCTU, particularly in the early years of the war, had typically spent very little time in the ranks and so had had little chance to learn the job of any of the soldiers he commanded. To compensate for this deficiency he heard lectures, witnessed demonstrations and took part in TEWTs – which can be likened to setting the field, deciding the length of the bowler's run-in and perhaps actually carrying out the run-in, but all without a batsman and a ball. Likewise, lectures on batting, bowling and wicket-keeping technique and demonstrations thereof are no substitute for actually doing it. Just as it is hard to conceive a cricket captain convincingly coaching his team on the basis of such limited training, it is hard to imagine an officer or NCO confidently training his men in techniques he may have read about, heard about and even seen, but not actually done himself.

That was the problem. But it was hardly a new problem to the British Army. Indeed the wartime policy of recruiting all new officers from the ranks can be supposed to have been an improvement over the peacetime practice of direct commissioning. At least the wartime system ensured that new officers had some military experience other than their time in OCTU. But in 1941 the War Office was content that the bulk of an officer's tactical education should take place in his regiment after he had been commissioned. Lieutenant-General Sir Robert Haining, the VCIGS, dismissing arguments for any change in the OCTU syllabus, said as much in January of that year.[40] As has been shown, battalions were not well placed to cope with the task. Indeed, they were failing to deliver what was necessary.

THE RISE OF BATTLE DRILL

A solution to the problem was found in the form of battle drill. Its modern origins lay in 1918 when Lieutenant-General Sir Ivor Maxse, Haig's Inspector-General of Training, codified tactical drills for use in battle.[41] The then Lieutenant-Colonel Harold Alexander ran a battle drill school in the last few weeks of the war. In 1919, as commander of a German force fighting Soviet encroachment in Latvia, he established such a school for his NCOs. Despite the heights of rank to which he ascended, Alexander's friends felt that at heart he remained a subaltern. He continued to take a keen interest in minor tactics when he attained general rank.[42] Commanding I Corps after Dunkirk, he urged his divisional commanders to consider the use of tactical drills in training 'both to save time and to cater for the officer who lacks training and initiative'.[43] That autumn, I Corps Tactical Notes, a pamphlet of tactical guidance based on Alexander's own sketches, appeared under the corps imprint. Each of the minor tactical actions illustrated in the pamphlet was described as a battle drill. The drills were taught to subalterns at the Corps Platoon Commanders' School at Lincoln Barracks, and to junior NCOs at divisional section commanders' schools.[44]

The two-week course at the corps school was designed around *I Corps Tactical Notes*.[45] Instruction took the form of lectures, followed in each case by an exercise. The latter were practical, rather than theoretical TEWTs. According to Alexander's biographer, who attended the Lincoln school himself, the course was greatly enjoyed by the students, not least because liberal quantities of live ammunition and thunder-flashes were used in the exercises. Even so, it is not clear that Alexander's initiative had much impact upon training in the units of I Corps. In 1st Division, for example, although the divisional commander thoroughly approved of battle drill, one of his COs, Lieutenant-Colonel R. Bryans of 1st King's Shropshire Light Infantry, returned from a visit to the corps school on 7 November 1940, 'NOT very impressed with what he saw'. Only for two of the division's nine battalions does the War Diary suggest that the kind of training practised at the corps and divisional schools might have been carried to the troops.[46] The likelihood is that for many graduates their time at the corps or divisional school represented a pleasant interlude free of irksome regimental duties but which bore little relevance to what they did beforehand or afterwards with their men.

Quite why Bryans took exception to the corps school is not certain, but it is likely that beneath his attitude lay reasonable and widely held objections to the concept of tactical drills. These will be explored below. How widespread such feelings were among the officers of I Corps is not known. It is at least possible that Alexander's initiative aroused only a lukewarm response among senior regimental officers. It is noteworthy that Alexander, who generally preferred to proceed by consensus rather than by command,[47] seems not to have introduced the idea in Southern Command when promoted there in December 1940. But the I Corps schools continued to operate, and Alexander's battle drill sired a much bigger movement that began to gather pace in the summer of 1941.

The seat of this new movement was 47th Division stationed in Sussex and commanded from April 1941 by Utterson-Kelso. In his previous command, he had taken 131st Brigade to France as part of 44th Division, and back home again through Dunkirk. During those proceedings he saw a lot of Alexander, an acquaintance he no doubt renewed when 44th Division came under I Corps soon after Dunkirk. Utterson-Kelso must have been aware of battle drill as taught at the corps and divisional schools. He shared Alexander's keen interest in minor tactics. Within days of assuming command of 131st Brigade in November 1939 he issued training instructions that stressed the vital need to train section leaders in their tactical functions. Underlining his personal interest, he signed them himself, the usual practice being for the brigade-major to sign such documents. He went by the sobriquet of the best platoon commander in the British Army.[48]

Early in July 1941, Utterson-Kelso launched a divisional school of battle drill. Located on the site of a prewar holiday camp at Chelwood Gate, the school quickly proved highly successful. Lieutenant-General B.C.T. Paget,

GOC-in-C South-Eastern Command was so impressed by its work that when made C-in-C of Home Forces that December he ordered that such a school be established in every division. To train instructors Paget set up a central battle school, located at Barnard Castle in County Durham and directly under the control of GHQ Home Forces.[49] As Chief Instructor at Barnard Castle, Paget selected Major Lionel Wigram, the founding commandant of the Chelwood Gate school.

Wigram, a Territorial officer of the Royal Fusiliers, had become acquainted with the battle drill idea through his brother-in-law, Lieutenant John Jockelson, an instructor at the I Corps school in Lincoln. Indeed, he was an enthusiastic advocate for that style of training even before Utterson-Kelso's arrival in 47th Division. When Utterson-Kelso assumed command, Wigram was serving on the divisional staff as GSO3 for Civil Liaison and so enjoyed relatively free access to the general. It is likely that the conception of the school was a joint effort between Wigram and his chief. There is no doubt, however, that Wigram's vigour and conviction as commandant made the school what it was. His personal commitment to the battle school concept is illustrated by the fact that he not only compiled a battle school manual-cum-propaganda tract but also financed its publication himself.[50]

Paget's singular confidence in Wigram and his methods is evident in the staffing arrangements at Barnard Castle. At least five Chelwood Gate instructors followed Wigram northwards, as did Jockelson. Not every officer of Wigram's station would have been allowed to employ his brother-in-law. As Commandant, Paget chose the CO of Wigram's former battalion. Wigram himself, a mere captain in July 1941, was promoted lieutenant-colonel in May 1942. The ideas that earned this high endorsement were inspired by the I Corps school at Lincoln and *MTP* No. 33. Before opening at Chelwood Gate, Wigram took his band of instructors to visit the Lincoln school. He himself also visited various other schools.[51] His object was to copy the best of what everyone else was doing. In that sense he was no innovator: he simply sought to learn from other people's successes and to make use of training literature published by the War Office. But that in itself was probably innovatory.

The Chelwood Gate course took two weeks. After hearing opening lectures by Wigram and Utterson-Kelso, students spent two days in mostly practical work on observation and fieldcraft on similar lines to *MTP* No. 33. The remainder of the course consisted mainly of lectures, demonstrations and practical exercises. There were a number of TEWTs, dealing largely with defensive preparations, but most of the work was practical. Students learned painfully why the area near Chelwood Gate was known locally as the Isle of Thorns.[52] Instruction was based around Alexander's battle drills. By October 1941 an important refinement had been added to these. Presumably in an attempt to simplify the teaching and learning of minor tactics, a number of battle drills were written up into parade ground schemes. A flag would be erected to represent an enemy post and a section would practise a diagrammatic representation of the manœuvres used to overcome such a post. The ideal was to assault from the enemy's flank with the covering Bren fire coming from his rear, perpendicular to the path of the assault. The section would divide into two groups which would then manœuvre by bounds, groups alternately covering each other's movement by fire until the section was suitably placed for the Bren group to cover the riflemen's final assault. Movement would preferably be at the double; if not it would be by marching. When students would have been firing, had the operation been for real, they stood to attention. To represent their action upon coming under enemy fire they bellowed 'Down–Crawl–Observe–Fire'. When the section was appropriately positioned, the riflemen ran into the imaginary enemy post as if assaulting it, while the Bren group stood to attention to represent the covering fire they would give until the riflemen reached the objective. Drills for platoon flanking and pincer attacks, in which one section provided fire to cover an assault by the other two, were also taught. Parade ground battle drills for these were published in October 1942.[53]

Parade ground battle drill, which must have been an absolute hoot to watch, seems not to have occupied more than two or three hours of the two-week battle school programme current in October 1941. Most of the course was conducted in more realistic tactical conditions. Precisely why it was introduced is not certain. It was probably because it was found too difficult otherwise to convey the central tenets of infantry minor tactics, not so much to the officer and NCO students at Chelwood Gate but to their men back in their units. Chelwood Gate students were expected to return to their battalions and pass on what they had learned to their troops. They were the ultimate target of battle drill training. Parade ground battle drill amounted to a theoretical tactical training in a practical fashion. With that background there would be more grounds to hope that the less bright among the soldiery would understand minor tactics when practised in realistic ground with all its inseparable topographical obstacles to vision and understanding.

Battle drill and battle school rapidly proved their value in 47th Division. The monthly training summary compiled by the adjutant of 11th Royal Fusiliers for August 1941 commented:

> Considerable benefit has accrued to the Bn from the 47 (Lon) Div School of Battle Drill . . . All Pl Commanders + Sergts have so far attended. The result is an unbelievable increase in the standard of training of the 'man in the section', whose liveliness and ideas on tactics have been revolutionised.[54]

The 11th Royal Fusiliers had on 21 June completed a four-month spell on beach defences near Chichester. Immediately all rifle companies started a period of intensive fieldcraft and minor tactical training, for which platoon commanders had attended lectures and demonstrations organised by battalion HQ.[55] But it was battle drill rather than the lectures and demonstrations, the standard tools of officer instruction at this time, that wrought the great improvement seen in August. For this, the highly practical nature of the course at Chelwood Gate, in contrast to the theoretical character of other methods of instruction, can be credited.

The 47th Division did not keep its battle drill innovation to itself. By October 1941, having trained all the division's subalterns, sergeants and corporals, Chelwood Gate began to admit students from other formations. The Canadians were particularly enthusiastic beneficiaries of this policy, and the Calgary Highlanders set up their own school modelled on 47th Division's example.[56] One of the reasons the Canadians took so readily to battle drill was that the order of priorities at Chelwood Gate conformed more readily to the purpose for which they thought they had crossed the Atlantic: to fight. For example, at Chelwood Gate the soldier's gas-cape was discarded because experiment revealed it as an impediment to fighting efficiency. The garment was virtually impossible to furl correctly, causing endless frustration to good soldiers pulled up for scruffiness. For similar reasons of efficiency, the gasmask and bayonet were worn on the back of the man rather than in their regulation positions on the chest and at the side. And the only inspection demanded was rifle inspection. The Calgary Highlanders found themselves out of sympathy with the more stuffy habits of military life, a fact they put down to the thrusting atmosphere of the New World compared to the Old.[57] It is likely that most British citizen soldiers were equally impatient with the Regular Army's conservatism. Wigram's success in 47th Division, and later in the wider Army, was in large part a reflection of his practical approach to the problems faced in training and reaction against the mindless habitual conformity to petty regulations accepted by regular soldiers. It helped, of course, that the British Army of the Second World War was a citizen army.

Despite the success of the 47th Division School of Battle Drill and its methods, and despite the enthusiasm and improvement in military knowledge the school bred among the soldiery, the War Office took against the initiative. In April 1939 the War Office had denounced the tendency to adopt tactical drills for use in battle.[58] Two and a half years later, 12 days after General Dill, the CIGS, visited Chelwood Gate, the War Office again warned against 'tactical rules', which it condemned as a menace to initiative.[59] Battle drill dealt in standardised solutions to standardised tactical problems. It could hardly avoid the charge that it encouraged stereotyped thought. As has been shown, the War Office was alive to the need for every private soldier to enjoy a certain level of tactical expertise so that he could function usefully when beyond the control of an officer or NCO. Many felt that drill-like tactics and drill-like training could not deliver this, that they would sap the initiative of the officer and man and drain them of tactical flair.[60]

Plausible though the War Office's objections to battle drill were, they were not unanswerable. Alexander conceived battle drill as a means of helping the officer who lacked training and initiative. Rebutting the critics who sniped at him from the War Office and from the corps of regular officers, Wigram developed Alexander's theme. If a man had initiative he would use it, regardless of what he had been taught. Otherwise he did not have initiative. In that case, it was better that he be taught something specific, for he would certainly not work out solutions to tactical problems for himself. In the absence of any ideas of his own or alternative orders from above, if he simply carried out woodenly the drill he had learned he would not do too badly.[61]

The same argument answered the criticism that battle drill led to stereotyped tactics: better stereotyped tactics than no tactics at all. But both Alexander and Wigram after him rejected the notion that it was undesirable to teach stereotyped tactics. Alexander likened the teaching of battle drill to the instruction of budding sportsmen in the standard strokes of their game. Having mastered the standard strokes, the talented player would adapt them or perhaps ignore them altogether and play some completely unorthodox shot to cope with the situation that faced him.[62] That the cricket textbook did not bind Don Bradman was no reason to abolish it. Not all players enjoyed Bradman's flair, and in any case Bradman started with the textbook. It is important to stress though that battle drill was not seen as the last word in tactical doctrine. All the relevant manuals emphasised that battle drill was merely a guide to action, the first rung on the ladder to tactical expertise.[63]

The evidence suggests that most men did not command sufficient initiative and military knowledge to make useful battlefield decisions when beyond immediate contact with a commander. In such circumstances, one remedy was for platoon and section commanders to issue detailed orders at the outset of each minor action. Wigram suggested that attempts to do so were quite common. He complained at the ludicrous sanctity attached to orders, writing that any orders issued in battle by a junior leader were likely swiftly to become irrelevant when the tactical situation changed before they could be implemented. In consequence the troops would not know what to do and so would do nothing. Battle drill, by ordaining and disseminating to each man a common doctrine, was intended to preclude that problem.[64]

In its reaction against battle drill the War Office in fact acquiesced in the problem that Wigram complained of, that is tactically incompetent troops who required detailed orders if they were to do anything useful. The evidence for this lies, ironically, in the War Office's publication, as an official manual, of Alexander's battle drill pamphlet. When Alexander published the pamphlet for use within I Corps, in the autumn of 1940, he made clear in a foreword that its purpose was to provide tactical guidance for the private soldier. It was not necessary for the other ranks to read the book; it was simply necessary that their officers who had read it teach them the drills. The War Office published the pamphlet in February 1941 under the title *Tactical Notes for Platoon Commanders*. Alexander's foreword was omitted and there was no indication anywhere that the troops were to be acquainted with the pamphlet's contents in any systematic way, by a drill or any other means. Indeed, the term 'battle drill' did not actually appear.[65] In other words, the pamphlet was intended as a guide for platoon commanders around which to take tactical decisions which they would communicate to their men by means of detailed orders. The whole point of Alexander's work had been lost.

Wigram noticed this retreat in War Office thinking from the aim of a tactically intelligent soldiery.[66] He might also have noticed that *MTP* No. 33 actually recommended the use of parade ground tactical drills to acquaint section commanders and their men with the fundamental principles before practising them on the ground.[67] Everything that Wigram did at 47th Division School of Battle Drill could be justified by reference to the example of Alexander, hardly a nobody in the military world, or to the recommendations of official publications the War Office might have preferred to forget.

Battle school teaching combined three elements: battle drill; vigorous, practical, physical action by all the students; and live fire. The battle drills, as has been shown, merely codified existing tactical doctrine. In that sense they opened doctrine up, rendering it intellectually easily digestible. It was far easier for a militarily inexperienced individual to understand what was meant by the term 'fire and movement' when it was shown in print and practised diagrammatically on the parade ground. But battle drill delivered more than an aid to understanding for the perhaps small minority of particularly backward officers and the majority of uncomprehending other ranks. Once everyone fully understood the theory, then they required only a minimum of instruction as to the application of that theory in specific real tactical situations. As has been shown, for all its rhetoric about the intelligent private soldier, the War Office preferred that every minor action be carefully planned by the officer responsible and orders issued to suit. Officers trained at battle schools found the battle drill alternative liberating. Denis Forman, who attended one of the early courses at Barnard Castle in 1942, describes a preposterous performance he staged for the delighted benefit of the umpires during an exercise in Scotland in 1941. Preparing to lead his platoon in an attack he delivered his orders in a prerehearsed crisp oration following the mantra 'Information – Intention – Method – Administration – Informative Any Questions', up to the 'Any Questions' when two intelligent prearranged questions were asked. None of this survived at battle school, where a rapid call of 'right flanking', 'pincers' or 'stay and cover' sufficed.[68]

Forman was a young man not long out of Cambridge University. He had seen what in wartime must have been morally the most repugnant side of military life: ten changes of uniform a day in the regimental depot of the Argyll and Sutherland Highlanders, and in his first battalion a second-in-command who became incontinently drunk on pink gin each evening.[69] Well might he welcome a less formal and more realistic approach to soldiering. But it was not only young Turks like Forman who welcomed the battle drill methods. Major J.G.E. Hickson, a regular officer of nearly 20 years' experience, reported much the same advantages for battle drill after attending a divisional battle school:

True, it is a flexible drill which can be altered to suit circumstances, but the orders required are stereotyped, and such that not only NCOs, but the private soldier can understand at once, so that he knows from the start what he is doing, which he rarely did before. Verbal orders are reduced to a minimum; within five minutes of sighting the enemy a platoon is off, like a pack of long dogs.[70]

Both Hickson and Forman were struck by the heavy physical demands of their battle school courses. Hickson dwelt at length on the training in methods of crawling – a vital skill if a soldier was to take advantage of minimal cover and keep his weapon free of mud and debris and so fit for action. Methods of crossing concertina barbed wire fences were also taught. One man threw himself face down over the wire forming a bridge for his colleagues to cross. Apparently, if done properly, this was not quite as uncomfortable for the 'bridge man' as it sounds. Students were shown that the best way to get through a hedge was simply to charge at it, relying upon kinetic energy to break through, a method that resulted in fewer painful cuts and scratches than any more cautious approach. Alan Wallace, a medical student destined for the RAMC, attended 3rd Division's battle school at Leighton Buzzard in mid-1942 while serving in the Home Guard. Even he, a fit young rugby player, found himself almost permanently drenched in sweat during the course. Forman described it as an 'attack on our bodies'. Wigram, the source of all this punishment, had been a solicitor and property developer before the war, with pastimes no more athletic than golf and the Savoy opera. Yet he was reputed to be the fittest man at Barnard Castle. If he could do it, he reasoned, then so could others. He was quite prepared to send any officer who objected to the violent physical activity, all of it carried out with each student carrying his share of the platoon weaponry, back to his unit.[71]

Live firing, the third element in the battle school formula, was part of an effort to inoculate the students against the sensations they would encounter in battle. Paget accepted that there would be casualties, and undertook to bear responsibility provided reasonable safety precautions had been observed.[72] He laid down safety rules for two types of live firing training: battle inoculation in which instructional staff fired live, to simulate fire by defending troops against students practising the attack; and field firing, in which the students themselves fired live ammunition.[73] There were casualties. Specific evidence is available of three fatalities at Barnard Castle. Divisional schools and field firing on the battle school model in units accounted for more. Non-fatal injuries, some of them from sheer physical strain rather than from stray shot and shell, added to the toll.[74] None of this was the battle school movement's innovation. Major-General J.A.H. Gammell, GOC 3rd Division, ordered a general weakening of the safety-first mentality in July 1940, promising to accept responsibility for casualties where reasonable precautions had been taken.[75] It is unlikely that he was unique in this, but that most senior commanders were so bold must be doubted in view of Paget's decision in 1942 to throw his weight as Commander-in-Chief behind efforts to loosen safety restrictions.

The dangers of extensive live firing compounded concerns over the wisdom of battle drill harboured by the War Office.[76] Apart from anything else, prescribed safety precautions were not always properly observed. But there was a further element in the battle school formula that caused very great unease. This was the hate training, practised at Chelwood Gate and Barnard Castle and at divisional battle schools. Hate training was an attempt to whip up among students an extreme hatred of the enemy. Quite whose brainchild it was is not clear, but Wigram, who was Jewish and thus had good reason for his apparently unusual degree of Germanophobia, undoubtedly favoured and promoted it.[77] Major A.E. Marshall, attending a Barnard Castle course in the spring of 1942, described a platoon attack exercise with live defending fire in which the urgings of the instructors were interspersed with cries of 'Kill! Kill! Kill!', 'The filthy Hun in England's green and pleasant land', and 'Hate! Hate! Hate!'[78] Such practices could become comical. The Times correspondent reporting on Chelwood Gate in November 1941 described a 'burly subaltern of the London Irish [almost certainly an instructor] who, his shirt torn to ribbons and brandishing a fighting knife at the heels of the pack, conducted a private hate campaign. "Hate! Hate!" he yelled – once in the face of two solitary cows.' The report continued: 'there was no doubting from their curses that the students' blood was up'[79] – the very purpose of the hate training. Further to inspire hatred of the Germans, students were shown photographs of German atrocities and heard special lectures on the subject. Closely connected to this was a variant of battle-inoculation training that endeavoured to acquaint students with the gore of the battlefield, for example by splattering them with ovine blood at the appropriate moments in bayonet training.[80] Students were also taken on trips out to local abattoirs. Lieutenant-Colonel T.F. Main, a psychiatrist attached to the GHQ Battle School, opposed such methods. Incidents of vomiting and fainting among students induced Barnard Castle to drop it in March 1942. But it continued at divisional battle schools. Blood and hate methods attracted considerable criticism from senior commanders, such as Montgomery and Lieutenant-General C.W. Allfrey, GOC V Corps, both of whom condemned it as un-British, and from politicians and clergymen. In May 1942 Paget ordered an end to it.[81]

It is easy now to mock blood and hate training. One commentator has dubbed it juvenile and ridiculous.[82] But blood and hate surely sprang from the fear that troops were being given no real preparation for the horrors of the battlefield. It was a citizen soldier initiative. Most citizen soldiers had not been in battle and could be forgiven for wondering how they would cope when they were. In the Great War, the static nature of the Western Front made it possible to acclimatise troops gradually to front-line conditions. In this war the entry into battle would be more sudden and the psychological shock greater. Such was the thinking behind blood and hate, and the live firing variety of battle inoculation too.[83] Many of the regular critics had been in battle, the older ones in the Great War and some of the younger ones in minor skirmishes in the course of colonial policing duties. They knew from personal experience what battle was like and they knew that they personally could handle it. Montgomery maintained that men resisted 'the wear and tear, and the buffeting of war, just in proportion to their character and will-power, and it is these qualities we must seek to develop'.[84] Needless to say, not everybody agreed with Montgomery. In August 1940, the War Office praised bayonet training at the Small Arms School for its '"blood, hate, fire and brimstone". It is "guts and gristle" instruction, with nothing peacetime or "pansy" about it.'[85] Whether the Small Arms School succumbed to pressure from fastidious critics such as Montgomery is not known, but one historian of the Normandy campaign has suggested that the aggressiveness of the British soldier might have benefited had 'the chaplains and bishops' been ignored.[86]

Not all COs and brigadiers at first welcomed the battle schools. Many felt that there were already too many courses which, by taking officers and NCOs away from their men, interfered with training. The 52nd Division had introduced a scheme whereby individual battalions were by turns isolated from all other calls on their manpower and allowed to get on with their training. Paget's demand for divisional battle schools forced its abandonment.[87] Both Alexander's Southern Command and Montgomery's South-Eastern Command initially proposed to train only NCOs at the divisional battle schools, sending subalterns to the Corps Platoon Commanders' schools. This scheme, probably the result more of convenience-driven inertia than insubordination, threatened to undermine Paget's intention for the divisional battle schools. The Commander-in-Chief wanted both officers and NCOs trained side-by-side, to the same syllabus, under the supervision of the divisional commander. Given that subalterns and NCOs would have to co-operate in the closest fashion in battle, and that corporals and especially sergeants were highly likely to find themselves temporarily in command of their platoon if the officer fell, Paget's wishes seem the merest common sense. It is a mark of the British Army's temperamental inability to treat realistically the subject of battle training that Paget felt obliged to issue specific orders to Montgomery, which he copied to all other Army commanders for good measure.[88]

Despite the physical rigours and dangers involved, the training techniques inspired by battle schools were widely welcomed by infantrymen. The first report of the War Office morale committee, presented to the Army Council in June 1942, noted that particularly strenuous training was appreciated by the men and reported wide agreement that the introduction of battle drill and field firing exercises had 'greatly improved morale'.[89] It was a message repeated in subsequent morale reports. For example, in December 1942 the committee reported that 'Hard training, battle drill, field firing, etc., continue to have the strongest possible effect in raising the men's confidence in themselves and stimulating morale generally.'[90] A 1944 tract on the British Army's progress in transforming itself from its contemptible prewar snobbishness and inefficiency into a 'People's Army' singled out battle schools as an example of the remarkable improvements in training since 1939.[91] Wallace went into the battle school sure in the knowledge that he could handle death and destruction around him (he had endured the blitz and was in any case used to corpses, being a medical student). He left it 'confident to dish it out as well'.[92] Senior commanders welcomed the great improvement in minor tactics and fieldcraft wrought by battle drill,[93] although some entered the caveat that it needed to be applied with discretion – a point to which we will return in Chapter 5. Montgomery relished the high standards of physical fitness demanded by the battle schools, delighting in the fact that many students found that they had to give up smoking and drinking in order to keep up.[94] In June 1942 Utterson-Kelso, recently installed as Paget's infantry adviser at GHQ, congratulated battle school commandants on their excellent work which was having 'a marked and most beneficial effect on the Infantry'.[95]

THE TRIUMPH OF BATTLE DRILL

The success of the battle school movement did not pass unnoticed in the War Office. That institution underwent a change of management at the end of 1941 with the dismissal of Dill and the advent of Brooke as CIGS. Brooke admired Paget, indeed it was at Brooke's recommendation that Paget succeeded him as Commander-in-Chief. And Brooke viewed the work of the battle schools with favour.[96] Three months after Brooke's arrival at the War Office, Major-General J.A.C. Whitaker succeeded Major-General J.L.I. Hawkesworth as Director of Military Training (DMT). Quite how much impact these changes had on the War Office's attitude is impossible to tell. Wigram was certainly not sorry to see Hawkesworth go, describing the general as his 'principal stumbling block'.[97] But the War Office remained suspicious of battle schools until at least the middle of 1942. By October, however, the atmosphere had changed completely. In that month the War Office issued a warm endorsement of battle drill,[98] a move apparently prefigured in July by the establishment under War Office auspices of the School of Infantry at Barnard Castle, which absorbed the GHQ Battle School.

Whitaker's appointment as DMT was followed swiftly by a revived interest in infantry matters by his directorate. *Infantry Training, Training and War*, published in 1937 and intended only as a provisional handbook, was still the current training manual, even though it was out of date in such basic matters as platoon organisation. The task of rewriting it fell to Major (later Brigadier) James Brind, a regular officer of the Somerset Light Infantry, who was summoned to the War Office in late April 1942. Previously unaware of the battle school movement, Brind had no experience of battle drill but was given to understand that these new phenomena did not carry full War Office blessing.

His orders were to reconcile battle school teaching with the officially approved doctrine, somehow eliminating the worst rigidities of battle drill.[99]

Within six months the War Office performed its volte-face on battle drill. The manual Brind prepared, *Infantry Training*, Part VIII, *Fieldcraft, Battle Drill, Section and Platoon Tactics*, published on 4 March 1944, drew heavily upon the Home Forces manual, *The Instructors' Handbook on Fieldcraft and Battle Drill*, prepared by Wigram and his colleague Major R.M.T. Kerr, published in October 1942. The inclusion of two parade ground battle drills[100] set the seal upon the War Office's acceptance of the training technique pioneered in 47th Division's School of Battle Drill two and a half years earlier.

It is impossible to tell with certainty why the War Office changed its mind. Lieutenant-Colonel J.W. Gibb, the official historian of British military training in the Second World War, cited battle drill as an example of the War Office's orderly procedure for evaluating new ideas and methods reported by field formations: '[Battle drill] went through its trials, proved itself and was accepted officially. The school at Barnard Castle was then transformed into a badly needed School of Infantry.'[101] Such contemporary evidence as is available, not least the fact that the establishment of the School of Infantry preceded the promulgation of the War Office's approval of battle drill by some three months, does not support Gibb's version of events.

The School of Infantry opened in July 1942 with Brigadier T.N.F. Wilson as commandant and Colonel James Mardall as his assistant. The GHQ battle school, of which Mardall had been commandant, became a wing of the new school with Wigram as its Chief Instructor. But this was not what had initially been proposed, unanimously, by an *ad hoc* committee of War Office and Home Forces representatives chaired by Whitaker. The committee recommended that a School of Infantry be established at Devizes, and that it should confine itself to the training of actual and potential company commanders. Barnard Castle was to remain at the apex of the divisional battle school system, concentrating on the training of section and platoon commanders.[102] This division of effort was no more sensible than the vetoed plans to segregate platoon commanders from their NCOs in extra-regimental training. When Brind was briefed for his manual-writing task in late April, the Directorate of Military Training still frowned upon battle drill and was unhappy at the methods of the battle schools. The committee sat on 4 May 1942 and it is unlikely that any shift in policy had taken place in the intervening few days. It can therefore be inferred that the DMT did not really want to assume responsibility for Barnard Castle. As for Home Forces, when Brind first visited Barnard Castle in May 1942, he formed the impression that the staff there rather resented what they assumed to be interference from the War Office.[103] Utterson-Kelso, who represented Paget on the committee, remained very close to the battle school movement. It can be supposed that he was content with Whitaker's reserve on the battle school issue.

Brooke overthrew this emerging *modus vivendi*. Because of his dissatisfaction with infantry training, he himself had proposed the establishment of a School of Infantry during his time as DMT in 1936–37, – a scheme blocked by the CIGS, Deverell.[104] He saw that the scheme now proposed was really no more than a central company commanders' school, and felt that any infantry school should have a much wider remit. The consequent incorporation of the GHQ battle school into the new School of Infantry was apparently negotiated by Whitaker and Paget on some occasion between 2 and 9 June 1942. It did not signify any conversion to battle drill methods on Whitaker's part.[105] Brigadier Wilson adopted a distinctly hostile attitude to Wigram and his work when he took up the post of Commandant in July, no doubt influenced by his Whitehall briefing. But his attitude changed dramatically after only a few weeks in the job.[106] Had he wished, he could quite easily have got rid of Wigram when the latter accidentally shot his new chief with a Verey pistol in August 1942. Wilson was not badly hurt. The flare caught the end of fingers. He had to spend some time in hospital but soon returned to duty. Much to the surprise of Brind, by then on the staff of the school, and other regular officers who witnessed the incident, Wigram suffered no disciplinary consequences, a sure indication of the esteem in which Wilson held his work.[107] Indeed Wilson spoke warmly of battle drill when he addressed the Royal United Service Institution in November 1943.[108]

There is no evidence of any formal proving trials preceding the War Office's change of mind on battle drill. It is difficult to envisage how such trials could have been conducted, because battle drill was simply a method of teaching tactics that had, theoretically at least, long been a part of the British Army's repertoire. What was obvious, so much so that no trial was needed to demonstrate it, was the effect battle school methods had upon the efficiency, confidence and morale of the infantry. Battle drill was an intrinsic feature of battle school training. It was part of the process by which those beneficial effects were achieved. The most likely explanation of the DMT's change of policy was that those beneficial effects could not be ignored. Nor could they be explained other than by reference to Barnard Castle techniques. The hostile attitude with which Wilson took up his duties at Barnard Castle probably represented a last effort by the War Office to suppress the battle school fever. Wilson's conversion announced that effort's failure, leaving the War Office little option but to acquiesce.

CONCLUSION

The British Army at home in 1941 was full of young men who knew that they faced a difficult and dangerous task in defeating the German Army and feared that they were not being properly prepared for it. Wigram, highly intelligent, vigorous, determined and entrepreneurial, with the patronage of a small number of senior commanders filled this gap in the market, the size of which can be gauged by the enormous success the battle schools enjoyed in 1942. The morale factor features largely in their good fortune. Army morale is often stated to have reached its nadir in 1942 and the Morale Committee found that hard, realistic training actually improved morale, noting in its September 1942 report that the new type of battle training had come 'just at the right moment'.[109] But it was not only a question of morale. Before the battle school movement got underway training in the British infantry was inadequate. Paget confided as much at a meeting of the Army Council in August 1942, and set great store by battle schools as the means of improving things. Colonel I.M. Stewart, one of very few distinguished veterans of the Malayan campaign, became Assistant Commandant of the School of Infantry in October 1942. His testimony to the official historians as to the Malayan garrison's training before the Japanese attack pulled no punches. He told Wigram a similar story, 'and in an address he gave to our students he simply pulverised the old regular army and all it stood for. He fairly dished it out'.[110]

There was less enthusiasm for admitting to such things in public. A BBC writer working on a proposed radio broadcast about battle schools found his script peremptorily vetoed by Wilson on the grounds that it gave the impression 'that the Army was no damned good before the war, and that it was only when some enthusiastic young upstarts got hold of the idea of Battle Drill that things began to get better'.[111] Whether this was a false impression or not is beside the point. The Army of 1941 was a different creature from that of 1939. It was vastly bigger for one thing, and manned mainly by civilians pressed into khaki, many of whom had little enthusiasm for things military and possibly little natural aptitude either. Battle schools helped greatly in the process of turning such men into fighting soldiers. In doing so they raised the British Army's game enormously.

5

The Failure of Infantry

As a result of the battle school movement, the British Army at home was better trained for war at the end of 1942 than it had been 12 months earlier. Nevertheless, questions do remain over the movement's achievements. According to the story as it has been narrated so far, the regular Army in general and the War Office in particular showed itself to be backward and reactionary in failing to embrace battle drill with enthusiasm. Fear of stereotyped tactics prompted their suspicion and conditioned the negative official reactions to the battle schools in which battle drill was taught. As has been shown, such objections were idle in 1941. At that time, progress towards the creation of an army composed of professionally skilled officers and men was so poor that any method that raised the troops to minimum levels of tactical skill should have been welcomed. But, as those responsible for its introduction acknowledged, battle drill represented only the minimum levels of tactical skill. Given that battle drill was a success in its particular context, did the British Army in training at home succeed in transcending battle drill by the time the bulk of it went into battle in Normandy?

Noting sharp differences of opinion among veterans of the Second World War, English, whose study of the Canadian Army contains the only scholarly treatment of the subject to have appeared to date, concludes that battle drill 'may have been a pedagogical dead end'.[1] Gudmundsson, revising English's *On Infantry*, steers the subject into something of a dead end himself. Arguing that British training methods in general and battle drill in particular, were 'mindless', he adduces the German General Bayerlein's verdict on the 'rigidly methodical technique' of the British higher commanders in North Africa in the winter of 1941–42, which apparently left no scope for the initiative of junior commanders.[2] Seemingly unaware that battle drill did not feature in the training programmes of the British Army at large until the spring of 1942, Gudmundsson confuses the habits of generals with those of subalterns and field officers. Of value only at sub-unit level, battle drill minimised the need for and discouraged the issue of highly detailed orders.

Although careful attention to his sources reveals the shallowness of Gudmundsson's analysis, his problem perhaps owes as much to poor advocacy as to an intrinsically bad case. Reports on battle experience that specifically mentioned battle drill were generally favourable. An article in *Notes from Theatres of War* on the destruction of a German coastal battery by commandos during the Dieppe raid observed that the fire-and-movement tactics used in the attack were precisely those taught at the School of Infantry.[3] In the Burmese jungle, battle drill helped junior leaders to retain control of their men even when unable to see them.[4] In the Tunisian campaign, according to a report endorsed by Alexander, battle drill paid a 'handsome dividend',[5] and an unidentified CO in 21 Army Group told his officers in October 1944 that 'Battle drill has proved itself.'[6] Yet all three latter reports cautioned against thoughtless appliance of battle drill. The War Office summarised the situation thus:

> It is important . . . that junior leaders should not regard battle drill as a universal panacea to be applied *in toto* in every situation. Battle drill teaching aims at teaching the 'basic strokes', and thus represents only the first rung in the ladder. The drills must be intelligently applied in accordance with the nature of the ground and the particular tactical situation. There were many occasions when unnecessary casualties resulted from poor leadership because junior officers followed a set drill and failed to apply it with common sense.[7]

Such reports cannot be ignored. Had such instances been isolated ones it is hardly likely that senior officers would have wasted their time and ink with such warnings. The process by which the glowing prospectus of battle drill, outlined in Chapter 4, was translated into lacklustre battlefield performance deserves close attention.

It was not a problem that became apparent only in battle. Montgomery and Allfrey, both of whom welcomed the introduction of battle drill in 1942, none the less cautioned against its unthinking application – a sure sign that, to adapt Montgomery's own injunction, battle drill too frequently served as tactical master rather than in its proper capacity of servant.[8] Some idea of what they meant can be gleaned from notes issued by Lieutenant-Colonel N.C.E. Kenrick, CO of 5th Wiltshire Regiment, in May 1943. Commenting on a recent training exercise, he noted that a direct frontal assault on one of the objectives would, for reasons of speed and reduced conspicuousness, have been far preferable to the flanking attacks platoons had carried out. The procedure for the platoon flanking attack must have been deeply engraved on the minds of junior leaders and their men because it was taught as a parade ground drill. The platoons of 5th Wiltshires appear to have been guilty of applying a well-known drill without first assessing its suitability to the circumstances.[9]

But other criticisms Kenrick made show that the problem in his battalion was more profound than that. He complained that too few leaders, from section commander upwards, made proper use of supporting fire, that sub-units advanced without covering fire, that platoons generally made too little use of fire, that only one platoon took full advantage of its two-inch mortar fire.[10] Compare such complaints with one of the principles for section and platoon tactics set out in the Home Forces battle drill manual:

> No advance is possible in modern war unless the enemy's heads are kept down by weight of metal – COVERING FIRE is essential to any advance. You must gain fire superiority so that the actual assault can be looked upon more as a mopping up operation than as an end in itself.[11]

So central was the principle of fire and movement to battle drill, and to autho-rised infantry doctrine before battle drill, that it defies credibility that, after nearly four years of wartime training, the officers and NCOs of 5th Wiltshires did not understand it. Kenrick's summary complaint was that 'there is too much of the letter and not enough of the spirit of battle drill',[12] implying that the problem was not so much lack of understanding as lack of fluency in action. Mastering the principles of section and platoon tactics by book-learning and parade ground practice was easy enough. Mastering the many minor details by which the principles could be translated into integrated battlefield tactics was not. Lieutenant-Colonel W.S.C. Curtis, commanding 4th Somerset Light Infantry, commenting upon his battalion's showing in field firing exercises in April 1942, referred to failings in weapons-siting and ammunition supply for section Bren guns. He also criticised his troops' un-satisfactory cohesion amid the confusion of the exercise caused by such realistic factors as uncertainty as to the enemy's whereabouts.[13] A training film produced by the School of Infantry in 1942 illustrated clearly the wide disper-sion of sections in the execution of a platoon flanking attack.[14] Since the platoon commander had no means of real-time telecommunication with his section commanders apart from prearranged flare signals and the like, the understanding between the two levels of command had to be of the closest intimacy, and the technical efficiency with which tactical manœuvre was carried out had to be of the highest to avoid hiccups. By providing a common framework around which all could base their own actions, battle drill sought to ensure that all were thinking along the same tactical lines; but thorough theoretical knowledge of battle drill was no substitute for extensive training in its practical application.

To judge from Kenrick's comments on his unit's showing in May 1943, 5th Wiltshires did too little of such training, or what they did was of inadequate quality, or both. The greatest value in training was to be gained when comp-letion of each scheme was followed swiftly by an independent objective assess-ment of what had gone well and what needed to be improved. As discussed earlier, large-scale, formally umpired exercises were not occasions for intensive attention to minor tactics. Minor tactical training fell most into the province of subalterns, captains and majors and was carried out, one assumes, on the innumerable days for which War Diaries recorded 'training under company arrangements' or something similar. Evidence as to what actually took place on those days is negligible. A set of company training programmes for 1st Motor Grenadier Guards in February and March 1942 show, typically, two to three days spent in tactical training exercises and related classroom work per five-and-a-half-day working week. Weapons training absorbed a good deal of the remaining working time. A variety of maintenance work, PT and sports, and current affairs training also featured. (In keeping with Brigade of Guards traditions, troops spent every morning of the week commencing 30 March 1942 doing spring drills on the parade ground – a use of time that Hitler would no doubt have welcomed had he been watching.)[15] One can only assume that officers and NCOs examined critically their men's work on such tactical exercises as there were, and took steps to effect improvements where necessary. Some individual soldiers would doubtless have sought to improve their performance without prompting when they noticed some aspect in which they were deficient. But as to regular external monitoring of the performance of platoons and companies by officers from other sub-units, if it took place there is no evidence of it.

How much interest COs and seconds-in-command took in this routine training under company arrangements is not clear. What is clear, however, is that such officers in Home Forces spent far too much of their time in their offices. This was not their fault. Higher HQs and the War Office imposed a steady stream of pointless paperwork on units. This tied senior regimental officers to their desks and prevented them from exercising critical supervision over minor tactical training in companies. That is why it was only in May 1943 that Kenrick of 5th Wiltshires went into print on his men's inadequacies.[16]

Indeed, documents such as Kenrick's memorandum in May 1943 and Curtis's critique of minor tactics in 4th Somersets a year earlier are conspicuous only by their rarity in unit War Diaries. This does not prove that other such documents were not issued (vast quantities of paperwork have not survived) or that minor tactical concerns were not exhaustively discussed in unrecorded training conferences and so on. But, if they were, there was little to show for it in 5th Wiltshires by May 1943. Kenrick had a particular reason for issuing his May 1943 memorandum. His battalion was shortly to take part in a three-day battalion exercise, codenamed NONSTOP, set by the divisional commander, Major-General G.I. Thomas of 43rd Division. Thomas intended the exercise 'as an arduous example of possible war time conditions'. Kenrick told his officers that the exercise would involve the battalion, with tanks and artillery attached for part of the time, 'in rapid action against sudden opposition'. He expected platoon battle drill to be a strong feature of operations.[17]

The involvement of divisional HQ in NONSTOP implied Thomas's strong interest in the battalion's minor tactical performance. Clearly Kenrick felt this keenly. It is in such exercises, designed to test minor tactics but organised, controlled and umpired by an HQ well above the level usually concerned with minor tactics, that one might expect the most objective attention to sub-unit performance. Unfortunately there is no evidence of how 5th Wiltshires fared.

Neither is there such evidence for the other two units of 129th Brigade, both of which were similarly exercised. What can be told is that such exercises were exceptional. NONSTOP was the only instance of such an exercise for 129th Brigade.

The scarcity of evidence makes it impossible to gauge the progress of units towards achieving fluency in minor tactics. But if one approaches the problem from a slightly different angle it is possible to elaborate a picture that accounts for the apparent lack of real fluency in battle. Battle drill was concerned with teaching infantry to work with the use of their own fire-power, that is without fire-support from extraneous sources such as the artillery, machine-gun battalions and heavy mortars. Quite rightly, much training effort was devoted to achieving effective co-operation with those other arms. This produced a dichotomy in tactical thinking that the War Office endorsed in the *Army Training Memorandum* in November 1944 as on the one hand, 'the broken battle . . . in which the infantry work forward supported by their own fire', and on the other, 'an attack supported by an organised fire-plan – in which the attacking troops must not stop to fire, and must understand that, from the moment they cross the start line until they reach their objective, they must go forward'.[18] This dichotomy was new. Official doctrine published in 1941, for example, recognised that covering fire would not always achieve its object of wholly neutralising enemy defences until the assaulting infantry were actually on the objective. The infantry might, therefore, have to complete the assault under their own covering fire.[19]

The section and platoon battle drills were taught as tactics to employ in discrete section and platoon actions in which other arms were not involved. The principles upon which they were based, however, were no less applicable when troops faced the task of crossing the last 200 yards or so of no-man's-land against revived resistance when the supporting barrage had lifted. Yet battle school teaching discounted such tactics in those circumstances. The battle drill movement grew from a conviction that infantry were good for a much more adventurous form of fighting than the 'leaning on the barrage' model of the Great War. As has been shown, such a belief was not out of line with official doctrine. *The Instructors' Handbook on Fieldcraft and Battle Drill*, however, distinguished between attacks by 'infiltration', in which sections, platoons and companies would feel their way into the gaps between enemy localities and execute flanking and pincer movements against them, and cases in which there were no usable gaps between enemy localities and which therefore demanded frontal attack behind a barrage.[20]

There were plenty of examples of what one might dub the barrage approach to battle working and working well. Geoffrey Picot describes in his memoir of the North-West Europe campaign how, commanding a rifle platoon in such an attack, he heartlessly drove his men forward behind a barrage, denying their pleas to fall out to tend wounded comrades. His resolve found its reward with the unopposed occupation of the objective.[21] In March 1945 the

War Office published, under the heading 'Leaning on the Barrage', an account of an attack, apparently in company strength, behind a barrage, which reached the objective with minimal interference from hostile fire. Judging that the enemy had withdrawn, the commander sent two platoons 200 yards beyond the objective where they ran into and eliminated the defending Germans as they made their way back to their positions following the cessation of the bombardment. Later, the victorious attackers found 'several Spandaus in position, cocked and ready to fire. It was as well that we had so closely followed the barrage.'[22]

According to Major John North of the Directorate of Military Training, reporting from Sicily in August 1943, the barrage approach was the standard recourse of infantry commanders whatever the scale of enemy resistance. He characterised the practice thus:

> If a cabbage gets in your way – put down a thousand tons of shell; the whole divisional artillery cracks down on a single pill-box or company locality. Of course, there will always be plenty of survivors, but they will still be running around in circles if your own infantry hop in quickly.[23]

That was the essential accompaniment to the artillery barrage or concentration. Emphasis on the need for the infantry to keep close to the falling shells was a constant refrain of the official campaign lessons' publications, which repeatedly reminded readers that even the heaviest supporting fire inflicted few casualties if the enemy were well dug in. On one occasion in Tunisia 4,000 shells falling on a strong enemy locality claimed only six lives.[24] Attacking infantry were advised to accept casualties from friendly artillery fire, for the advantage gained by swooping on to the objective before the defenders returned to their weapons more than outweighed the losses. This meant the forward troops keeping between 50 and 200 yards behind the exploding shells.[25]

The barrage approach was fine in theory and, as has been shown, often worked. One can conclude from the regular repetition of the 'lean on the barrage' message that the theory was not universally applied. Indeed, in May 1945 the War Office complained that 'Even now it is clear that some commanders do not seem to realise that neutralising fire on the immediate front of the assaulting troops is greatly reduced in value if those troops . . . do not keep up as close as possible to it.'[26] GHQ Middle East made a similar complaint in September 1943, based on experience in Sicily, noting that, even with eight field and four medium artillery regiments in support, brigade attacks had sometimes been halted by light small arms fire and mortars, and that such failures were often due to the infantry's failure to lean on the barrage.[27] Sitting comfortably in Cairo or London, the staff officers responsible for such complaints were perhaps unaware of just how difficult it could be for the infantry to keep up with the barrage in difficult terrain. Drawing lessons from its experience with Eighth Army in North Africa and Sicily, 152nd Brigade concluded that against dug-in troops even the high standard of artillery support they enjoyed was 'not nearly so effective as one would have imagined'. Infantry had to accept that they would have to deal with many enemy with their own weapons. This was especially true in hilly theatres such as Tunisia and Sicily.[28]

Allegations of ignorance of the need to keep up with the barrage were clearly unfair, and doctrinal dichotomy between the barrage approach and the infantry fire-and-movement approach quite misleading. If the infantry failed, for whatever reason, to lean on the barrage properly, they then faced the need to complete their approach to the objective without the benefit of the fire-plan. If accompanied by an artillery forward observation officer (and if that officer did not become a casualty and his communications remained effective) then renewed extraneous support was a possibility. If not, or if the infantry kept up to the barrage but the enemy troops returned to their weapons so smartly after its cessation that they managed to resume the defence before the advancing infantry overran their position, then fire-and-movement tactics were the proper means of making further progress. Here was required the highest degree of initiative from officers up to company commander level. In such circumstances the plan had failed, that is to say that the infantry could not simply advance on to the objective behind extraneous fire-support and mop up. A new plan had to be made on the spot, probably under fire, and put into effect quickly. For such circumstances battle schools taught two methods of approach: the lane method and the pepper-pot method.

The latter was predicated upon the principle that it took a rifleman or light machine-gunner a few seconds to perceive a target, take aim and fire. If no man remained on his feet for more than a few seconds, then the defenders would struggle to hit more than a few, especially if the attackers sprinted when they were on their feet. In the pepper-pot method, therefore, upon coming under effective fire each section was to divide into three groups: the Bren group (two or three men); two riflemen; and three riflemen. Each group would advance separately, 20 yards at a time, and then drop to the ground. As one group dropped, another would get up. The Bren group would move on the flank so as to get a clear field of fire when on the ground. The pepper-pot method was useful only when the ground afforded suitable cover.[29] Moreover, it involved the enforced idleness of LMGs when they were either moving or unable to acquire targets without causing friendly casualties. As the backbone of platoon fire-power, the longer the Bren guns could be kept in action the better.[30] The lane method of attack was designed to make fuller use of them.

As the figures show, it demanded that the path of the attack be divided into lanes for movement and lanes for LMG fire. Riflemen and LMGs across two platoons had to co-ordinate their movement, fire and assault. By this method, LMGs could deliver local fire-support until the moment the assaulting riflemen stepped on to the objective. This was a far more responsive means of support than could be delivered by high-trajectory weapons firing from beyond visual range.

FIGURE 1. THE LANE METHOD OF ATTACK: PHASE I

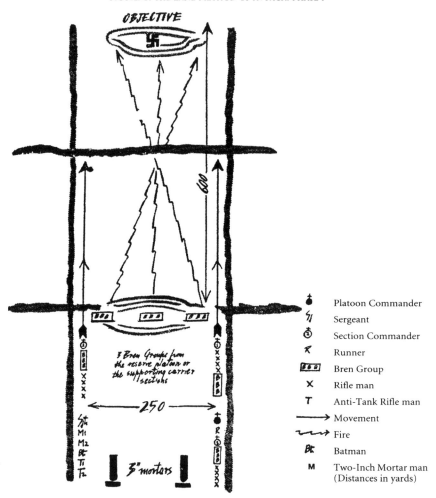

♦	Platoon Commander
𝓢/	Sergeant
③	Section Commander
✗	Runner
[▣▣▣]	Bren Group
X	Rifle man
T	Anti-Tank Rifle man
⟶	Movement
⤳	Fire
Bt	Batman
M	Two-Inch Mortar man (Distances in yards)

The objective is pounded by three-inch mortars and the rear areas by artillery fire. Three Bren groups open fire. The leading platoon forms up in dead ground in 'snake' formation and moves straight forward. (Flank platoon doing a similar manoeuvre is not shown. They would have three Bren groups similarly firing centrally between their sections.)

The lane method was a far more complex procedure than the pepper-pot. Reporting on experience in Tunisia, 1st Division contended that it was quite impracticable.[31] Its complexity was such that it required a plan to be made and communicated to those involved before the start of an operation, even if only as a contingency arrangement to be put into effect if circumstances demanded. The School of Infantry instructional film on the lane method showed a company carrying out such an attack to a preordained plan, each

FIGURE 2. THE LANE METHOD OF ATTACK: PHASE II

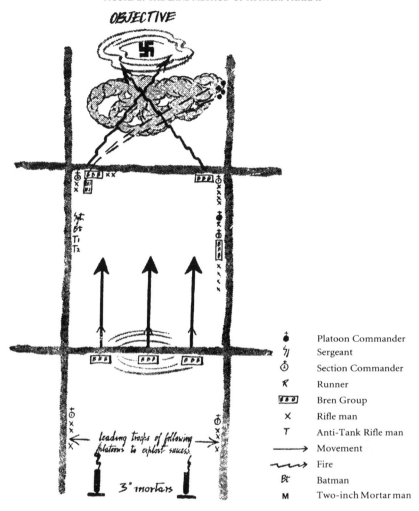

Brens of the leading sections are now on the ground and they open fire. The three rear Brens now move forward covered by smoke from the two-inch mortar and cross-fire from leading Brens.

man knowing exactly what he had to do.[32] To achieve that degree of precision from an improvised plan contrived under fire was not feasible. The only successful lane attack known to the author was executed by a company of an unidentified unit of 53rd Division near 's-Hertogenbosch on 22 October 1944. In that case, however, the tactic constituted the entire plan for a discrete action in which artillery support could not be used for fear of hitting other friendly troops in the vicinity.[33]

FIGURE 3. THE LANE METHOD OF ATTACK: PHASE III, THE ASSAULT

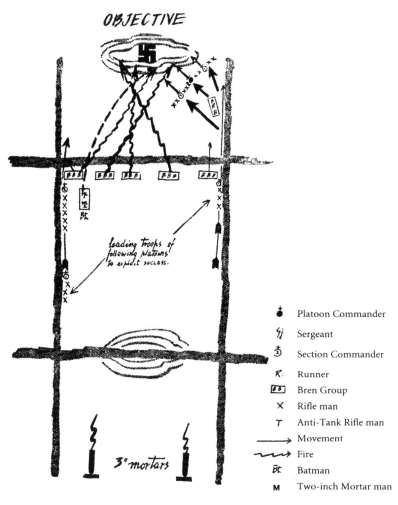

Platoon Commander	
Sergeant	
Section Commander	
Runner	
Bren Group	
Rifle man	
Anti-Tank Rifle man	
Movement	
Fire	
Batman	
Two-inch Mortar man	

Source: The Instructors' Handbook on Fieldcraft and Battle Drill (GHQ Home Forces, October 1942), pp. 164–6. Reproduced by permission of the Trustees of the Liddell Hart Centre for Military Archives, with acknowledgements to the Ministry of Defence.

Both the lane and pepper-pot methods were based upon the principle of infantry fire and movement, but the complexity of the lane method rendered it unsuitable for impromptu application. The pepper-pot, by contrast, was fire and movement in a very rudimentary form. Conducted in small groups of two or three men each, not all of which included a formally recognised leader, the emphasis of the pepper-pot method was on forward movement rather than manœuvre. Its purpose was to mesh in with timed tactical plans based upon artillery, so constant forward movement was essential and the scope for sub-unit and junior leader initiative correspondingly minimal. It shared this characteristic with the infinitely more complicated lane method, whose very complexity diminished the scope for on-the-spot initiative. Beneath both methods lay the assumption that sub-unit manœuvre along the lines comprehended by the section and platoon flanking attack battle drills was impracticable in a barrage-led attack.

But this underlying assumption was quite invalid. Paul Bryan, the highly successful second-in-command and then CO of 6th Royal West Kent Regiment in North Africa, Sicily and Italy, contributed numerous tactical tips to the *Army Training Memorandum.* He advised against platoon flanking attacks on the grounds that German positions were always placed to render infiltration between them quite impossible. Frontal attacks were best, Bryan counselled, and both platoon and company commanders should place one section/platoon forward and move with the two reserve sections/platoons. That way they could observe the source of the fire drawn by the leading sub-unit and manœuvre the reserve accordingly.[34] Although Bryan also recommended that troops training at home practise pepper-pot attacks, his reference to commander-directed manœuvre of sub-units confirms that more sophisticated tactics were practicable. Although flanking attacks would seldom be possible, if the commander took the time and trouble to exploit the natural features of the ground he could achieve much the same fire-and-movement effect. Reporting on his first battle experience from Sicily, Wigram insisted that where it was attempted (which was not often) battle drill fire and movement to secure further progress when the supporting artillery fire lifted invariably worked.[35]

These tactics were as useful in Normandy as they were in Italy. When George Taylor assumed command of 5th Duke of Cornwall's Light Infantry (DCLI) in Normandy in mid-July 1944 he instituted a programme of training in fire and movement and battle inoculation. He also laid down a battalion doctrine. Attacks would always be carried out in depth, with no more than one sub-unit forward and the remainder held back in reserve. Within a platoon the rear sections would move at least 300 yards behind the leading section, except in close country where the gap would be smaller. Taylor described the leading echelon of an attack as the 'opening bid'. Depending upon the enemy's response to it, he, or the company or platoon commander concerned, would decide how to manœuvre the reserve. Taylor grasped that at battalion level and below troops rarely knew the exact positions of the enemy they were attacking. By tempting the enemy to open fire – and thereby disclose his positions – on only a small proportion of the attacking force, Taylor retained the power to deploy the fire-power of his main force in whatever way seemed most advantageous given information that became available only after the battle started. The more troops he staked in the 'opening bid', the fewer he retained with which to shape events during the action. Taylor remained CO for the rest of the war, winning the DSO and Bar. His battalion failed to carry its objective on only one occasion.[36]

Predicated on the assumption that artillery fire-power did not guarantee a safe passage to the objective, Taylor's method applied the principles of infantry minor tactics, as set out in battle drill, to the setpiece attack behind gunner support. The principle of holding two sections in reserve for deployment only after the platoon commander had 'read' the battle aroused by the leading section was enshrined in platoon battle drill.[37] But platoon battle drill dealt with flanking and pincer attacks intended for use in infiltration operations. They were thought quite impracticable when troops were expected to lean on the barrage delivered under a prearranged fire-plan. Taylor was, in effect, telling his men to forget about the barrage – if they were under effective fire then manifestly it had not done its job – and fight forward with their own weapons. Clearly, Taylor's thinking had not featured in 5th DCLI's tactics before he came to the battalion. Evidence of attack line-ups in other cases suggests that battalion 'opening bids' of two and even three companies were normal.[38]

Brigadier James Hargest, a New Zealander who observed the fighting in Normandy until 10 July 1944, bemoaned the frequent reluctance of British infantry to rely upon their own weapons. Too often they called for artillery support when held up in circumstances where they might well have made progress without it.[39] It is surely no coincidence that the ethos of exercise umpiring, as discussed in Chapter 3, militated against the generation of the unexpected, and that where some setback was allowed to rear in an exercise its purpose was usually to test the forward infantry in obtaining on-call artillery support.

The effectiveness of 5th DCLI under Taylor's command suggests that the deficiencies identified by Hargest were not universal. Another example of what could be achieved given effective leadership under pressure came on 16 July 1944. During an attack on the village of Cahier, about a mile north of the River Odon eight miles or so above Caen, 'C' Company of 1st Oxfordshire and Buckinghamshire Light Infantry came under heavy small arms fire from the fringes of a wood at about 50 yards range. The battalion was operating without artillery support. In this unpromising situation, a plan was made for the riflemen to storm the wood covered by the fire of the Brens, which were pushed out to the flanks for the purpose. Delivered with fixed bayonets, the assault prevailed, although while the troops were digging in, having mopped up the enemy within the wood, heavy machine-gun fire compelled a withdrawal.[40]

But the deficiencies Hargest found were widespread enough seriously to hinder British efforts. The way in which 15th Division's advance on the first day of operation EPSOM fizzled out in the face of the fire of 'a handful of determined teenagers toughly arrogant at the havoc they were causing'[41] is a case in point. It was not that the British forces were too weak, nor that the troops were not brave. One officer observed (not in particular reference to EPSOM) that the problem was 'the tendency to sit still and be petrified – not with fright but with bewilderment about the course of action to be adopted'.[42] What was lacking was the initiative among junior leaders to organise effective action at sub-unit level, the expectation among all ranks that such action would be attempted, and prior training in the art of putting it together 'on the hoof' rather than before zero hour.

Gerald Templer, in a memorable address at a junior leaders' course in 1942, described an initially peaceful platoon advance along a quiet lane:

> 'Suddenly all hell is let loose. You look up, and your platoon sergeant's guts are hanging on a tree beside you. The platoon is turning to run – it is then, gentlemen, that you must grip those men.' He paused in absolute silence and, holding out his arm, tightened his fist slowly to give graphic illustration to his words. It was superb theatre and we sat enthralled.[43]

One is tempted to conclude that platoon commanders took him at his word, but no more. There was plenty of grip when events turned against British troops. Casualty figures in major offensives testify to that. But good fieldcraft coupled with effective offensive action, the wherewithal to make effective tactics out of confusion, was less common. Where did the British Army go wrong?

Firstly, ease of concealment in the Norman bocage presented acute tactical problems that had not been foreseen in training. The Down–Crawl–Observe–Fire sequence taught in battle drill as the action to take upon coming under fire assumed easy discovery of the enemy's whereabouts. In Normandy it was often impossible to ascertain the source of enemy fire.[44] Similar problems had arisen in Sicily and 50th Division had argued that infantrymen should use their rifles as weapons of neutralisation rather than marksmanship if definite targets were not apparent.[45] This, however, risked considerable wastage of ammunition. Indeed, that concern was an obstacle to the acceptance of battle drill's Down–Crawl–Observe–Fire imperative, and there were arguments on the subject at battle schools. However, as one platoon commander in North-West Europe put it, to get the men's heads up and firing 'is a moral victory worth infinitely more than a few rounds of small arms ammunition'.[46]

Concealed enemy undoubtedly contributed to the bewilderment factor, but given that the topography of the invasion zone could not be publicised in advance it is hard to see how it could have been universally addressed in training. In any case, the advantage in bocage fighting by no means lay entirely with the defence. Lieutenant-Colonel J.R. Bowring of XXX Corps observed that the bocage was 'probably the best possible country for infantry to operate. They can move out of view of the enemy because of the cover afforded by the hedges and trees in almost any direction.'[47] It should not have been impossible to use such cover to obscure forward movement by infiltration or to provide jumping-off places for minor fire-and-movement operations by sections, platoons and companies.

However, to take advantage of the opportunities presented by the bocage in a barrage-led setpiece attack demanded the incorporation, as an integrated component, of sub-unit manœuvre along the lines of platoon battle drill. The notion that such integration was impracticable led to a general failure to rehearse it in training. The closest any of the battalions whose War Diaries have been examined for this study came to it was a platoon exercise set by the second-in-command of 1st Herefordshire Regiment and carried out separately by each of the 12 rifle platoons in May 1944. The exercise postulated a two-battalion attack, with the divisional artillery in support, in which 1st Herefords was on the right with two companies forward. The platoon concerned was the right-hand platoon of the left-hand company and as the exercise opened the entire attack had become stalled by heavy enemy fire from the objective. Two lessons were intended of the exercise: 'Movement without fire produces unnecessary cas[ualties]' and 'Fire without movement is useless.' It was a bit late to be teaching such lessons: within a month the battalion would be in Normandy. Perhaps, even after nearly five years of war, this battalion had not grasped the elementary principles of tactics. More likely, however, is that the real purpose of the exercise was not to teach such principles, which must have been well known by then, but to test the platoon commanders in the use of a faculty that tended to be neglected among the fire plans of higher tactics. The code name of the exercise was INITIATIVE.

It is impossible to be absolutely certain of what was expected of the platoon commander in INITIATIVE. The map references show that his platoon was held up somewhere between 300 and 600 yards short of the objective and he had lost the benefit of the fire-plan as a result. No other troops took part in the scheme. The exercise's code name allows the fairly sure speculation that the platoon commander was to be asked: how are you going to continue the attack using your own fire-power?[48]

To present a subaltern with such a problem in training was exceptional. In battle it happened all the time. It was not that suitable tactics were not known. Battle drill saw to it that they were. The error was to assume a rigid distinction between battles where sub-unit manœuvre tactics were appropriate and setpiece artillery-dominated actions where they were not. At a conference of battle school commandants in June 1942, Wigram (Chief Instructor of the GHQ Battle School and founder of the movement) stated that at Barnard Castle the emphasis was on infiltration tactics (i.e. section, platoon and company flanking attacks and the like), but that methods for frontal attack were also taught.[49] Clearly he recognised the (false) distinction between the two. The fact that he accepted heavy restrictions upon infantry sub-unit tactical scope in the setpiece attack behind a barrage, restrictions that he and other talented infantry officers later found to be unnecessary, demands explanation.

For Wigram the battle drill movement was in part a revolt against the regimentation of the barrage-laden ethos with its rigid fire-plans, zero-hours, start-lines and inter-sub-unit boundaries. Writing in 1941, he derided pepper-pot tactics as a pathetic excuse for fire and movement.[50] He conceived flanking attacks and pincer movements as the only real application of the fire-and-movement principle. Encouraged by a shift in British defensive doctrine away from continuous defensive lines towards strong defensive localities, and by the manœuvre warfare practised by the Germans, he predicted that flanking and pincer attacks against individual localities would supplant broad frontal attacks in higher tactics and operations. Wigram did not discount artillery support, but preferred it in the form of brief concentrations and smoke, responding to the actual progress of operations on the ground – as indicated by flare signals and gunner observers – rather than inflexible barrage fire-plans that attempted to dictate progress. Notwithstanding artillery support, small arms fire delivered by (in a battalion attack) one company to cover the movement of the assaulting companies was a central feature of Wigram's teaching.[51]

In predicting the demise of the setpiece, barrage-led frontal attack Wigram was certainly premature – a fact he must have realised by the time he prepared *The Instructors' Handbook on Fieldcraft and Battle Drill* in 1942, for that manual ordained the lane and pepper-pot methods for use in such attacks. Although at the June 1942 conference mentioned above Lieutenant-Colonel M.W. Roberts of 53rd Division Battle School asserted that section and platoon battle drill 'could be applied in practically all circumstances' (presumably including the setpiece attack),[52] *The Instructors' Handbook* published four months later suggested otherwise. Roberts was undoubtedly swimming against the tide but he was swimming in the right direction, as the later battle experience of Wigram and others demonstrated. It would not be unreasonable to contend that Wigram and his battle school colleagues were guilty of fundamental error in ruling the improvised sub-unit manœuvre tactics of battle drill out of the setpiece barrage-led attack. Were they not largely responsible for the be-wilderment that overcame so many British troops in Normandy when the barrage failed to put them on their objective? The terrain did not always permit the pepper-pot and the lane method was quite impracticable. But did the spurious dichotomy really originate in the battle school movement?

Fortunately we have what might be described as a control sample, evidence from a formation, 50th Division, that went overseas in the spring of 1941 before battle drill swept through Home Forces. After serving in Iraq and Syria, the division joined Eighth Army, fighting in the advance from El Alamein to Tunisia and then in Sicily. The division then produced a battle lessons pamphlet, which included the following:

> However effective the arty sp [artillery support] in an attack it must always be expected that some Spandau and riflemen will be left and will fight to the last. These, often isolated, Spandau must be overcome in the

quickest possible time by the Inf with the use of their own weapons. Minor tactics for this type of op, whether it is to be performed by a Sec, Pl or Coy, requires more trg [training].[53]

That such a statement should be necessary after an extended period of active operations is a remarkable reflection on the thinking with which the division entered battle and suggests that it was not only the battle drill-masters who had underrated the potential of and need for sub-unit manœuvre in the setpiece attack. The battle drill movement can be indicted for underestimating its own potential. Wigram's mistake was to accept too readily the dictates of artillery-dominated tactical planning. As an attempt to shake off the constraints of gunnery, battle drill failed: Wigram was beaten down by the barrage. And, with his embarkation for the Mediterranean in 1943, the residue of his efforts began to wither.

Wigram went overseas in May 1943 and apart from a brief visit after the Sicily campaign had nothing more to do with the School of Infantry. He was killed in action in Italy the following February. Battle drill remained on the British Army's curriculum. Indeed, in May 1944 the War Office issued a fresh endorsement of it as a training technique.[54] However, by that time there were definite signs of atrophy in the battle drill movement. None of the original team of battle drill instructors remained at Barnard Castle. In the spring of 1944 a paper produced by the school's operational research team doubted that the technique of intrasection fire and movement could be practised 'in the type of deliberate set-piece attack now in favour'.[55] In the summer of 1944 the battle drill wing at Barnard Castle, of which Wigram had been chief instructor, was dissolved[56] and in November the Directorate of Military Training announced that battle drill was no longer taught at the school.[57] With the School of Infantry no longer training battle drill instructors, it is perhaps no coincidence that one newly commissioned officer serving with 10th Black Watch who attended a divisional battle school in the late summer of 1944 stressed in his memoirs the heavy physical demands of the course but did not mention battle drill.[58] The diary of another officer who attended a different battle school in June 1945 similarly makes no mention of battle drill.[59] It is not that tactics were neglected at such schools. They certainly were not. But battle drill was a means of rationalising tactics and packaging tactical doctrine for the consumption of the private soldiers that battle school students commanded when they returned to their units. Without it, tactics was a closed book to the troops.

It is unlikely that the misgivings of many regular officers at the very idea of tactical drills ever fully went away. In some cases, however, such misgivings extended beyond the fear of stereotyped tactics to embrace fundamental doubts over the moral fitness of the typical infantryman to apply fieldcraft and battle drill to common tactical ends. While some objected to the Down–Crawl–Observe–Fire routine on grounds of excessive ammunition expenditure, others held that once down soldiers would refuse to get up again.[60] Such fears were not unfounded. In Sicily, Wigram was dismayed to find that only around a quarter of the men in a typical platoon were reliable in battle. This was a problem that had to be overcome if any degree of sophistication in infantry minor tactics was to be achieved. Wigram proposed a more efficacious distribution of leadership within the platoon for that purpose.[61] A pretence that the barrage would render infantry minor tactics superfluous perhaps convinced many officers that they could avoid the problem altogether. Ultimately battle drill failed to rescue infantry minor tactics from the barrage-laden ethos.

Writing in *Army Quarterly* in 1948, Major-General C.H. Boucher contended that the proper role of infantry in the attack was to close with and destroy the enemy and nothing more. Until they were at very close quarters, fire was no business of the infantry and they should be armed only with automatic rifles sighted for up to 200 yards and an edged weapon: 'if fire is required its production is not the job of the Infantry, it is the job of the other arms, particularly of the Royal Regiment [of Artillery] and of the MG Battalions'.[62] In effect Boucher was arguing that the section, platoon and company fire-and-movement tactics comprehended in battle drill were wrong in principle, and that the role of the infantry should be little different from the role they had been intended to perform on 1 July 1916. There can be little doubt that infantry tactics tended towards the Somme model during the Second World War, and that it was the vast improvements in the capabilities of the other arms, chiefly the Royal Artillery, that prevented disasters of the magnitude seen during the Great War. But artillery was no complete substitute for infantry combat effectiveness, the supply of which was too short in North-West Europe. Boucher's thinking was part of the problem.

The criticism to which battle drill has been subjected, both at the time and by modern historians, namely that it suppressed initiative, is not baseless, but it is unfair. It was not only battle drill that promoted the suppression of initiative. The whole offensive technique of the British Army, with its emphasis on timed fire-plans, tended to suppress individual initiative because it claimed to render the infantry minor tactics comprehended by battle drill redundant. This notion was deeply embedded in the training exercises carried out at battalion level and higher. It was deeply pernicious. It was not too much battle drill that deprived the British infantry of the power of initiative, but too little.

6

The Armoured Arm

Whereas infantry tactics and technology made no radical leaps between the wars, tank technology took enormous strides. Vast technical improvement over the primitive machines of the Great War brought a far more extensive battlefield role within the ambition of the champions of armour. Some forecast that mechanisation would bring a revolution in the conduct of land warfare. Naturally, others disagreed. There being no opportunity between the wars to test in battle either the technology or the tactical and operational theories devised for its use, this controversy burned on up to the outbreak of war in 1939.

There is a further general contrast between the infantry and the armour. A tank could fight only by the continuous collective application of the various technical skills of the crew in driving, gunnery and wireless. Although also a collective activity, infantry fighting was technologically primitive by comparison. Like the infantry, however, the tank was intended to fight if not at close quarters with the enemy then certainly within visual range. Simultaneously with the exercise of its technical functions, therefore, the tank's tactical faculties had to be continuously active, no less so than those of the technologically less-advanced infantryman. A clearer sense of this distinction can be gained by comparing tanks with field artillery. Aiming the guns, loading and firing them was entirely a matter of mathematics and mechanical activity. The tactical element came in deciding at what to fire and from where. This was a separate process, often undertaken some time before the technical processes of aiming and firing and usually by different people. In the infantry the tactical had never really married the technical. In the artillery they were divorced. In the armour, however, the two lived together, although not necessarily in complete marital bliss. On account of this, armoured forces presented a rather more complex training problem than infantry did.

At the outbreak of war, the British Army possessed two armoured divisions and five independent Tank Brigades (only one of which was regular). The prominence of German armour in the conquest of the Low Countries and France in the summer of 1940 prompted massive expansion of Britain's armoured forces. But it did not end the disputes over how those forces should be organised and used. Neither did the battle experience the British Army gained over the next few years. Indeed, when the British Army returned to France in 1944, there was no greater consensus over armour than there had been five years earlier. The disagreements involved rather different issues and, where they were debated at all, were not discussed in public. None the less, they ranged from higher organisation to minor tactics. The tactical issues will be fully explored in the following two chapters. As a background to that, this chapter will explore the controversies over higher organisation, having first investigated the ramifications of the general armoured training problems alluded to above.

ARMOURED TRAINING

Before going any further, it is as well to describe briefly the sub-unit structure of armoured forces. During the Second World War there were two different categories of fighting tank in the British Army: those designed for infantry support, known as infantry tanks, and those intended for mobile operations, which were known as cruiser tanks. Correspondingly, there were two categories of unit, armoured units equipped with cruiser tanks and the self-explanatory infantry tank units. This distinction formed one of the organisational controversies mentioned above and will be explored in greater detail later on in this chapter. Sub-unit designations in armoured units used the cavalry terminology 'troop' and 'squadron'. Infantry tank units adopted this terminology in April 1941 to replace the infantry nomenclature 'section' and 'company' that they had used hitherto. Official War Establishments specified three tanks to the troop, although this figure was varied locally from time to time (four tanks to the troop being the most common alternative). The troop was a subaltern's command. He rode in one of the tanks. The other two were each commanded by an NCO. The squadron was a major's command and (except in armoured units between April 1940 and May 1941 when four troops were specified) comprised five troops and a squadron HQ. The latter comprised four tanks in armoured units and three in infantry tank units. In each case two of the HQ tanks were Close Support tanks. Close Support variants of most infantry and cruiser tank designs were produced. Instead of the standard two-pounder (later six-pounder) main gun, they mounted a three-inch howitzer capable of firing high explosive (HE) shells and smoke shells – the standard tank armament being suitable only for solid-shot armour-piercing (AP) rounds. Three squadrons made up a unit, which was known as either a battalion or a regiment depending upon its origins.

The crew of each tank varied in numbers according to the space available and the number of weapons to be manned. The turret, the fighting compartment of the tank, ideally accommodated three men: the gunner, a gun-loader-cum-wireless operator and the tank commander. In some tanks, however, there was room for only two in the turret, so the duties of the loader–operator were shared out between gunner and commander. The driver sat in the hull of the tank. In some tanks there was also a hull machine-gun, manned by a co-driver. It was not only operations that demanded the technical skills of the crew. Mechanical and electrical maintenance, without which the tank would not long remain battleworthy, was a matter of daily routine. Technical training, therefore, loomed large in the concerns of the Royal Armoured Corps (RAC).

Recruits went first to a Training Regiment RAC. There, after basic military training (until this was removed to Primary Training Centres in mid-1942), they did specialised Corps training that consisted primarily of technical instruction. The training regiments were organised in specialist wings for (1) driving and maintenance, (2) gunnery and (3) wireless, with a further wing for (4) crew training and troop tactics. The latter, the first stage of collective training, can only have been of a basic nature, probably to teach troop formations and evolutions. It is important to note, however, that although it was the work of the driver and the gunner in a tank that produced fire and movement – the foundation of all tactics – tactical decision-making was the preserve of the tank commander. No crew-member sat more than a few feet from him and telephonic communication within the tank cemented this physical closeness. Whereas in the infantry the need for dispersal of the smallest sub-unit produced a demand for tactical knowledge in every private soldier, such conditions just did not apply in tanks. Therefore, although a kind of battle drill for armoured units did appear in official manuals in 1943, it was aimed at tank commanders rather than the private soldier.

None the less, it was certainly desirable that crewmen achieve some degree of tactical competence during their training, if only to ease their commander's burden. However, closed down for action their vision, and thus their knowledge, of what was happening outside was severely restricted. Although in theory tank commanders maintained a periodical commentary over the intercom, in practice they had much else to do. In any case, the need to keep the wireless set adjusted for external communication precluded free communication within the tank. 'The result', as one unit War Diarist observed, 'is often bored and mechanical execution of orders with no notion of what is really happening'.[1] There was, in other words, a disjunction between the technical tasks by which a tank operated and the tactical judgement that decided from minute to minute the purpose to which it operated. To labour the metaphor used earlier, the tactical and the technical shared a roof but not a ceiling. The seeds of this disharmony appear to have taken root in the RAC Training Regiments. All trainees must have taken part in the limited collective tactical training that took place there. Such evidence as is available, however, suggests that only those earmarked for command were actually conscious of receiving tactical instruction.[2]

The absence of tactics from the training syllabus for, and indeed from the minds of, most men in the ranks is perhaps characteristic of the tank as (what we now call) a weapon system rather than simply a weapon. The effectiveness of the tank depended upon collective effort. Provided each man played his part properly the tank could operate effectively even if some of them failed to see the jigsaw beyond their own modest piece. Of course, it was not in the training regiments that real collective proficiency developed, but in the field units to which men went at the end of their Corps training. Here they continued to perfect the trades to which they had been introduced during Corps training while learning to co-operate with colleagues in a permanent tank crew as part of a tactical sub-unit.

As explained in Chapter 3, large-scale exercises were not occasions on which regimental officers and their men gained much training in actual fighting. Nor were they occasions on which superior performance necessarily won reward, especially in exercises above regimental scale. However, as became increasingly clear as the war went on, tanks were not in themselves battle winners. Success could come only through co-operation with other arms. It was in the large exercises that the tanks and the other arms practised the framework of that co-operation. The following two chapters will, therefore, dwell extensively upon such exercises, for they show how commanders understood the battlefield functions and limitations of armour. Training in fighting on the other hand, that is using the tank's weapons against realistic targets in realistic ground, could be gained only at the tank battle practice facilities at the small number of centrally run armoured fighting vehicle (AFV) ranges. Typically, units got two to three weeks at one of these ranges each year. They got more time at the less well equipped local ranges run by Commands, but these rarely provided for much more than static firing practice.

The best appointed of the wartime RAC ranges was that at Linney Head on the Pembrokeshire coast in South Wales. It was to Linney Head that the armoured units of Guards Armoured Division went for their first range practices in the spring of 1942. Evaluating these practices, G.L. Verney, commander of one of the units concerned, wrote of the bewildering variety of responsibilities facing the troop commander. Directing one tank was onerous enough. Reading the map, reading the ground, spotting targets and directing fire all competed for attention. The troop commander had not only to direct his own tank, but also that of the two others in his troop. He had to maintain contact with them and with his squadron commander, each on a different wireless wavelength. He had to do all this while withstanding constant jolting and crashing as the tank negotiated the rough terrain.[3] If a few of the Guards' troop commanders were overwhelmed at first it would not be surprising. Most of them had been infantry platoon commanders but nine months earlier and this was the first time they had commanded their troops in anything approaching realistic battle conditions. Indeed, the lack of local range facilities was one of the reasons cited for the Guards' backwardness in a survey of the training of field force formations presented to Paget in May 1942.[4]

When the Guards next visited Linney Head in September 1942, tanks were put through a battle practice individually, which proved to be 'of surprising value, particularly for Troop Leaders whose only way it is of finding out their [subordinate tank] Commanders' abilities at fire-orders and crew control'.[5] This commentary, written contemporaneously by the War Diarist of the 2nd Armoured Irish Guards, is revealing. First, it strongly suggests that some tank commanders had been found wanting. More importantly, it indicates something of the difficulties to be overcome if the collective performance of a tank crew was to be judged. Plainly it was not possible to do this in the half-squadron battle practice runs that had taken place during the previous visit to Linney Head. On that occasion the half-squadron's collective gunnery performance could be judged by the number of hits on the mock-up targets; its use of ground could be judged by the CO who trailed each run in his own tank.[6] But weak performance by an individual tank crew could easily be obscured by the better performance of others.

That need not surprise us. Most forms of collective human endeavour present opportunities for the idle or incompetent to secure a free ride. What is interesting for our purposes is the evident difficulty of spotting the weak links without focusing very specifically on each and every potential case. Could this be done other than in individual battle practice runs at a suitably equipped range? Not according to the War Diarist quoted above. An objective measurement of the number of hits on the mock-up targets, complemented by a somewhat less objective assessment of the tank's use of ground, afforded perhaps the closest possible replication of the ultimate test, the real battle. Live firing could not be practised in a two-sided exercise, which precluded any truly objective measurement of performance, although the presence of live enemy produced stimuli quite absent when the targets were nothing but pulley-operated mock-ups. To judge a tank crew's performance in a two-sided exercise required an umpire with each tank monitoring movement and simulated gunnery. GHQ instructions specified just two umpires per squadron and two at unit HQ.[7] Even if a unit's full umpiring complement supervised a single-squadron operation, the ratio of umpires to tanks would still be lower than one to two. Clearly minor tactics could not be tested in a major exercise. But the War Office recommended that for small-scale exercises there should be an umpire for each tank and – somewhat improbably – that he should ride on the back of it.[8] Given the lack of passenger space inside a tank, this was the only place from which an umpire could possibly monitor the tactical and technical performance of the commander and crew. None the less, it would have been a risky activity for the umpire, whose observation of tactics and gunnery must have been heavily diluted by his efforts to hold on. Surfing was not an army sport. No evidence that the tank-riding method of umpiring was ever practised has been found in the records examined for this study.

So minor tactics could not be tested in major exercises, which is to repeat with tank-specific detail the general conclusion of Chapter 3. The War Office guidance for umpiring AFVs, while demanding that all relevant factors such as relative strengths, the formations used by units of tanks, the siting of anti-tank guns, the range at which fire was opened, and so on, implied that umpires should make a general judgement that could not possibly account for the detailed behaviour of individual tanks.[9] Practical considerations rendered the effective umpiring of minor tactics in smaller exercises very difficult too, which set armoured training at a handicap when compared to infantry training. (There was little physical problem in placing an umpire with each infantry section if necessary.)

The practical bar to umpiring tank minor tactics was of particular significance because minor tactics were a far weightier factor in the prospects of armour than for infantry. Heavy reliance upon extraneous fire-power rendered infantry minor tactics superfluous, theoretically at least, for much of the duration of an engagement. Artillery fire-support assumed increasing importance in armoured divisions too as the war progressed. However, tanks in a mobile armoured role could not be tied rigidly to artillery fire-plans. The increasing effective range of tank and anti-tank weapons erased any distinction there might have been between close-quarters fighting – the realm of minor tactics – and longer-range combat where supporting weapons of other arms were the only effective instruments. A tank could come under effective fire from an enemy anti-tank gun at 2,000 yards. Even at that range, if carrying a useful HE-firing gun, a tank could respond with its own weapons. So minor tactics and gunnery were important. By contrast, infantry under effective fire at such ranges had little effective recourse with their own weapons, and so could take only the tactically essentially passive measures of digging in, moving elsewhere or perhaps smoke. Any more active response depended upon supporting weapons, perhaps the medium mortars held by each battalion, but more likely the artillery.

So, just as with infantry hand-to-hand fighting, rapid reaction and technical efficiency were fundamental to all tank action. The first major exercise of 11th Armoured Division saw the two armoured brigades fight each other in an all-tank battle. Umpiring strength was one per squadron. In his remarks at the post-exercise conference the divisional commander, Major-General P.C.S. Hobart, who was not known for insipid judgements, commented in detail upon the manœuvres the two brigades had carried out. However, he could conclude only with the rather lame: 'it seems possible that the 30 Armd Bde were now in a position to deal a very effective blow'. The reason for his uncharacteristic uncertainty was this: 'Victory depends upon split-second manœuvre and gunnery. Can only be decided by shooting.'[10] Of course, there had been no actual shooting. In an infantry attack, whether or not the attacking troops got to close quarters with the objective depended largely upon the quality of the covering fire-plan decided well beforehand in comparative leisure and easily umpired. In an armoured attack, 'split-second manœuvre and gunnery' could make all the difference between failure a thousand yards short of the objective and sweeping success. The impossibility of umpiring those factors rendered all exercises inherently unrealistic.

ARMOURED ORGANISATION

As doyen of the Royal Tank Corps in the 1930s, Hobart fully shared its conviction that armour would be the paramount arm in future warfare. This vision stemmed from a plan conceived in the spring of 1918 for the defeat of Germany the following year. The brainchild of Major (later Major-General) J.F.C. Fuller, a general staff officer at Tank Corps HQ in France, 'Plan 1919' envisaged the use of masses of the latest medium tank to sweep virtually unsupported into the enemy rear areas, smash his command headquarters and thus cause the German Army's collapse. This, according to one recent historian of British armoured warfare, was pure fantasy.[11] Victory by more prosaic means in the autumn of 1918 ensured the plan's stillbirth. Perhaps the very fact that it was never implemented gave the plan a totemic influence that it could not otherwise have commanded. Be that as it may, Fuller's notion of a powerful armoured force in which tanks were the principal, if not the only, arm inspired Hobart and many others in the Royal Tank Corps between the wars.

Hobart had been passed over for the command of Britain's first armoured division in 1937. His appointment the following year as founding commander of the mobile division in Egypt (later re-designated 7th Armoured Division) assuaged his frustration and crowned his career with an important field command. It also appeared to open the door to official acceptance of Hobart's bullish estimate of his arm's potential. To Hobart's dismay, his tour in Egypt ended in dismissal. After clashes on doctrine with his superiors, he was relieved in the autumn of 1939 and retired soon afterwards.[12]

It was precisely over his excessive faith in the abilities of armoured forces that Hobart fell out with his chiefs in Egypt. Naturally, he felt vindicated when Hitler's panzers cut through the combined might of the British and French armies in a matter of a few weeks in the summer of 1940. A massive expansion of Britain's armoured forces followed the Dunkirk débâcle. Between then and the end of 1941 six new armoured divisions were added to the existing three and the number of tank brigades rose from five to nine. This expansion alone was not enough for Hobart. In the autumn he circulated a paper calling for the formation of an armoured army as a discrete entity within the British Army. Its commander, Hobart believed, should sit on the Army Council alongside the chiefs of staff.

Although Churchill took a keen interest in Hobart's idea, his senior military advisers, Brooke, C-in-C Home Forces, and Dill, CIGS, rejected it. They insisted that the armoured arm should be integrated with the older arms to form a homogeneous army. Although Hobart was recalled to raise 11th Armoured Division in March 1941, there would be no armoured army. Instead Dill decided to set up an HQ Royal Armoured Corps under the leadership of Lieutenant-General G.LeQ. Martel, hitherto GOC 50th Division. Martel took up his new duties in December 1940 with the title Commander,

Royal Armoured Corps (CRAC). Precisely what HQ RAC and CRAC were for is unclear. The historian of the RAC maintains that they were intended simply to deflect Churchill's enthusiasm for Hobart's scheme, and the War Office found it impossible to define Martel's responsibilities in writing. Martel later claimed that although administered by the Commands in which they were located, all the armoured formations in Britain came under his command in all other respects until they were ready to take their place in the field army.[13] In fact there is little sign in the War Diaries of armoured formations that they considered themselves to be under Martel's command. As CRAC Martel did play a role in the development of doctrine and organisation for armoured forces. But it will be shown in the following chapters that his powers cannot have been so strong as to ensure that doctrine was observed. Indeed, it was not until after he vacated the post in September 1942 that some semblance of doctrinal conformity descended upon armoured divisions.

From his HQ at Hammersmith in west London, Martel could hardly exercise close control over formations scattered up and down the country. Realising this, he demanded the establishment of a number of Armoured Corps HQs to command armoured divisions under his direction. Brooke refused. As a compromise, three Armoured Group HQs, each under a major-general, were set up in October 1941, one each in Northern, Eastern and South-Eastern Commands.[14] Their functions were set out in a letter to Command HQs:

(a) They will come under the orders of the Army to which they are posted for all matter[s] except those under para . . . (c) and will establish their HQs in close proximity to Army HQ.

(b) They will command and train Armd Formations in the Command, except when it may be necessary for operational or other reasons to place these formations under the orders of Corps operating within these armies.

(c) They will in all cases exercise direct control of the technical side of armd forces and in particular those connected with Signal and Ordnance duties, thus providing a direct line of control through RAC channels on all such technical matters between RAC HQ and Armd Units.

(d) The commanders of Armd Gps will act as Advisers to Army Commanders on all matters dealing with the employment, training and administration of Armd Forces.

(e) They will also assist Army Commanders in developing the study of the co-operation between armd and motorised forces under various conditions of warfare.[15]

If armoured forces were to be commanded by Armoured Group commanders, who were in turn under the orders of Army commanders, Martel could
exercise little authority over them. That is how Brooke wanted it. But neither
did he want Armoured Group HQs to exercise command authority. To put an
end to confusion on the matter, in November 1941 he explained that the
Armoured Groups' functions 'were more in the nature of advice and assistance to army Commanders than actual command of armoured formations
in operations'.[16]

It was only in technical matters that a clear line of authority existed down-
ward from HQ RAC, through Armoured Group HQs when they were formed,
to armoured formations. Dealing with his tenure as CRAC in his memoirs,
Martel seemed to attach the greatest importance to his success in attracting,
training and retaining the right kind of man for technical duties.[17] In the War
Office, the existence of Martel and his HQ was seen as an antidote to the
mechanical backwardness of the prewar Army. Like all antidotes, this one was
needed only so long as the evil it was intended to redress remained.[18] By
September 1942 Brooke, now CIGS, clearly felt that HQ RAC was redundant.
He sent Martel on a world tour, supposedly to learn from armoured operations in active theatres overseas. Since Martel received no opportunity to
apply whatever he had learned in any systematic way when he returned six
months later, this was probably simply a way to be rid of him. No new CRAC
was appointed. Instead Paget, the C-in-C, got an RAC adviser attached to his
HQ staff, an appointment filled by Major-General C.W.M. Norrie, formerly a
corps commander in Eighth Army. The Armoured Group HQs all expired
between June and October 1942. In one case, the commander was posted
away without replacement three months before his HQ was dissolved.[19]

There is little evidence that either HQ RAC or Armoured Group HQs had
any impact upon tactical training in armoured formations. Their unhappy
existence was clearly the product of a struggle between Brooke and Dill on the
one hand and the interwar armoured enthusiasts on the other over the organisation by which armoured forces should be controlled. Brooke prevailed and
it was probably a good thing that he did. None the less, as will be shown in the
following chapters, considerable doctrinal confusion was to afflict tactical
training in both tank and armoured units as late as the end of 1943. Had HQ
RAC been vested with real authority, it might have been able to prevent that.

Whether a powerful HQ RAC could have extinguished the controversy
over the distinction between infantry tanks and cruiser tanks is another
matter altogether. The essentially limited task of helping the infantry cross no
man's land had been the job for which the tank had been invented. That is
why 'Plan 1919' counted as a radical departure. Despite the ambitions Fuller's
plan aroused in the Royal Tank Corps, the original infantry support function
never went away. The infantry continued to demand armoured assistance to
help them cross no-man's-land and the high command remained minded to
provide it.

In 1932 the Tank Brigade was ordered to include training in infantry support duties during its annual exercises. Such training, in Liddell Hart's view, 'did not repay the effort'.[20] The Royal Tank Corps preferred the glamour and potential strategic decisiveness of an independent mobile role. However, the differing tactical conditions to be expected in the two roles threw up contradictory technical requirements. A tank engaged in infantry support duties perforce had to move slowly and thus enjoyed limited opportunity to exploit cover afforded by the ground against enemy anti-tank weapons. The latter were certainly to be expected if the defences were strong. So the tank needed thick (and therefore heavy) armour. Because its role did not demand great speed or agility the detrimental impact on those performance values of the increased weight did not much matter. A tank engaged in independent mobile operations, on the other hand, needed a good turn of speed. Thickness of armour was less important because hostile defences would be less intense and the agility consequent upon lighter weight would in any case help such a tank evade tank-killing fire.

British tank designers found it impossible to reconcile in one vehicle these conflicting demands. So in the mid 1930s the General Staff decided to recognise two classes of fighting tank: infantry tanks for infantry support work and cruiser tanks for mobile operations.[21] Accordingly, two classes of armoured formation featured in the British Army's order of battle. On the one hand were the tank brigades, whose principal function was to support infantry and which were equipped with infantry tanks. On the other were the armoured brigades, the main striking force of the armoured divisions, intended for fluid, mobile operations. They were equipped with cruiser tanks.

The differences in armour thickness, weight and top speed that resulted from the infantry tank/cruiser tank distinction are shown in Table 1. But it was not only the tanks in the two types of armoured formation that were different: the tactics were too. Their training followed quite different lines. A unit that formed part of an armoured brigade was unlikely to be able to meet the demands of infantry support duties without retraining. A unit in a tank brigade was equally unlikely to be able to step readily into the role of an armoured unit. And it was more than a narrow question of training. It was a question of attitude too. In an armoured division the tanks were the principal arm that the other arms were there to support. Infantry tanks, however, were support weapons, there to assist the infantry.

The policy that produced this dichotomy remained until early 1945, when tank brigades were re-designated as armoured brigades. However, for two years and more before that change the policy had aroused dissent, most notably in Montgomery. He addressed the matter during January 1943 in a letter to Brooke. Writing with the authority of five successful months at the helm of Eighth Army, he argued that only one class of fighting tank was necessary, capable of both infantry support and mobile operations.[22] He never changed that view and commentators have tended to sympathise with him,

TABLE 1: BRITISH TANKS OF THE SECOND WORLD WAR

	Year of introduction	Maximum armour thickness (mm)	Weight (tons)	Maximum speed (mph)
Infantry Tank Mark I	1938	60	11	8
Infantry Tank Mark II Matilda	1939	78	26.5	15
Infantry Tank Mark III Valentine	1940	65	16	15
Infantry Tank Mark IV Churchill III	1942	102	39	15.5
Infantry Tank Mark IV Churchill VII	1944	152	40	12.5
Cruiser Tank Mark I	1938	14	12	25
Cruiser Tank Mark IIA	1940	30	13.75	16
Cruiser Tank Mark III	1939	14	14.75	30
Cruiser Tank Mark IV	1940	30	14.75	30
Cruiser Tank Mark V Covenanter	1940	40	18	31
Cruiser Tank Mark VI Crusader III	1942	51	19.75	27
Cruiser Tank Mark VIII Cromwell I	1943	76	27.5	38
Cruiser Tank Mark VIII Cromwell VII	1944	101	28	32
Comet I	1944	101	32.5	32

Sources: B. H. Liddell Hart, *The Tanks: The History of the Royal Tank Regiment and its Predecessors Heavy Branch Machine Gun Corps and Royal Tank Corps* (London: Cassell, 1959), Vol. 2, pp. 486–93; B.T. White, *Tanks and other Armoured Fighting Vehicles of World War II* (London: Peerage Books, n.d.) pp. 114–15, 120–4, 133–5, 140–1, 154–5, 267–70, 273–4, 322–3; E. Grove, *World War II Tanks* (London: Orbis, 1976), pp. 71–87.

seeing the distinction between the infantry tank and cruiser tank roles as an unworkable luxury.[23] At the time, however, as Montgomery acknowledged, most commanders-in-chief were content with matters as they were, and he made little headway with the War Office on the issue. Indeed, in January 1944 the War Office reiterated that technical considerations precluded the production of a general-purpose battle tank.[24]

It was not in Montgomery's nature meekly to accept disagreeable doctrine. He brusquely rejected urgings to incorporate a brigade of the heavily armoured Churchill infantry tanks in his order of battle for the attempted breach of the Mareth Line in March 1943.[25] From Sicily, he told the VCIGS, Lieutenant-General A.E. Nye, that he would not have tank brigades in Eighth Army and that he was converting the one that he did have into an armoured brigade. At that time he dubbed the dual-purpose class of tank he favoured the 'capital tank' and named the American Sherman as the most suitable machine for the role.[26] The Sherman was generally better armoured than the cruiser tanks it had supplanted in British service. It was, however, more lightly armoured than infantry tanks.

Where the Sherman scored over the latter was in its top speed, which, at 25 mph, was 10 mph faster. In Montgomery's capital tank concept, speed held a far greater importance than weight of armour. It was not until the Normandy campaign that he first had tank brigades – equipped with Churchills – under his command in battle. In October 1944 he complained that the Churchill's slowness (coupled with its inadequate gun – a failing that was not unique to the Churchill) rendered it unsuitable as a capital tank. Once the German front in Normandy collapsed, the Churchill brigades simply could not keep up in the pursuit.[27] He had written much the same in his 'Memorandum on British Armour' of 6 July, although at that time, for obvious reasons, he made no reference to the pursuit.[28] Undoubtedly, Montgomery's capital tank concept was a function of his overall command style. In particular, it suited his stress on maintaining balance at all times if his armoured forces were capable of both types of action. As it was, the Churchill-equipped tank units were unsuitable for the mobile role by dint of their low top speed. There was little Montgomery could do about it except complain to the War Office, which he did. But what of the armoured units equipped with cruiser tanks?

Montgomery's capital tank conception demanded that cruiser tanks take part in attacks on strong defences. In War Office philosophy, such attacks were the province of infantry tanks. The defining technical difference between the two classes of tank lay in the greater weight of armour carried by the infantry tank. The principal objection in War Office doctrine to the use of cruiser tanks for infantry tank work was that they were ill-protected against the stronger anti-tank defences bound to be encountered. Montgomery cannot have been unaware of this. One can only conclude that for him the advantages in convenience to higher commanders of the dual-purpose capital tank idea outweighed the increased risks run by cruiser tank crews.

Montgomery was not alone in his concern for operational flexibility. Those responsible for the training of the armoured forces in 21 Army Group before he took command appreciated that operational conditions would not always recognise the distinctions between the two types of battle tank. From the autumn of 1943 onwards, both infantry tank brigades and armoured brigades carried out a certain amount of training in the functions of the other variety. But the scale of such training, even after Montgomery took over, was quite inadequate. The different attitudes that went with the different roles were too deeply ingrained for a few days here and a few days there of alternative training to remove them.

Moreover, organisational differences severely limited the suitability of cruiser tanks for infantry tank work. In this regard, Montgomery completely failed to measure up to the situation. By 1944, the establishment of a British armoured division consisted of one armoured brigade and one infantry brigade together with artillery and engineer components. This gave the division the resources necessary to mount infantry attacks in brigade strength or lower with tank support. But the organisation of the division did not allow for the intermingling of armour and infantry necessary to achieve a properly co-operative attack. In the tank brigades, where co-operation with infantry was a primary function, decentralisation for operations so that, for example, a tank squadron worked with a particular infantry battalion, was a matter of routine. Indeed, the brigading of infantry tank units was primarily for administrative convenience rather than operational need. Tank brigade commanders frequently found themselves acting as tank adviser to a divisional or corps commander rather than as commander of their troops in battle. By contrast, the armoured and infantry brigades in an armoured division were regarded as discrete entities with separate, albeit complementary, roles. For the most part, the work of armoured divisions in training reflected the separate functions of the armoured and infantry brigades. These functions were conceived with the mobile role – exploitation or pursuit – in view.

In Normandy, however, there was little scope for mobile operations. Armoured divisions found themselves committed to setpiece attacks against strong enemy defences. Bloody experience persuaded them to effect a complete reorganisation of the division to allow intimate armour–infantry co-operation. Not until December 1944 was this recognised in doctrine, and then only in a pamphlet published by 21 Army Group over Montgomery's signature.[29] This was at least a year too late. The delay stemmed partly from inexperience but mainly from the failure of Montgomery and the War Office to agree over what armoured divisions were for.

This was not the only aspect of armoured organisation on which Montgomery clashed with the War Office. He also objected to the reorganisation of infantry divisions in the summer of 1942 to include an infantry tank brigade in place of one of the three infantry brigades. According to Martel, who had a hand in this reorganisation, its purpose was to get co-operative

training started.[30] Indeed, the records of tank brigades show very little training with infantry before their incorporation in infantry divisions. Scheduling
such training when the two arms lay at the ends of separate chains of command that met only at corps command level or above cannot have been easy.
Investing divisional commanders with power over the training timetable of
their tank support simplified matters enormously. Accordingly, much valuable
work in devising drills for combined tank and infantry tactics was carried out
during the life of the mixed divisions. In some respects this was a mixed blessing because the arrangement allowed individual divisions to evolve their own
techniques that bore little resemblance to those practised elsewhere. But it was
not for that reason that the mixed division experiment was unpopular with
some. In December 1942 Brigadier G.N. Tuck of the War Office's Research
Branch pointed out that with only two infantry brigades a British division
could not emulate the Russian practice of keeping the enemy under constant
pressure through day and night.[31] Montgomery claimed never to have liked
the mixed-division concept, and in January 1943 pronounced himself 'quite
certain that it is wrong'.[32] Only one division, the 4th, actually saw action as a
mixed formation, as part of First Army in Tunisia. The division reverted to
conventional infantry organisation before going to Italy in 1944. The mixed
divisions in Home Forces remained until the late summer of 1943 when they
too reverted to the three-infantry-brigade pattern and their tank brigades to
corps or army troops. Whether Montgomery's views on the mixed divisions
were decisive in securing their abolition is not known.

CONCLUSION

The general difficulties under which armoured training in Britain laboured
during the war can be divided into two categories, those that were inescapable
and those that the British Army imposed upon itself. There is space here to do
no more than mention the numerous shortages that afflicted armour in training. Most were inevitable in a small country engaged in a total war and fall
firmly into the first category. The War Office set limits on track mileage to
save wear and tear, to the extent that units were sometimes unable to take
their tanks out for months at a time. Similarly, gun-barrel wear was held in
check by severe limits on the number of rounds per gun fired. Shortages of
training land in the early years of the war made field training almost impossible for units that were not located close to the few training areas. The creation
of a number of large armoured training areas from 1941 onwards ameliorated
this problem. The number of RAC ranges also increased markedly, although
the allocations to units did not, presumably because of the expansion of the
armoured arm and the arrival of Allied armoured formations. Two to three
weeks per year on a fully equipped range was by no means a generous
allowance.

On top of administrative deficiencies lay the impossibility of achieving realism in armoured training. Again this falls firmly into the inescapable category. No army, no matter how well endowed with land and material, could have avoided it. For that reason its significance should not be overstated: the Germans must have had the same problem. Nor should the realism achievable in infantry training be overstated. Ultimately there was no substitute for the test of battle, whatever the arm. Even the sophisticated electronics that now assist the business of armoured training cannot replicate the unique stresses imposed on soldiers in battle. None the less, realistic tactics were slow to take root in the British Army's home training, as the following chapters will show. The particular problems of armour do perhaps help to explain why. They do not, however, provide the whole answer. For that, one must also consider the self-imposed handicaps that afflicted the British Army, those relating to organisation.

A consensus was achieved on the place of the tank brigades in the order of battle. Or at least War Office policy did move into agreement with Montgomery. However, there was no such agreement on the limitations of the tank brigades' role and the concomitant limitations on the functions of armoured brigades and divisions. Montgomery's disagreement with the War Office over the infantry tank/cruiser tank question was highly regrettable. The rights and wrongs of the dispute are not the point. What matters is that armoured divisions in particular trained according to the War Office conception of their role but ultimately had to function in battle according to Montgomery's different policy. That was a self-imposed failure. And it was not the only one. As the following chapters will show, disagreement over armour ran far deeper than Montgomery's misgivings over higher organisation. It descended to the very methods by which the different types of tank should carry out their assigned functions: the British Army could not even agree on how the various tactical functions of armour should be performed. Although official doctrine laid down by the War Office was frequently wrong, units often ignored it in their training even when it was right.

That doctrine for armoured operations should have been misguided is forgivable given the youth of the armoured arm and its complete lack of inter-war battle experience. Clearly, what was missing was an institution within the British Army that commanded both the resources to formulate doctrine that did meet the need and the authority to see that field formations trained by it. No doubt Martel would have liked his HQ RAC to wield those powers. Brooke's undermining of Martel flowed from his readily comprehensible anxiety to ensure a clear chain of command. The fact remains, however, that he failed to install an alternative mechanism to ensure that sound doctrine was observed in training. The resulting confusion and dissent revealed in the following two chapters made a sure recipe for trouble. Chapter 9 will explore the consequences realised in Normandy.

7

Armoured Divisions

THE ROLE OF ARMOUR

Until recently, historians' understanding of the British armoured arm between the wars has been governed by what might be called the 'Liddell Hart paradigm'. Liddell Hart claimed that the Army's high command adopted a wholly backward-looking approach to the question of tank warfare and failed to promote officers of the Royal Tank Corps (RTC) who, had they been placed to make full use of their expertise and vision, could have prepared the Army much more effectively to meet the German onslaught in the early years of the Second World War.[1] Scholars such as Bond, Winton and Larson have refined that analysis considerably, showing that the financial neglect that the whole Army suffered in the 1930s and uncertainty over the role the Army was to perform in a European war also hindered the proper development of doctrine for armoured forces. Indeed, the Army and the high command were far less hostile to mechanisation than Liddell Hart had claimed. None the less, these historians have accepted Liddell Hart's thesis that the Army misguidedly rejected the strategic ideas for the use of armour promoted by, among others, Liddell Hart himself and generally accepted in the RTC. Larson, in particular, has argued with admirable clarity that Liddell Hart and his friend Fuller expounded a distinctive theory of armoured warfare whereby armoured forces would not do battle with the enemy's main forces but instead destroy his command and communication facilities, thus paralysing the fighting components. Instead of adopting this theory as a strategic tenet, the British Army preferred to incorporate armoured forces in the attritional concept of warfare that had at length delivered victory in the Great War. Armoured divisions thus took on the role cavalry formations had filled in the nineteenth century. Had the British Army embraced the theory of armoured warfare, its showing against the Wehrmacht, particularly in the desert, would have been rather more successful than it was.[2]

Harris has mounted a vigorous challenge to the Liddell Hart paradigm. In his analysis, British failures in the desert stemmed not from rejection of RTC thinking but from its excessive acceptance. The tactics in which Major-General Hobart trained the Mobile Division in Egypt in 1938–39 set the pattern for the tactics that would bring defeat after defeat at Rommel's hands in 1941 and 1942. In Harris's judgement a coherent and relevant theory of armoured warfare never actually existed.[3] Where Hobart went astray was in conceiving the decisive battle of the future as an all-tank affair and in consequence neglecting interarm co-operation. Hobart also supposed, wrongly, that large armoured formations could operate effectively even if dispersed by units over a large area. It was not, therefore, a failure of strategic imagination that undermined British arms in the first half of the Second World War but a failure of tactical thought.[4]

Harris's explanation of the causes of the British armoured arm's problems in the desert war is the more satisfactory if only because any condemnation of the British Army's failure to adopt Larson's theory of armoured warfare must be based on the speculation that it would have worked had it been tried. As Larson himself concedes, not even the Germans tried it.[5] Harris's interpretation is more closely linked to battlefield realities in 1941 and 1942, and his account of the deficiencies in British armoured tactics was prefigured by no less an authority than Field Marshal Carver.[6] None the less, the Liddell Hart school was correct in claiming that a neo-cavalry role was laid out for armoured divisions. *MTP* No. 41, *The Armoured Regiment*, published in July 1940, directed that armoured formations should concentrate their attentions on the destruction of enemy armoured forces and mobile unarmoured forces. As for static enemy positions, wherever possible they should bypass them.[7] However, this very limited conception of the fighting role of armoured divisions did not survive for long. As Ogorkiewicz observes, from the first offensive in the North African desert British armour played a more versatile part.[8]

Indeed, in May 1941 the War Office outlined nine suitable roles for the armoured division in a new pamphlet on the subject. They were: (1) engagement of enemy armoured formations; (2) attacking enemy infantry formations except where holding an organised position; (3) outflanking movements and operations against enemy lines of communication; (4) maintenance of momentum in an attack after a breakthrough (i.e. exploitation); (5) pursuit; (6) reconnaissance in force; (7) counterattack in defence; (8) denial of ground to the enemy during a withdrawal; (9) action against enemy airborne forces.[9] In its increased emphasis upon unarmoured enemy as potential subjects of attack, this list of tasks represented considerable progress upon the previous year's guidance. However, that it appeared in the restricted-circulation *Army Training Instruction* series constrained its influence. A more widely distributed manual on armoured troop tactics published in September 1941 maintained that armour's primary role was to destroy enemy armoured forces.[10] It was this outdated doctrine rather than the more apposite list of May 1941 that can most be seen at work in armoured training over the next 12 months.

During this phase, armoured divisions not only trained according to a mistaken concept of armoured warfare, but also took markedly differing approaches to what was in effect the wrong problem. Such disorder was typical of the Royal Armoured Corps. Armoured training entered a new phase during 1942 in response to the lessons of battle experience in North Africa. No longer was armoured warfare diagnosed as exclusively an armoured business. It is no coincidence that the most radical of the many changes made in the composition of British armoured divisions took place in mid-1942. As the diagrams show, armour steadily lost its predominance as the war proceeded, the unit ratio of armour to infantry to artillery shifting from 6:2:2 in 1939 to 4:4:4 in 1945. May 1942 saw the armoured division lose an armoured brigade, gain an infantry brigade and double its artillery component. This rebalancing of the armoured division reflected the fact that enemy tanks were not the only, or even the principal, threat with which armour had to contend.

Correct diagnosis of the problem did not in itself ordain the right cure: British armoured divisions strayed up a few doctrinal dead ends during their training. The chief puzzle to be solved concerned the proper role of the expanding infantry component of the division. Intimately connected with this, though, was the problem of equipment unsuitability, that of tank armament in particular. The main guns in British cruiser tanks produced before 1944 were designed as anti-tank weapons. They were of limited value for other purposes. By good fortune rather than by good judgement, an American tank that filled what would otherwise have been a gaping hole in the British armoury became available just when it was needed. This was the Sherman, whose main gun was suitable for use against both armoured and soft-skinned targets. Home-based British armoured divisions were re-equipped with Shermans in the summer of 1943, thus opening a third phase in armoured training. Astonishingly though, the War Office promulgated no guidance for the Sherman's tactical employment. Armoured divisions were left to work it out for themselves. Naturally, some of them got the wrong answer.

The following three sections explore those three phases in the training of armoured divisions, concentrating mainly upon the armoured component rather than the other arms in the division. What, though, of the infantry, whose strength grew so prodigiously? There were two types of infantry in the armoured division: the motorised (or motor) battalions and the lorried infantry battalions. The latter were identical in organisation to conventional infantry battalions. They differed only in that they had motor transport for all men and equipment, whereas in conventional infantry units most personnel marched. The motor battalions had a different organisation and each fighting section rode in its own truck along with its weapons and basic administrative equipment. Because their transport organisation matched their tactical organisation, motor battalions were often described as 'tactically mounted'. Their trucks, however, were not fighting vehicles. They had limited off-road mobility and although some carried armour plating this was proof only against conventional small arms. The issue of American armoured half-tracks to replace the section trucks in the spring of 1944 greatly improved cross-country mobility but again their armour was easily penetrated by anti-tank weapons.[11]

DIAGRAMS 1–6. THE ORGANISATION OF ARMOURED DIVISIONS
IN THE BRITISH ARMY, 1939–44

1. Armoured Division, May 1939

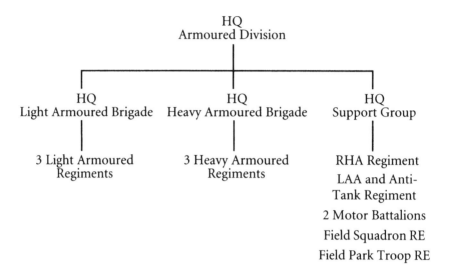

2. Armoured Division, April 1940

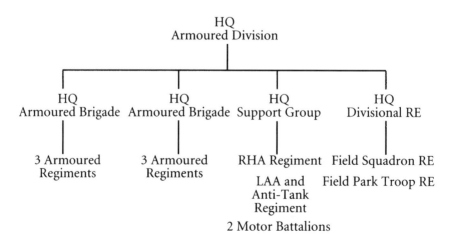

3. Armoured Division, October 1940

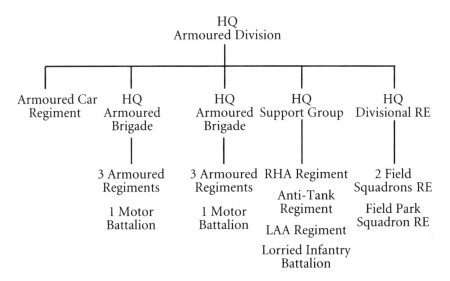

4. Armoured Division, May 1942

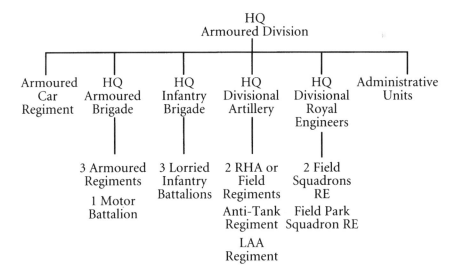

5. Armoured Division, April 1943

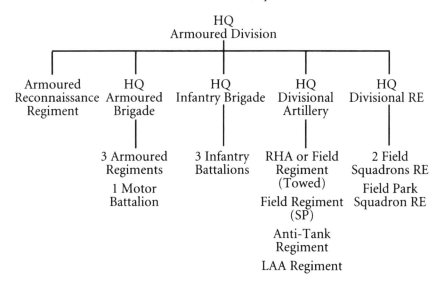

6. Armoured Division, March 1944

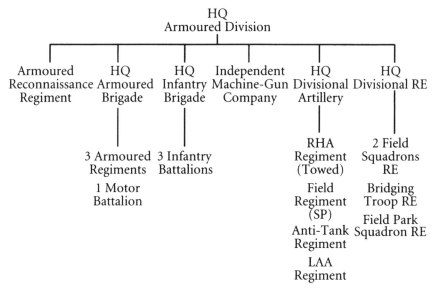

Source: H. F. Joslen, *Orders of Battle. Second World War: 1939–1945* (London: HMSO, 1960), pp. 3–10.

Each motor company included a reconnaissance platoon mounted in carriers, which considerably enhanced the company's tactical self-containment. A motor company was readily capable of operating decentralised from the parent battalion, attached to one of the armoured regiments. However, in official doctrine co-operation between tanks and infantry in an armoured brigade was very limited. The motor infantry's main function was to restore mobility to the armoured units when they met anti-tank defences that were beyond the ability of armour alone to handle. This meant not a combined attack in which the tanks supported the infantry but a single-arm infantry attack by troops from the motor battalion. Other tasks foreseen for the motor battalion included forcing an obstacle for the armour, mopping up after the armour, holding important locations and defiles seized by the armour and holding localities as a pivot for armoured action.[12] All were tasks for which armour was considered unsuitable. None involved intimate tank-infantry co-operation.

The lorried infantry had a still more distant relationship with the armoured units than their motorised brethren. Their functions included all the tasks that might be expected of the motor battalion, which latter the lorried troops were to relieve to allow the continuation of operations by the armoured brigade. One other function that fell to the lorried infantry was to protect the armoured brigade when it was in harbour, defensive work from which the motor battalion was apparently exempted. The divisional field and anti-tank artillery was mainly intended for the support of the infantry battalions in operations. Artillery was not thought to be of any assistance in tank-versus-tank battles. The Support Group as a whole, comprising the lorried infantry and the artillery, might also be used to occupy ground, particularly as a pivot from which the armoured brigades could manœuvre.[13]

This conception of armoured operations, which is summarised from *ATI* No. 3 of May 1941, clearly shows the order of primacy in the armoured division. The armour alone was regarded as the main striking force of the division. A realisation that tactical and topographical conditions would at times prevent the employment of armour led to an enormous strengthening of the proportion of infantry in the division. But in regard to the tactical relationship between the two arms, doctrine remained constant. The motor battalion in the armoured brigade had the closest relationship with the armour, but the co-operation between the two extended little beyond the armour handing over to the infantry to mop up, or the infantry moving aside from a gap they had forced in hostile anti-tank defences to allow the armour through. It was the armour's independent action, respectively before and after those two handovers, that constituted the primary work of the armoured division. All the other arms were there to prepare the way or clear up afterwards. Any tactical task that could not be accomplished by either the armoured brigade acting alone or the infantry brigade with support from the artillery was not a task for an armoured division. Although modified to the extent that artillery support for armour became essential to counter the Germans' prolific use of towed anti-tank guns (explaining the strengthening of the artillery in the division), that thinking prevailed in the War Office's policy on armoured divisions until and beyond D-Day.[14]

Segregating the armour and the infantry in adjacent but separate spheres of operation preserved the armour's mobility and thus served the division's overall purpose. Despite the expansion in the range of tactical tasks expected of armoured divisions, their place in the War Office's concept of operations remained the mobile role. The following description of the armoured division, published in July 1943, succinctly summarises the intended role for such formations.

> It is a mounted, hard-hitting formation primarily constituted for use against hastily prepared enemy defences, for exploitation of initial success gained by other formations, and for pursuit. It is designed for use in rapid thrusts against the enemy's vitals, rather than hammer blows against his organised defences. It is the rapier in the hands of the higher commander, rather than the bludgeon.[15]

DOCTRINE AND TRAINING, 1940–1942

Three British armoured divisions took part in the Normandy Campaign. Of these, one, 7th Armoured Division, was a veteran formation repatriated from Italy at Christmas 1943. The other two, 11th Armoured Division and Guards Armoured Division, had been raised in Britain in 1941. Neither saw action before Normandy. Their training forms the basis of this chapter.

The early tactical training of both divisions revolved around the assumption that armoured operations would be primarily tank-versus-tank operations. The 11th Armoured Division's exercise BULL in September 1941 is a good example. After a divisional advance southward across the North Yorkshire Moors, Major-General Hobart, the GOC, took his troops across the River Derwent before manoeuvring the two armoured brigades (29th and 30th) into opposing positions. Thenceforward, the exercise took the form of a battle between those two brigades on the Yorkshire Wolds. The infantry and artillery played a negligible role in this climactic action. Hobart pronounced himself generally satisfied with that, maintaining that unarmoured troops were usually a handicap in a tank-versus-tank engagement. However, in parallel with German tactics in the desert (official news of which did not reach Home Forces until six months later) he did suggest that in BULL anti-tank artillery could perhaps have been used to ambush hostile tanks pursuing retreating friendly tanks. Hobart dismissed 29th Armoured Brigade's limited use of its field artillery. Conforming with the advice of official doctrine, he held that 'little result is likely from HE [high explosive] against tanks', although he conceded that at ranges below 1,000 yards armour-piercing (AP) shot from the 25-pounders might have been effective.[16]

A demonstration laid on for General Paget (the recently appointed C-in-C Home Forces) when he visited Guards Armoured Division on Salisbury Plain in February 1942 presents an interesting comparison with BULL. An armoured squadron with a supporting field battery, anti-tank troop and infantry company formed the focus of events. Moving on the right flank of an imaginary divisional advance across the Plain, at Breach Hill the squadron came under fire from enemy tanks positioned hull-down 1,200 yards ahead on the other side of a valley. The programme of events ordained that a troop of field guns engage the enemy with direct fire at about 1,500 yards range from a position protected by the anti-tank guns, the infantry, and mines laid hastily by a sapper detachment. Meanwhile close-support aircraft bombed the enemy positions. This having failed to suppress the enemy, who continued to block the squadron's advance, a second field troop was to lay a smoke screen to cover the tanks' advance, in close formation, to close quarters. During this advance the armour was to thicken the screen with smoke from the close-support tanks. When the enemy armour had been defeated, other enemy tanks launched a counterattack upon the gun positions, which was easily resisted because the guns were in an anti-tank locality.[17]

Although the Breach Hill demonstration involved a tank-versus-tank battle, albeit on a smaller scale than BULL, the Guards armour relied far more on the support of other arms, principally artillery, than Hobart thought useful. The division had existed for less than six months and the Guards had not practised operations such as those shown at Breach Hill in their regular training. As such, the demonstration represents a somewhat groping exploration of the possibilities for all-arms co-operation within the armoured division. Presumably the field troop fired HE, since AP ammunition would not have been effective at such long range. In fact 25-pounder HE could not be expected to destroy enemy tanks, but direct hits and near misses would damage the vulnerable suspension and track parts, and flying shell fragments would drive enemy tank commanders back into their turrets. At this time, the use of field artillery against tanks was quite contrary to doctrine. The use of smoke laid by the field artillery to cover the tanks' advance to close range perhaps had some potential for favourable results, but good reasons to question the wisdom of the tank tactics demonstrated at Breach Hill will be explored later. The central flaw in the demonstration was its postulation of an all-armoured enemy. That alone renders it almost worthless as an example of realistic thinking and realistic training. This was no aberration. When Guards Armoured Division visited the RAC ranges at Linney Head in April 1942 machine-gun strikes on the mock-up anti-tank guns distributed around the battle practice course were not reckoned in the scoring. Although rectified when the Guards next visited in September, this speaks volumes for the RAC's early failure to appreciate the threat that anti-tank guns posed.[18]

This presumption that the operations of armoured divisions would be primarily tank-versus-tank actions continued to inform training exercises in both divisions until mid-1942. Actions against other types of enemy were not entirely neglected, but such major exercises as there were – and there were not very many – postulated some kind of all-tank clash. Although it is impossible to tell the role of the infantry in such exercises with certainty, it is reasonable to suppose that, where that arm took part at all, it played no more active a role than it had in the Breach Hill demonstration. And the infantry did not always take part in armoured exercises. Armoured units of Guards Armoured Division's 5th Guards Armoured Brigade took part in two exercises in May 1942: BIBURY on 8–9 May and STEWART on 22–23 May. The motor battalion, 1st Motor Grenadier Guards, took part in neither. It was not until exercise DERBY on 5–6 June that the brigade actually went out as a whole.[19] Indeed, there was no co-operative training between 1st Motor Grenadiers and the armoured battalions of 5th Guards Armoured Brigade before the autumn of 1942, despite official doctrine's specific message that sub-units of the motor infantry would normally be decentralised to armoured units in battle. One might almost draw some derisive amusement from the fact that exercise WHITSUN, scheduled for 25–26 May but cancelled owing to wet weather, which was to involve the 1st Grenadiers and 2nd Armoured Irish Guards, in fact involved the two units in opposition to one another rather than on the same side.[20] Had it taken place, however, the exercise would have represented a much-needed departure in the direction of training in armour versus unarmoured enemy.

The summer of 1942 saw the dramatic reshaping of the armoured divisions. At two brigades, the armour had previously dominated the divisional structure. Now one of those brigades was abolished. With the lorried infantry component uprated from one battalion to a full brigade and the field artillery component doubled, the balance of fighting arms within the armoured division came into approximate parity. However, this did not signify any fundamental reassessment of the functioning of the armoured division. It was motivated purely by the perception that the armoured division needed a more substantial infantry force if it was to overcome tactical problems arising in battle for which armour was not suited. Accordingly, the revised doctrine for the armoured division published in 1943 ascribed to the infantry brigade much the same roles as the 1941 doctrine had envisaged for the single lorried battalion. The presence of the brigade did not endow the armoured division with the capability to attack well-organised enemy defences. Moreover, the new doctrine ordained that the infantry brigade would normally be employed as a whole directly under the hand of the divisional commander rather than be decentralised to armoured units.[21] So at the minor tactical level, the new organisation changed nothing. The lorried infantry component had the same tasks, but was now of a strength better suited to their accomplishment.

It is all the more surprising, therefore, that 159th Infantry Brigade's arrival in 11th Armoured Division in June 1942 should have been followed in July by a series of combined camps in which companies joined armoured squadrons of 29th Armoured Brigade and artillery sub-units.[22] Relations within 29th Armoured Brigade between the armoured regiments and the motor battalion, 8th Rifle Brigade, had never extended to such intimate training. The same was true of 5th Guards Armoured Brigade. It was not until the autumn that armoured regiments in both brigades practised co-operation in battle with sub-units of the motor battalions with which they had been associated ever since the brigades' creation. Before turning to that it is necessary to examine more closely the training of the armoured regiments within these two divisions and the relevant official doctrine during the period up to mid-1942.

Whereas in the infantry fire and movement were complementary but separate activities, the armour on the face of it enjoyed greater potential for combining the two. Hobart, among other enthusiasts for armoured warfare in the 1930s, had maintained that tanks could and should produce accurate fire from their main armament while in motion.[23] British doctrine in 1941 was rather less positive on this point. Both in 1940 and 1941 official manuals stressed that since fire from a moving tank was less accurate than from a stationary vehicle, tanks should seek and use stationary fire positions whenever possible. The 1941 manual, however, added that the fluid character of inter-tank engagements demanded that tanks develop fire on the move so that they could exploit fire opportunities arising during the pursuit of enemy tanks. Accordingly, the specified open-range practices for tanks and armoured cars published in 1942 required motile firing.[24] Evidence on the efficacy of motile fire is inconclusive. On the one hand, Liddell Hart cites a number of examples of effective motile fire from British tanks against the Italians and the Germans in desert battles.[25] Contemporary advice drawn from experience in North Africa, however, tells a different story. In May 1942 the War Office pointed out that a fast-moving gun was unlikely to hit even a stationary target. Twelve months later the War Office stressed that experience showed motile fire with the main gun to be unusual and inadvisable at all but the shortest ranges. This, the War Office conceded, was a change in doctrine.[26]

In a lengthy training memorandum shortly after the birth of 11th Armoured Division in 1941, Hobart demanded that tank gunners be trained to fire on the move. Accomplishment in this field was as much dependent on the driver as the gunner. No tank was to move, Hobart ordered, without both the commander and the gunner in place. The gunner was 'the best judge and best critic of the driver, who must think of his gunner and drive so as to ensure the best possible gun platform'. An appendix, entitled 'Notes on Tank Fire', asserted that by keeping the tank steady the driver could boost fire effect by at least 50 per cent. In August 1941 an almost identical document was issued in the nascent Guards Armoured Division.[27]

For his unshakeable faith in the efficacy of motile firing, Hobart has recently been savaged by Harris, an authority on British interwar armoured doctrine.

But even Harris, no admirer of Liddell Hart, concedes the factual accuracy of the latter's history of the Royal Tank Regiment, which includes examples of successful motile firing.[28] Clearly such a technique could be effective. It is surely an unjust slur on Hobart's character to suggest that he should have persisted with a technique that was technically impracticable. Had it been so he would surely have known. In any case, certainly by 1941, Hobart was not addicted to motile tank fire. His 'Notes on Tank Fire' described the intertank battle of the future as:

> a series of fights for local and temporary (almost momentary) fire superiority. They will be decided by the ability of Tp, Sqn and Regtl Commanders to gain fire superiority for a few minutes in one place, and then in another. This will not be a matter of total numbers of tanks, or of blind charges by masses of AFVs.

> ... we must try to get ... simultaneous opening of fire from all available tanks under best conditions as soon as possible after first exposure. Tanks should therefore usually approach crest line (or cover from which they are to deliver fire) in line or line ahead ... with turrets already swung to the hull down or other fire position.[29]

Clearly, Hobart appreciated the advantage conferred by stationary firing. He appears to have conceived armoured engagements as ideally a competition of wit, in which the opposing commanders would attempt to manœuvre the other's forces into places from which they could be engaged by tanks in commanding fire positions. This concept, in which the operational offensive and defensive had no clear counterpart at the minor tactical level, did not work with the Germans, whose great reliance upon towed anti-tank guns demanded that they establish a position and entice their enemy to attack it. But Hobart's misapprehension as to the nature of armoured warfare should not damn the man completely. Motile firing, for Hobart, was simply one of several fire tactics for which his men should be technically competent.

Unfortunately, the records of 11th Armoured Division do not relate whether firing was practised at the halt or on the move. However, when the armoured units of Guards Armoured Division trained at Linney Head for the first time in the spring of 1942 tanks halted to fire their main guns.[30] It can reasonably be inferred that this was standard procedure. Battle practices at RAC ranges were standardised. There was certainly competition to achieve the best results within units and formations,[31] and the range staff are bound to have gossiped with the personnel of visiting regiments about particularly good or bad scores. In such circumstances it is hard to see inaccurate motile shooting surviving very long. In Guards Armoured Division, stationary firing seems to have been the rule long before official doctrine changed in 1943.[32]

The term 'hull down' was central to minor tactical doctrine. A hull-down position was one in which the hull of the tank was protected from enemy fire by cover, only the more heavily armoured turret being exposed. Because the main armament was mounted in the turret, a hull-down position combined a high degree of cover with the capacity for fire action. All the relevant manuals stressed its value as the prelude to a charge of some kind. The hull-down, preferably behind a crest and therefore with a height advantage over the enemy, was a position from which to surprise the enemy by fire, establish a moral advantage over him thereby, and then to chase him as he fled.[33] This somewhat one-dimensional conception of an armoured battle gained a good deal in sophistication from the manual on armoured troop tactics published in September 1941. Here there was rather less stress on the charge, and more on the fire-fight. Troops would conduct the latter from a succession of hull-down positions, moving from one to another in order to baffle the enemy as to the precise locations of his assailants. Moreover, in the troop training manual, much more stress was laid upon the skill and initiative of the individual tank driver, who was to be trained to get his vehicle hull-down when necessary without waiting for orders from the tank commander.[34] This postulates a somewhat more fragmented effort by troops, squadrons and regiments to that implied by the manuals on regimental and divisional tactics. Nevertheless, the conception of the hull-down fire-fight followed by the charge is the context in which the demand for motile fire must be seen.

Evidence of the type of tactics actually practised in armoured training during this period is not plentiful. It is reasonable to believe, however, that in 11th Armoured Division training reflected the preconceptions in Hobart's training instruction. His address on exercise BULL in September 1941 explained the tactics used by the opposing brigades in the final armoured battle. It is plain from his remarks, and from an accompanying map showing the movements of 30th Armoured Brigade, that both sides used fairly sophisticated tactics, including outflanking and pincer movements at brigade and regimental level. Although Hobart said nothing substantial on lower tactics, it is evident that he and his staff had established the movements of all the elements of the opposing sides. Had squadrons failed to act in the spirit of Hobart's doctrine, one can be sure that he would have said so. He did not.[35]

As a means of illustrating Hobart's approach to the tank-versus-tank action it is worth quoting Liddell Hart's exciting description of a 'battle' between 2nd RTC, then under Hobart's command, and 5th RTC, commanded by Lieutenant-Colonel J.C. Tilly, during the 1932 training season.

> Running on parallel courses they opened fire at 1,500 yards range. The 5th gained an initial advantage, but the 2nd retorted with a clever move – dropping out of sight by a somersault-wheel down a slope to the westward, they came back and 'peeped' their guns over the crest, thereby profiting from well-aimed stationary fire. The scales changed again when, as the battle moved on, Tilly cornered a company of the 2nd between two of his own. But Hobart brought a still intact company

round on to their tail, with a decisive bite – showing that in tank battle the value of the 'last reserve' was likely to be even greater than it had been in Napoleonic Battle.[36]

This was the kind of battle Hobart orchestrated in exercise BULL. It corresponded very well to the teaching of the training manuals.

Instead of the artful tangos that Hobart favoured, the approach in Guards Armoured Division better resembled British Bulldogs. Although the Breach Hill demonstration of February 1942 shows that the Guards envisaged better co-operation between armour and other arms than Hobart, their armoured action invariably took the form of a massed charge. At Breach Hill this was in squadron strength only, covered by a smoke screen[37] – not a wholly reliable means of protection. Breach Hill was no isolated instance of the massed charge. On 22 May 1942 the armoured regiments of 5th Guards Armoured Brigade went out on exercise STEWART which culminated in a massed charge by the whole brigade on a narrow frontage. The diarist of 2nd Armoured Irish Guards described this 'Balaclava' as a tactical 'nightmare'. But on 6 June, in exercise DERBY, the brigade carried out the same manœuvre against imaginary armour occupying high ground. Again, on 20 June, the Irish Guards carried out a massed charge during exercise DIGBY. Later that month, on becoming CO, Lieutenant-Colonel C.K. Finlay immediately announced the demise of the 'Balaclava' charge. Commented the battalion's diarist: 'it has survived so long, and is so obviously suicidal, that everyone was delighted to hear it is now right "out"'. But it was not right out. The Irish Guards' final engagement on interbrigade exercise LILO on 9 July was 'distinguished by an old-fashioned mass charge by the irrepressible No. 2 Sqn'. Moreover, Major-General Sir Allan Adair, Guards Armoured Division's longserving commander, proudly recalled in his memoirs 'a tank gallop through the best of the hunting country near Towcester' with which his division ended the Home Forces exercise SPARTAN in February 1943. Neither the umpires nor the local farmers shared Adair's pleasure in this at the time.[38]

Clearly the massed charge died hard. And it was not solely a Guards fetish. On exercise SARUM in July 1942, 2nd Armoured Irish Guards witnessed a massed charge by the enemy 20th Armoured Brigade that passed diagonally across their front. The enemy's tanks would have been easy targets had the Guards been armed with a better gun than the two-pounder. Much to their regret, at more than 1,000 yards range the umpires judged the 20th Brigade to have suffered few casualties.[39] As C-in-C of Home Forces, Brooke had condemned the charging tactics 9th Armoured Division used during interarmy exercise BUMPER in September 1941, which brought heavy casualties but achieved nothing.[40] It is remarkable that ten months later armoured divisions in their training were still practising such ill-conceived tactics. It is doubtful that Adair ever fully grasped their flaws.

Of course, Hobart's wonderful tangos represented a deeply flawed approach to battle with the Germans. In the desert British armour found German anti-tank guns to be the chief cause of tank casualties. For an armoured commander to hurl his troops around the battlefield in pursuit of enemy tanks was to invite disaster. Armoured battle had to comprehend other arms if such disaster was to be avoided. We shall examine the developments in doctrine and training that stemmed from the realisation of this later. However, it is appropriate here to mention what became of the tank-versus-tank battle in British doctrine. The tango conception was completely absent from the new edition of *MTP* No. 41 published in 1943. Not that the British Bulldogs beloved of the Guards found any official favour. A rather sedate polonaise filled the gap; indeed it could be argued that the British armoured arm was advised in 1943 not to take the floor at all when a German suitor asked for the pleasure. Instead, the new teaching advised the armoured commander to arrange his troops in well-concealed hull-down positions in some locality that the enemy would wish to control. When the enemy ventured to do so he could be attacked with stationary and obscure fire.[41]

The inspiration for this teaching, published in February 1943, became clear four months later with the first official lessons from Eighth Army under Montgomery. In a lengthy section on armour in the mobile role (if you please) the pamphlet adduced the battle of Alam El Halfa to show that in tank-versus-tank engagements the side that remained stationary and forced the enemy to attack enjoyed a great advantage. It would therefore be a 'cardinal principle' that: 'Whatever . . . may be the final role allotted to an armoured formation [presumably an allusion to a later pursuit role], its task initially will be to seize ground that is so vital to the enemy that the enemy armour will be forced to attack.'[42] That Alam El Halfa was a defensive battle, for which there had been no need for the British armour to 'seize' the vital ground, was not mentioned. It is improbable that such a scheme could have worked in offensive operations because in defence the Germans would have held any vital ground themselves, rather turning the tables. It is hard to view the stationary battle concept of tank-versus-tank combat as anything but the pursuit of the chimera of an all-tank battle. Not even Alam El Halfa had been such a thing. To the credit of troops training in Britain, they seem hardly to have practised such a battle after mid-1942, and when they did it was in its proper place as a defensive operation.[43]

To return to 1941 and 1942. Although Hobart's tango conception of armoured warfare was unrealistic, it bred excellent sub-unit training. The use of ground and general minor tactical sophistication by small units of tanks even when taking part in a 'big battle' exercise was far superior to that needed for the British Bulldogs' tactics of Guards Armoured Division. None the less, minor tactics were not entirely neglected by the Guards. On 2 January 1942, sub-units of 2nd Armoured Irish Guards trained in the action of a troop upon coming under fire from an anti-tank gun. In armoured jargon this was known as 'ant action' and involved a flanking movement against the enemy position by two tanks of the troop using natural cover, smoke and the fire of the third tank to mask their movement. The War Diarist thought fit to record it because Lieutenant-General Alexander, the Army Commander and himself an Irish Guardsman, happened to be visiting that day and saw the training in progress.[44] One can only assume that such training was practised on a proportion of the many days when the diarist of the Irish Guards, and in other units, merely recorded 'troop training' or some such. Similar tactics at squadron level were also practised in the Irish Guards, although not very often to judge from the diary entry recording one such occasion.[45]

The techniques of co-operation and communication essential to make such tactics work were highly important ones. But the emphasis on massed charges in brigade and regimental tactics left little scope for such skills, little scope for troop and squadron tactics at all. When Brigadier C.M. Dillwyn-Venables-Llewellyn took command of 5th Guards Armoured Brigade in May 1943 he laid down a similar troop 'ant action' drill to that prescribed in official doctrine. The mere fact that he did so suggests that such tactics were not a strong feature in the brigade's training. The spectacularly-named brigadier himself advanced a good reason for the Guards' backwardness in this respect. He maintained that it would be exceptional to use such tactics in battle, but claimed that the training was excellent practice 'in quick thinking and control'.[46]

Why should such an action be exceptional? Presumably because the extent of troop frontage necessary for it to be feasible without interfering with neighbouring troops was no longer envisaged. One might add that fire and movement within the troop would be a very vulnerable tactic because a single lucky strike by the enemy could deprive the flanking tanks of their fire-support. Official thinking came to discourage the notion that an armoured troop might function as a divisible unit in the manner suggested by Dillwyn-Venables-Llewellyn. An early draft of the 1943 armoured regiment training manual included several troop 'ant action' schemes, none of which survived in the published edition.[47] So Dillwyn-Venables-Llewellyn was not out of line to suggest that troop fire and movement would be extraordinary in action. But neither was he wrong to demand that his men practise it. It is clear that in Guards Armoured Division during the summer of 1942 the tactics practised at regimental and brigade level gave no scope for the application of troop and squadron manœuvre. All the emphasis was placed upon the controlled display of armour in mass. No account was taken of enemy action, the disruption to higher control that this would cause and the consequent need for officers at troop and squadron level to take the initiative. Although, as will be shown, the Guards moved cautiously away from charging tactics in the autumn of 1942, to judge by Dillwyn-Venables-Llewellyn's intervention in May 1943 they did little to foster fighting initiative at junior levels of command.

So the picture of British armoured divisions training at home in this middle part of the war is a mixed one. The 11th Armoured Division, under the leadership of Hobart, rejected the idea of interarm co-operation in battle, but within the severe limitations of that approach adopted a sophisticated and realistic approach to tactics in the intertank battle. Guards Armoured Division recognised the role of other arms, although evidence that such recognition extended to practical training is lacking. But the Guards' approach to intertank battle virtually precluded minor tactics – a shortcoming apparently shared by other armoured divisions.

ARMOUR AND INFANTRY:
BATTLE LESSONS AND HOME TRAINING, 1942–1943

Although the CRUSADER offensive in the Western Desert in the winter of 1941 produced no enduring strategic gains, it did teach some important lessons about armoured operations. As Eighth Army struggled to stem Rommel's advance during the first half of 1942, those lessons filtered back to the regimental libraries of Home Forces, courtesy of the War Office's new *Notes from Theatres of War* series. Two crucial points emerged from the first few editions. Firstly, armoured warfare was not exclusively tank against tank: a German enemy invariably included a component of towed anti-tank guns. Secondly, to overcome such an enemy, tanks needed the support of other arms.[48] The War Office summarised the position with stark clarity in May 1942: 'The recent fighting has shown beyond doubt that the tank cannot win battles. In the armoured division, tanks must act in the closest co-operation with infantry and artillery in order to defeat the German armoured forces.'[49] Although the War Office claimed, without serious mendacity, that experience in the Western Desert showed its previous training literature to be sound, the fact remained that armoured divisions training in Britain needed to change their ways. Until the summer of 1942, official doctrine went unheeded on the training grounds of England. It took the lessons of vicarious experience to transmute doctrine from printed page to training reality.

None the less, the War Office was not entirely candid in its reportage of battle lessons. Until May 1942, when the American Grant tank entered service in North Africa, the British Army lacked a tank that could fire a useful HE round. Later that summer, benefiting from further American generosity, Eighth Army received the first operational Sherman tanks, mounting 75-mm guns capable of firing both AP and HE ammunition. War Office advice to troops at home failed to underline the handicap that any tank suffered if it could not throw HE against anti-tank artillery. Consequently, although by the end of 1942 armoured divisions training at home had integrated their infantry tactically, their new habits still reflected an overestimate of the fighting power of the tanks themselves. They recognised and corrected this error in 1943 and the armoured brigade's motor battalion gained a prominence in offensive operations that it had lacked in the previous year's training. This was probably an over-correction, the occasion for which disappeared when home-based armoured divisions received Sherman tanks in the summer of 1943. Accordingly, the infantry role abated once more. This was confused progress, but it was progress none the less, and this section will explore its meanderings.

Reacting quickly to the early *Notes from Theatres of War*, Guards Armoured Division produced a lengthy training memorandum on 3 April 1942. Appreciating the trend in armoured warfare towards intimate all-arms co-operation, divisional HQ directed that all arms be available for co-operation training with armoured units. This heralded a shift in tactical method. Numerous objections can be raised about the methods of attack set out in the document. Mass charges of tanks remained the principal offensive stroke, for example. Yet the idea that objectives would be defended by enemy anti-tank guns and infantry in addition to tanks featured centrally in the Guards' doctrine. This represented a major advance. All attacks were to enjoy artillery support. Similarly, attacks by the tanks were to be followed up by motor infantry (although, harking back to Breach Hill, an illustrated example had the infantry remaining behind to protect the guns).[50]

It was not until the autumn that units of Guards Armoured Division practised anything resembling the attack schemes outlined in the April training memorandum. The primitive quality of the Guards' thought on these matters is evident in the course that events took when 2nd Armoured Irish Guards exercised with a company of the motor battalion and artillery sub-units under command on 19 October. The tanks led the attack but, because it was wooded, were unable actually to go on to the objective. Instead they were to orbit the objective, suppressing enemy fire while the infantry charged in over a distance of about 600 yards to mop up. In the event the tanks completed their circuit and retired to a rally point long before the infantry arrived. As the unit's War Diarist observed, the infantry would have been easy targets for any surviving enemy machine-guns as they approached the wood. Moreover, as they executed their circuit of the wood, the tanks would have been vulnerable to any surviving anti-tank weapons.[51]

These tactics were riddled with problems. None the less, the exercise did begin to bring training in Guards Armoured Division into line with official doctrine published nearly 18 months earlier and indeed with a divisional training instruction that was already six months old. In one particular, though, the Irish Guards introduced an important departure from the divisional doctrine. Whereas in the latter all available tanks participated in the assault, in the Irish Guards' exercise only two of the three armoured squadrons did so. The third remained behind and, in company with the attached artillery, provided covering fire for the squadrons making the assault. This use of tanks as self-propelled artillery appears to have become standard in Guards Armoured Division. A training instruction issued a few weeks later in 1st Armoured Coldstream Guards embraced a similar practice.[52]

For those tanks that did take part in the assault, the Coldstream's training instruction marks a shift away from the mass charging tactics used at Breach Hill. Each of the two squadrons conducting the assault was to form a separate wave, preferably assaulting from different directions. The progression from the massed charges of hitherto lay in the requirement for troops to operate a rudimentary form of fire and movement during the assault: 'one or two tps in each Sqn halting and firing two or three rounds per gun, while the other tps move forward to close the range'. The leading squadron was to overrun the objective and then withdraw to a rally point, while the second squadron remained at or near the objective until the motor infantry arrived to mop up and consolidate. Meanwhile, the support squadron was to exploit forward to forestall counterattack, accompanied by an artillery forward observation officer.[53] These tactics were much more to the point than those practised by the Irish Guards.

However, as will be shown, the use of armour as self-propelled artillery was deeply questionable and would become controversial by late 1943. It is note-worthy that 11th Armoured Division seems to have avoided the practice during 1942. Armoured regimental group training took place for the first time in that division at about the same time as in the Guards. Detailed evidence as to the tactics practised is limited but does suggest that, although the motor company was used in the same way as in Guards Armoured Division, all the armour assaulted and none of it operated exclusively in a fire-support role.[54]

By introducing co-operation between the armour and the motor infantry, 11th Armoured and Guards Armoured Divisions' exercises in the autumn of 1942 represented a great advance in tactics. That it took so long for both divisions to practise a proper level of interarm co-operation evinces a serious failure to apply the doctrine laid down by the War Office. Hobart's many critics would undoubtedly blame his allegedly persisting faith in the all-armoured idea for the inadequacies in his division. Even his devoted bio-grapher later backtracked on his defence of Hobart on this point.[55] In fact, while in command of 11th Armoured Division, Hobart clearly recognised the roles of other arms in the armoured division as set out in official doctrine. Indeed, he went beyond official doctrine in foreseeing the need for intimate armour–infantry co-operation in close country.[56] But before October 1942, when Hobart relinquished command, 11th Armoured Division did not realise this vision in training. Hobart's ill-health during 1941 and 1942 cannot have helped, but question marks over his thought and conduct must remain.

Like Hobart, the leadership of Guards Armoured Division clearly under-stood the need for interarm co-operation. That much is evident in the April 1942 training instruction. Getting brigadiers and colonels to understand was perhaps a different matter, and it was to those officers that the immediate responsibility for training fell. From the division's creation in August 1941, the GOC had been reluctant to interfere with his subordinates' training responsibilities.[57] The consequences of such reticence can be seen in the query raised by the War Diarist of the 2nd Armoured Irish Guards in June 1942 concerning the actions of tanks once they got on to an enemy infantry position. Methodical mopping up, necessitating a period of virtually static action, was clearly too dangerous. Attempting to mop up without halting the tanks was likely to be ineffective and result in collisions. 'For the first time one really misses the slow-but-sure tactics of the bayonet and Tommy gun.'[58] What at the time was perhaps regarded as an unseemly outburst of nostalgia was in fact a highly progressive notion in Guards Armoured Division at that time. Nothing was wrong with the bayonet and Tommy gun. They were necessary weapons and the motor battalion existed alongside the armoured units precisely to use them. It is remarkable that by the summer of 1942 the Irish Guards had not grasped this.

But the official doctrine, belatedly taken on board in these two armoured divisions, was itself gravely flawed, or at least it required different weapons and equipment from those then available. Until re-equipped with the Sherman, 11th and Guards Armoured Divisions operated British cruiser tanks mounting either a two-pounder or a six-pounder gun. Designed as anti-tank weapons, neither fired a useful high explosive round. An HE shell did not need a direct hit to be effective. A near miss could destroy unarmoured equipment and its flying shell fragments were damaging to equipment and lethal to men over a much wider radius. HE shells thus had substantial neutralising value even when they did not kill – a quality that armour-piercing ammunition just did not have.

The AP round projected a solid shot that harnessed kinetic energy to penetrate armour. To cause any damage it needed actually to strike the target. No gunner could count on a direct hit at long range upon a small (compared with a tank) and easily concealed object like an anti-tank gun. Accordingly, RAC weapons-training doctrine published in 1940 implied that against artillery the two-pounder could be effective only at short range.[59] The open-range practices published in 1942 went further, specifying the use of two-pounder and six-pounder guns against tank targets only. All other types of target, including anti-tank guns, were to be engaged with the tank's machine-gun.[60]

Even if accurate, machine-gun bullets would no more destroy an anti-tank gun than an inaccurate armour-piercing shot. However, as the open-range practices specified 40 rounds per target their neutralising effect was vastly greater. But the effective range of tank machine-guns was limited. The War Office reckoned it at 400–600 yards. All but one of the machine-gun targets specified in the 1942 open-range practices were at or below that maximum. The German 50-mm anti-tank gun, first issued in 1941, could penetrate 53 mm of armour at 1,000 yards, thicker than on any British cruiser tank in service before the Cromwell and thicker too than the hull armour on a Sherman. The heavier 75-mm and 88-mm weapons were even more lethal. Clearly, the machine-gun was no substitute for a dual-purpose gun.[61]

Field artillery was the weapon upon which armoured units relied for protection against hostile anti-tank guns at long range. An eight-gun battery, the standard allotment for an armoured regimental group, was by no means a generous volume of fire-power against an enemy locality likely to measure tens of thousands of square yards. To be sure of disabling all hostile anti-tank weapons, accurate information on their positions was necessary – an unlikely luxury given that in mobile operations the time available for reconnaissance would be limited. Although an artillery forward observation officer accompanying the assaulting squadrons could call down fire on to threatening anti-tank guns that disclosed themselves during the attack, a time-lag inevitably attended the process of passing target information back to the guns and the gun crews acting on that information. Even a few moments delay would be enough for the offending weapon to claim new victims. A more immediately-to-hand form of support was available from the two close support tanks held in each armoured squadron, but the range and HE blast effect of their howitzers was limited and they were used mainly for smoke[62] – another possible protection against the unforeseen anti-tank gun. Apart from the close support tanks, the regular tanks could lay local smokescreens using the two-inch smoke bomb throwers mounted outside their turrets. Smoke, however, was an unreliable tool, dependent upon wind conditions and liable to hinder as much as help.

Apart from the problem of the tank's unsuitable armament, the feasibility of the motor infantry's role in the attack is suspect. As mentioned earlier, in the Irish Guards' exercise on 19 October 1942 the infantry did not reach the objective to start mopping up until after the tanks had withdrawn to rally. This was characteristic of an exercise that was ill-conceived from start to finish. However, the problem of ensuring that the infantry reached the objective very soon after the armour was a general one. Failure to solve it meant that the tanks had to remain dangerously exposed on the objective – a flaw that tainted the scheme of attack outlined in 1st Armoured Coldstream's training directive just as much as it did the Irish Guards' ludicrous exercise. The problem was that the motor infantry had to dismount for action. Although some of their vehicles carried thin armour plating, they were too conspicuous and, being wheeled, too slow across country to be used in an assault.

The problem persisted until the spring of 1944 when motor battalions received American half-track armoured personnel carriers. In the meantime, one possible solution, suggested by the Irish Guards' diarist, was for the tanks to carry the infantry to about 100 yards from the objective. But this would stop the tanks from swinging their guns and thus heavily restrict their fighting power. There is no evidence that Guards Armoured Division ever tried it. The 11th Armoured Division did try it in 1943, but found that the infantry suffered great discomfort from the tanks' engine heat. The infantry also worried about their desperate vulnerability while perched on tank decks, deprived of their normal agility and removed from the minimum cover that the ground affords even an upright man. Experience in North Africa highlighted that problem and the War Office discouraged the practice in official lessons published in June and October 1943.[63]

Exercises held in the spring of 1943 obviated the problem by giving the motor battalion the leading role in attacks. A good example is exercise BLACKBULL, a demonstration for the Secretary of State for War by 11th Armoured Division held in May. One feature of the performance was the failure of an armoured regimental attack due to an unexpectedly strong anti-tank defence. This was followed by an attack by the motor battalion with fire-support from the armoured regiment whose earlier attack had been repulsed. Exercises in Guards Armoured Division during this period showed a similarly forward role for the motor battalion.[64]

In extending the role of the motor battalion into tasks that had previously been the preserve of the lorried infantry component, these exercises merely applied the lessons of operations in the desert during the first half of 1942 published by the War Office in October of that year. 'It seems that much greater use must be made in the future of infantry in close co-operation with anti-tank guns [an odd choice of weapon, and surely a mistake that should have read "artillery"] and the tanks to destroy the German anti-tank defence before our main tank attack is put in',[65] ran the advice in *Notes from Theatres of War*. There was no contradiction between that teaching and the official doctrine of 1941, which foresaw that the armoured brigades' motor battalions and the lorried infantry unit would have to deal with stiff anti-tank resistance.[66] But the words used suggest that the infantry had been little used for such tasks in the desert and also that the emphasis was now upon the use of infantry in most cases where anti-tank defences confronted the armour instead of only in the most severe instances.

Another passage from the official lessons of these operations, however, ran counter to the call for greater use of infantry to deal with anti-tank defences. This concerned the Grant tank (which first saw action at Gazala in May 1942) – a peculiar machine in that it mounted two main guns. In addition to a turret-mounted 37-mm weapon firing AP shot, the Grant carried a medium-velocity 75-mm gun mounted in a hull sponson. This fired HE, smoke and AP ammunition, albeit with a field of fire heavily limited by the gun's 30-degree swing. The lesson the War Office drew was that Grants

> should support one another with fire against targets not destroyed by the artillery, which open fire when the pre-arranged fire or smoke has lifted. Squadrons and troops must then cover one another's advance to decisive range, one squadron or troop engaging the enemy while the others take advantage of the effect of such fire on the enemy to advance, and so on, until the enemy tanks can be engaged at decisive range or his position overrun.[67]

By singling out the Grant tank for this tactic, the War Office can only have had in mind the capability which that tank and no other standard tank in British service had – the HE-firing gun. One can infer only that the primary use of infantry to overcome anti-tank defences was not necessary if the attacking tanks were Grants. What the War Office recommended specifically where Grant tanks were involved was little different in principle to the tactics followed in home-based armoured divisions using British cruiser tanks mounting two-pounders and six-pounders, which underlines the unreality of their training.

Unrealistic though the habits of armour–infantry co-operation practised in the autumn of 1942 were in regard to the capability of the armoured elements, the employment of the armoured brigade's motor infantry to deal with substantial anti-tank defences practised the following spring rather overestimated the stamina of the foot-soldiers. Frequent resort to infantry attack to overcome defences for which the tanks were not suitably armed would result in rapid depletion of the motor battalion's strength. In the words of Major-General G.P.B. Roberts (who had extensive experience of armoured regimental and brigade command in North Africa) when he took command of 11th Armoured Division in December 1943, 'I doubt if the Mot Bn would have lasted for more than 48 hrs.'[68] However, the arrival of the Sherman tank obviated the problem. With its high-velocity 75-mm gun the Sherman could throw both HE and AP, so it matched the capabilities of the Grant. Indeed, given the gun's all-round traverse, it exceeded them. Its fire-power and its reliability (in marked contrast to the British vehicles that it replaced) made it a great success in the desert.

Both 11th Armoured Division and Guards Armoured Division were re-equipped with Shermans in the summer of 1943, at last giving them a tank that could engage hostile anti-tank guns at long range. Thenceforward, training witnessed the motor battalions of both in a similar role to that they had played the previous autumn, i.e. mopping up and consolidation.[69] In Guards Armoured Division there were instances of the motor battalion engaging in somewhat more independent operations such as were envisaged in official doctrine.[70] The latter maintained that the unit might be used for a variety of offensive tasks in front of the armour, including mine-gapping, forcing obstacles and establishing a bridgehead. Doctrine also allowed setpiece attacks on objectives that were too strong for the armour to cope with but not so strong as to demand the services of the infantry brigade.[71] Roberts, however, envisaged that the infantry brigade rather than the motor battalion would be used in all cases where a setpiece infantry attack was required.[72] A comparison of the employment of the motor battalions of Guards Armoured Division and Roberts' 11th Armoured Division during the major intercorps exercise EAGLE in February 1944 illustrates the contrast. The Guards' motor battalion was used to breach a secondary minefield and destroy the enemy covering it and to effect a major river crossing. The War Diary of 8th Rifle Brigade, 11th Armoured Division's motor battalion, meanwhile recorded that the unit passed the entire exercise decentralised by companies to the armoured regiments – not an organisation conducive to major setpiece attacks.[73]

There is no need here to make a great issue of this variance. Both Roberts and the War Office held that infantry of one sort or another should take over from the armour when the latter encountered tough anti-tank defences. The limit of tank-and-infantry co-operation within the armoured divisions was quite simply the matter of the one arm handing over to the other tasks for which it was not the better suited.

It is clear that both 11th and Guards Armoured Divisions began their training in 1941 with quite unrealistic expectations of armoured warfare. In early training the notion that hostile anti-tank guns would be a significant foe did not feature. The object of all operations was the tank-versus-tank clash. In 11th Armoured Division little role in such an engagement was foreseen for arms other than the armour. Although marginally less backward in that respect, Guards Armoured Division favoured the armoured charge against hostile tanks in good positions, completely artless by comparison with 11th Armoured Division. Neither division considered the problem of the combined-arms enemy in early training. It was not until the middle of 1942 that such problems were considered, and only then did training begin to marry armoured units with an infantry component. This development in training at home corresponded closely with the official lessons of experience in overseas theatres published by the War Office. However, while those lessons prompted a more satisfactory quality of interarm training, they reflected little that was not clear in previously published, but ignored, doctrine.

In responding to the lessons learned overseas, commanders of home-based units were confounded by the wholly inadequate properties of their weapons. Tactics that worked in the desert were practised in Britain, but the lack of an HE-firing tank-gun rendered such tactics a nonsense. From mid-1943, however, when divisions training at home received Sherman tanks, tactics and equipment were at last mutually suitable. Although the role Roberts foresaw for the motor infantry was far more restricted than that envisaged in official doctrine and practised by Guards Armoured Division, no further change occurred in the division of tactical responsibility between infantry in general and armour before D-Day.

SHERMAN GUNNERY AND SET-PIECE ATTACKS, 1943–44

It is noteworthy, but perhaps not surprising, that the War Office neglected to confess the shortcomings of the weaponry installed in British tanks. Morale among the officers and men expected to fight with the second-rate equipment available might well have plummeted had the War Office been honest. It is surprising, however, that the War Office's doctrinal publications paid virtually no attention to the arrival of Sherman tanks in Home Forces. Not only was there no trumpeting of this tremendous improvement in armoured fighting power, but there was no explanation of its tactical implications. As if that were not enough, shortly before the Shermans arrived the War Office published new doctrine that, because written with the obsolete tanks in view, misled readers as to Sherman gunnery tactics. The timing can be put down to bad luck. That the bad doctrine went uncorrected for 15 months can be ascribed only to carelessness. In these circumstances, 11th Armoured Division's tactics went awry during 1943, but the arrival of a battle-experienced GOC six months before D-Day brought remedy. The Guards, however, found that on tank gunnery the new and misleading doctrine blessed their existing practices. They therefore maintained them.

In 1943 the War Office produced a three-volume manual on armoured operations under the designation *MTP* No. 41. The first to appear was Part 2, *The Armoured Regiment,* published in February and undoubtedly under preparation well before the British Army received its first Shermans. This manual ordained that the use of one part of the available force to pin down the enemy with fire from covered or hull-down positions was the basis of all tank tactics against a static enemy. A series of diagrams illustrated the application of the technique.[74] This teaching presumably accounted for the facts that direct hits by tank guns on anti-tank artillery were unlikely and that individual solid shots had little neutralising effect. Massing the fire-power would magnify the latter even if kills remained few.

The attractions of that practice to a unit equipped with HE-firing Shermans are obvious. Each squadron held 16 75-mm gun tanks, equivalent to two field artillery batteries. For a brigade-level attack, the gun-power of one supporting armoured regiment was equivalent to two field regiments supplementing whatever support was available from the Royal Artillery. Major-General M.B. Burrows of 11th Armoured Division undoubtedly relished these prospects. In a training instruction issued in April 1943, shortly before the Shermans arrived, he instructed that special attention be given to indirect shooting, such as might be appropriate for the supporting element in an armoured attack.[75]

If a third of the available tanks participated in the attack by bombarding the enemy from static fire positions, the process of choosing those positions and moving into place lent the whole operation a highly deliberate 'set-piece' flavour. Upon receiving Sherman tanks, 11th Armoured Division's tactics shifted in that direction. The BLACKBULL demonstration in May 1943, shortly after the Shermans arrived, which rehearsed the armoured brigade's battle drill for the attack, illustrates this. Upon receipt of information from the armoured reconnaissance regiment as to the enemy's locations and strength, the brigadier was to order an assault by two armoured regiments with the third giving supporting fire. The regiments concerned were then to move to positions from which to perform their role. This process, from receipt of initial reports to zero hour, was to take around 40 minutes. The attack had a definite beginning: it was a set-piece operation.[76]

Such stately progress was far too slow for Roberts. Addressing his officers shortly after taking command of 11th Armoured Division in December 1943, the newly promoted general asserted that armoured operations did not generally include set-piece attacks. He preferred a much less ceremonious entry into battle. Having penetrated a breach in the enemy's main defences made by other formations, Roberts maintained, the leading armoured regiment would quickly find itself in contact with the enemy. While that regiment engaged the enemy with fire in an effort to force him to disclose his locations, the brigade commander would send his other regiments around one or both flanks and they would similarly engage the enemy. Meanwhile, the armour would move forward under cover of artillery concentrations on centres of resistance. Fire and movement was the key. Tanks would move forward, profiting by the fire of the artillery and neighbouring troops and squadrons. Nobody would remain stationary if advance was possible. Roberts attached little importance to careful and deliberative reconnaissance. In the earliest stages of armoured operations, while the armour was pouring through the gaps in enemy defences made by preceding infantry formations, he proposed to use his armoured reconnaissance regiment to protect his flanks. Although once contact with the enemy was lost he would send reconnaissance troops ahead of the armoured brigade to report on the going and gather information about the enemy, only in exceptional circumstances would he await their reports before pushing his armoured brigade on. Saving time was far more important.[77]

It is important not to overstate the variance between Roberts' way of armoured warfare and the set-piece alternative. Roberts did not envisage a casual launch into battle. He did envisage manœuvre of units around flanks. He did envisage the setting of pieces in a limited sense. What he did not want was a long pause between first contact and the launch of the attack – a distinctive feature of the set-piece approach. Instead Roberts wished the first contact to be maintained and the enemy kept under pressure even while the manœuvres and preparations necessary for a flanking attack were made. It is not difficult to imagine the probable benefits in speed and economy of effort. By maintaining frontal pressure on the enemy his overthrow might be effected without flanking attacks by other units. Even if that happy outcome did not come to pass, then the pressure would hamper the enemy's efforts to improve his defences, with a corresponding beneficial effect on the prospects of the escalated brigade attack when it came. No competent enemy would have wasted the 40-minute lull demonstrated in BLACKBULL.

If the Sherman's fire-power encouraged the set-piece approach, the latter encouraged a regression to one feature of the tactics practised by Guards Armoured Division at Breach Hill back in early 1942: the charge. The 11th Armoured Division, which had never before been given to 'Balaclava' tactics, began to practise them after getting Shermans. A complaint made by an armoured regiment of 11th Armoured Division concerning operations during exercise CRUSADER in June 1943 conveys both the highly regimented flavour of a set-piece attack and the essential role of the assaulting tanks in such an operation.

A Bde [brigade] attack was put in on the left by ourselves and 24L[ancers] with the 23H[ussars] pinning from the right and the [8th] Rifle Brigade following the armour to mop up. There was a lag between the end of the gunners' concentration and the arrival of the armour which could be avoided if the Armd Regts were told the zero hour and allowed to move up to attack independently. Only those on the spot can estimate the going and as the plan sounds, it will be difficult for the Bde Comdr to order in his armour attack to coincide with the arty fire. On this occasion, we had to wait for the order to attack from our assault positions and had a lot of ground to cover. We could have moved up during the arty fire and waited in dead ground nearer the objective.[78]

Whether these complaints were justified cannot be judged. But the implication of this account is that the assaulting armour was expected to cover the distance from the assault position to the objective in accordance with a predetermined timetable, around which the fire-plan was constructed, and therefore with little mind to its own protection. That the timetable had taken no account of the topographical impediments did not help, but the central fact was that the assaulting armour's task was to charge the enemy.

We mentioned earlier Brigadier Dillwyn-Venables-Llewellyn's efforts to train 5th Guards Armoured Brigade in 'ant action' when he assumed command in the early summer of 1943. The brigadier, who had commanded 2nd Armoured Grenadier Guards during 1942 before serving as second-in-command of 29th Armoured Brigade in 11th Armoured Division, was undoubtedly trying to spread good habits learned in that latter appointment. Ironically, 11th Armoured Division then let those virtues slip. It is no surprise that Guards Armoured Division should have done so too. In fact, despite Dillwyn-Venables-Llewellyn's efforts, it is doubtful that the Guards ever really escaped from the 'British Bulldogs' tactics with which they started. His emphasis on initiative at the lowest levels of command sits uneasily with the predilection for set-piece attacks that the Guards certainly shared with 11th Armoured Division during the second half of 1943. Indeed, the plodding deliberation of the set-piece approach was even more pronounced with the Guards than in 11th Armoured Division. The 5th Guards Armoured Brigade easily trumped the 40-minute pause rehearsed by 11th Armoured Division in the BLACKBULL demonstration. A forecast of events prepared before exercise MOON in November 1943 envisaged a period of nearly three hours between the reconnaissance regiment's first contact with the enemy and the launch of the brigade attack.[79]

Having received Sherman tanks, the Guards maintained their habit of using a large proportion of their armour in an artillery role.[80] This basic misuse of armour had consequences. After exercise EAGLE in February 1944, Lieutenant-Colonel R. Myddelton of 1st Armoured Coldstream rebuked his men for failure to observe the principle of fire and movement, which he said would often be necessary within a squadron to accomplish forward movement.[81] Myddelton observed that such matters were of long standing. Assuming, generously, that the Guards had ever learned sub-unit fire and movement, they had since forgotten it. Fire and movement had been promoted to a unit- or brigade-level technique, allowing lower commanders to lapse into the old bad habit of massed charges, indeed demanding that they do so. This was the real price paid for using tanks as artillery in deliberate set-piece attacks. Although Myddelton clearly had some idea of what was wrong, there is no evidence of the clarity of vision at the top of Guards Armoured Division that Roberts brought to 11th Armoured Division.

Until armoured divisions had worthwhile HE fire-power in their tanks, that deficiency in weaponry confounded their tactics. They cannot be blamed for their misinterpretation of the proper role of their new HE fire-power when they got Shermans, for War Office doctrine appeared to endorse it. The result was that, until Roberts arrived to correct matters in 11th Armoured Division, in both formations tactics confounded the capabilities of the weaponry. Both misused their Sherman tanks as the agents of massed neutralisation fire, properly the function of artillery rather than armour, to provide cover for armoured charges. Roberts knew this to be a tactical blind alley that stressed the fire-power of the tank to the partial exclusion of its mobility. Keen to discount its value as a neutralising weapon, he pointed out that the Sherman's magazines carried too few rounds to make extensive neutralisation firing a sensible option. More dubiously, he claimed that the 75-mm shell's HE burst effect was too weak, when trials had shown it to be superior to the 25-pounder.[82]

Roberts was not alone in his anxiety to discourage tank crews from behaving like gunners. Indeed, a lively controversy on the question was whistling within the War Office in the autumn of 1943. In August, Major-General E. Fanshawe, responsible for armoured training at the War Office, had written to Commanders-in-Chief to clarify tank gunnery policy following the widespread issue of Shermans. Fanshawe advised that indirect HE fire would usually be by single tanks but that occasionally it would be more effective to combine the fire-power of a troop of three tanks for the purpose. He claimed that combined shoots by more than one troop had proved impracticable in operations. Finally, he stressed that the tank remained an assault weapon: turret-down shooting was a useful technique when within the range of hostile anti-tank guns but, he implied, was to be continued only so long as was needed to eliminate a specific enemy threat.[83] This policy was reiterated and slightly hardened in October by Major-General R. Briggs, the War Office Director of the Royal Armoured Corps:

> although ... 'turret down' shooting bears some resemblance to indirect fire as practised by the Artillery, it is not the intention of the General Staff that armoured formations should usurp the functions of the Royal

Artillery. The limit of control by one commander for turret down shooting will be his own troop of three tanks and this form of shooting will be used only when tactical conditions make it desirable.

The primary function for armoured formations is to combine fire and movement, and any tendency towards static roles is to be discouraged.[84]

If Fanshawe and Briggs were concerned that armoured units were falling into artillery habits, their concerns were well justified, as we have seen. Writing to Fanshawe later that year, Major-General C.W. Norman of GHQ Cairo cited cases of successful supra-troop HE shoots in recent operations in the Mediterranean theatre. Norman suggested that official disapproval of such practices be relaxed. He also mentioned that he had heard (correctly, as we know) that squadron and regimental shoots featured in the training of armoured units in Britain.[85] Commenting upon Norman's letter, Major-General Whitaker (the Director of Military Training and Fanshawe's chief), who had recently returned from a lengthy tour of the Mediterranean theatres, cited 15 Army Group 'who I found strongly deprecated tanks devising good reasons for sitting behind hills'.[86]

Whitaker's line remained the official policy for the time being. However, squadron HE concentrations featured in gunnery training carried out by 2nd Fife and Forfar Yeomanry of 11th Armoured Division in September 1943.[87] If the War Office's policy was made known to that division, evidently it was ignored. Roberts' strictures on Sherman gunnery would not otherwise have been necessary. Probably the first opportunity regimental officers had to scrutinise official thinking came in January 1944 when the War Office published the policy in an appendix to the *Army Training Memorandum*.[88] By that time Roberts had already educated 11th Armoured Division in the lessons of his battle experience, which accorded with official thinking at that time. However, the policy was about to change in the light of more recent battle experience.

Not all Whitaker's colleagues in the War Office favoured his downright rejection of Norman's suggestion. Briggs took a more indulgent attitude, accepting that squadron shoots had 'come to stay and are of proved value'. He felt that while stressing that collective shooting was not armour's primary role it was right to endorse occasional supra-troop shoots.[89] A major tank gunnery conference held in January 1944 concluded that squadron and regimental shooting should not be ruled out even though the troop should be regarded as the basic sub-unit for the control of indirect fire.[90] The War Office accepted the conference's recommendations in March[91] and published its new policy in the *Army Training Memorandum* three months later.[92] Few officers of 11th Armoured Division can have had time to read it. In any case, it did not endorse a return to the tactics ante-Roberts. Squadron and regimental shoots were sanctioned only as occasional departures from a norm that did not embrace control of fire above troop level. When recommending the relaxation of official policy, Norman suggested that the collectivisation of armoured fire-power above troop level was to be reserved for static tactical conditions as a means of restoring fluidity.[93] His comments resonated with the tactical conditions on the Italian front. The 11th Armoured Division was supposed to be training for fluid battle. Not that Whitaker's sneering remark about tanks preferring to sit behind hills was a fair reflection of the practice in 11th Armoured Division before Roberts assumed command. The division's practice was for only one-third of the tank strength to give supporting fire while the rest of the tanks advanced. It is in the manner of that advance that the most biting significance of the collective HE shooting lies, at least so far as the divisions training in Britain are concerned.

Because the 75-mm gun made neutralisation fire tactics possible, and because the latter greatly improved the prospects of a charge, there is a clear link between the introduction of the Sherman and the armoured tactics practised by 11th Armoured Division in the second half of 1943. Guards Armoured Division had practised such tactics even earlier, in the autumn of 1942 long before taking delivery of Shermans. However, as has been mentioned, the field army could point to War Office doctrine published in February 1943 that endorsed neutralisation fire tactics with a series of illustrative diagrams.[94] In May 1944 the War Office cancelled those diagrams and their accompanying narrative, explaining that new tactics now applied as a result of changes in tank armament.[95] This was a belated response to the arrival of Sherman tanks in the home-based armoured divisions a year earlier. Careful readers of the *Army Training Memorandum* and *Notes from Theatres of War* might have been able to discern what the War Office was getting at, for both had carried accounts of armoured battle that read consonantly with Roberts' teaching.[96] Yet the War Office published no guidance to the new tactics, neglecting even to refer readers to those other publications. At that stage, with units heavily occupied with final preparations for OVERLORD, accurate teaching might not have made much impression. It would, however, have justified a verdict that the War Office got the doctrine right in the end. As it was, such a verdict would be wrong.

CONCLUSION

In the early training of both 11th and Guards Armoured Divisions the importance of the infantry was grossly underestimated. It was not until lessons learned in North Africa showing that armour could not win battles alone were officially promulgated that training in the two armoured divisions considered here began to comprehend the techniques of using infantry to mop up after the armour. It is not the purpose of this study to criticise the tactics of Eighth Army, but it cannot be overlooked that the lessons learned in operation CRUSADER ought to have surprised no one familiar with the doctrine for armoured operations published in May 1941. Officers fighting battles can be excused lack of familiarity with such literature. Those engaged in the comparatively leisurely activity of training at home cannot. It is clear that they had not read the doctrine.

Recognition of the important role to be played by infantry went hand in hand with proper consciousness of the limitations of the tank as an instrument of battle, particularly its vulnerability to unarmoured enemy. Whereas in the spring of 1942 enemy tanks were the principal concern of tactical training in armoured units, by the autumn enemy infantry positions bolstered by anti-tank guns and perhaps some armour featured as the objectives in field exercises. The inference to be drawn from battle experience overseas, as reported in official publications, was that the stationary anti-tank gun was the tank's chief enemy. The War Office made this explicit in October 1943 and battle-experienced officers disseminated the bald truth that three-quarters of the armoured division's fighting was against anti-tank guns.[97] Although the general drift of this truth was clear to the forces training in Britain by the end of 1942, considerable confusion remained over the tactics it demanded.

At the heart of the problem lay the unsuitability of the guns mounted by British tanks for action against unarmoured targets. Following War Office advice, in the spring of 1943 both 11th Armoured Division and Guards Armoured Division resorted to the extensive use of their motor infantry battalions. Use of the motor battalion to deal with all forms of anti-tank opposition certainly preserved the armour, but at the expense, in real battle conditions, of unsustainable infantry casualties. The issue of Sherman tanks in the summer of 1943 overcame that problem. For the first time the two armoured divisions had equipment capable of dealing with all natures of enemy threat, although in armour-piercing capability the 75-mm gun fell short of that necessary to counter the German Tiger tank. Armoured units took to employing their new tanks' HE capability as mobile artillery. They were far more suitable for such employment than the old two-pounder- and six-pounder-equipped vehicles. When the War Office cancelled the doctrine that part of any armoured force should be used in a pinning role, the new tactics (which were not actually specified) were ascribed to the capabilities of the new tank armament. In fact, the old armament was quite unsuitable for the old tactics and the new armament was eminently suitable, facts that an honest administration would have admitted. It is hardly surprising that the old tactics remained in favour within armoured units. By comparison with the tactics Roberts favoured, the old tactics emphasised the fire-power of the tank and underplayed its mobility. They placed armour in either a static fire-support role or in a mobile assault (or charging) role. Roberts preferred that alternation between these two roles should take place rapidly and frequently during each attack and be organised at squadron or even troop level. The tanks should use HE shells against specific targets identified during an operation, leaving the task of area neutralisation to the artillery.

The progress of Guards and 11th Armoured Divisions during the three years of training preceding their deployment in Normandy can hardly be regarded as smooth. Both formations passed from one conception of how to prosecute their tactical tasks to another, and then to another, roughly reflecting the lessons learned by their colleagues fighting overseas. Their progress was confused because the process of correcting the flawed tactical conception of armoured warfare with which the British Army started the war was confused. Nevertheless, by mid-1942 recognition that armoured warfare was not exclusively a tank affair was well established in Britain, and by the end of that year training reflected that recognition. It could have come sooner, but only if those fighting in the North African littoral had first distilled the necessary lessons from their experience. It has been shown that the important lesson about the effectiveness of German anti-tank guns in the desert was disseminated in Britain in the spring of 1942 following operation CRUSADER. It was no fault of anyone in Britain that Eighth Army did not learn this lesson in operation BATTLEAXE six months earlier.

So far as Guards and 11th Armoured Division were concerned it did not matter that lessons from the desert took many weeks to pass up and down the chains of command between Britain and North Africa. Although they did not know it then, neither division would see battle for two years. Such delays in the dissemination of lessons from Tunisia the following year were more critical. In important respects the lessons themselves, at least as published by the War Office, were less helpful than they might have been. This was because they did not properly account for the Sherman tank with its dual-purpose gun. That the War Office failed to publish (rather than merely announce in a circular to higher HQs) a proper doctrine for the use of this weapon was perhaps its greatest failure of the war in the field of doctrinal dissemination.

It was particularly unfortunate that the issue of Sherman tanks in Britain coincided with the publication of a new edition of *MTP* No. 41 that had been written with six-pounder-armed vehicles in mind. This encouraged both Guards and 11th Armoured Divisions to continue with the old tactics when their weapons facilitated much better, more mobile, tactics. Roberts' arrival in 11th Armoured Division, and his swift correction of the division's neutralisation tank gunnery and setpiece attack habits demonstrates the benefit conferred by the marriage of battle-experienced commanders with unblooded troops. Guards Armoured Division enjoyed no such benefit. Given the highly restricted choice of divisional commanders available (he had to be a Guardsman) it is difficult to see how it could have done. Montgomery did try to sack Adair in February 1944 on the grounds that he lacked drive, but was thwarted by the refusal of the corps commander (the recently escaped PoW, Lieutenant-General R.N. O'Connor) to submit an unfavourable report on him.[98] Whoever Montgomery had in mind to replace Adair, the Guards appear not to have been advised to drop set-piece attacks and neutralisation gunnery. Therefore, they went to Normandy without having had the opportunity to acquaint themselves with lessons that had been learned more than a year earlier in North Africa. This goes some way to explain why it was Roberts' 11th Armoured Division and not Adair's Guards Armoured Division that earned the reputation as the best British armoured division in North-West Europe.[99] Having said that, 11th Armoured Division had little time to practise the tactics that Roberts brought with him. Thus the conclusion on the training of these two armoured divisions must be that neither was as well prepared for the role that they were intended to perform as they might have been.

8

Tank Co-operation with Infantry

During operation BATTLEAXE – Wavell's failed offensive in North Africa in June 1941 – a squadron of Matilda infantry tanks led an attack on the German position at Halfaya Pass. The plan was for the infantry to remain behind the start-line until the tanks had seized the objective. The Matildas, however, were torn to pieces by 88-mm guns sited behind sangars, and the attack failed miserably.[1] Three years later, on 11 June 1944, Sherman tanks from 4th/7th Dragoon Guards led an attack by 6th Green Howards on the village of Cristot in Normandy. A similar disaster ensued. The tanks crossed fields and entered the orchards surrounding the village. The infantry followed a little later. They were held up by enemy infantry who had lain low in hedges and ditches when the tanks passed earlier. The Green Howards never reached the orchards, where the tanks were suffering heavy casualties to anti-tank gunfire. Of nine tanks that penetrated to the orchards, only two survived to withdraw when the attack was abandoned.[2]

Despite the passage of three years, and the enormous topographical difference between the Western Desert and the Norman countryside, the chief tactical lesson of both these failed attacks was identical. It was that tanks were incapable of helping the infantry in the attack unless the infantry furnished reciprocal support to the tanks. Effective tank–infantry co-operation was a mutual exercise. If it were treated simply as a matter of the former supporting the latter, operations would fail.

One of the chief purposes for which the tank had been invented during the Great War was to engage enemy machine-gun posts from behind bullet-proof protection and thus enable the infantry to advance unmolested. Essentially this remained the principal task of infantry tanks throughout the Second World War. To do this, tanks had to overcome the threat presented by anti-tank weapons. Anti-tank artillery, either towed or tank-mounted, was the main perceived threat in 1939. Most armies also possessed anti-tank small arms, such as the anti-tank rifle and hand-thrown or rifle-launched anti-tank grenades. Although such weapons threatened lightly armoured vehicles, infantry tanks carried heavy armour and remained fairly safe, although not immune, from small arms until the introduction of the Panzerfaust later in the war. The British Army did not anticipate another anti-tank weapon that became a major menace by the middle years of the war, the anti-tank mine.

Technical improvement formed one means by which to overcome such dangers. Thickness of armour increased in response to the ever-increasing power of anti-tank guns. Gun power also improved. The Mark I infantry tank, which carried no more powerful weapon than a turret-mounted machine-gun, was withdrawn from service after Dunkirk. This left the obsolescent two-pounder as the main armament of British tanks, which the six-pounder gradually replaced from 1942 onwards. A British-made version of the American 75-mm gun supplanted the inadequate six-pounder in a proportion of Churchills from late 1943 onwards. But, as in every other sphere of military operations, technical capability was not enough. Its effective application was a tactical matter.

All tanks of this period shared a number of inherent weaknesses. The crewmen inside a tank were half-blind. Narrow vision slits and optical instruments with a limited field of view were their eye on the battlefield. Spotting the usually well-concealed enemy machine-guns against which the infantry demanded the tanks' help was not easy, especially when the tank was pitching and rolling as it moved. Enemy anti-tank guns presented similar problems of detection, and for most of the war German anti-tank guns were capable of destroying British tanks at ranges of many hundreds of yards. British tanks could not hope to prosper unless those guns were identified and dealt with.

Not only were tank crewmen half-blind in their steel shells, they were half-deaf too. No man sat more than a few feet from the engine. Its noise quite overwhelmed the reports of firearms and explosions that might otherwise have helped to compensate for limited vision. Slow to detect danger, tanks were also slow to react when they did. Even the lightest tank was a clumsy device. It could not fall flat on the ground, stop, start or change direction in a split second, as a man could. A rut in a track might be enough to protect a man from direct fire; a tank required at least ten feet of depth. From his rut, an infantryman would see and hear what was happening on the battlefield around him with far less hindrance than a tank commander. Although the latter might put his head out of the turret, silhouetted against the sky he presented an irresistible target to enemy snipers. If he eluded that peril and spotted a target, traversing the main gun took precious seconds, whereas a rifleman or light machine-gunner could have his weapon pointing towards a target almost immediately.

In areas where the tank was weak – sensory perception and agility – the infantryman on the ground was strong. Fire-power and bullet-resistance, faculties in which the tank was strong, were weak links for the infantryman. These comparisons formed the starting point for the elaboration of effective tank–infantry co-operation tactics such as can be seen in the second attack on Cristot, mounted five days after the first. Attacking over exactly the same ground, this time the tanks and the infantry moved in closer proximity to one another, swapping the lead as the changing topography demanded. The attack succeeded with three men dead, 24 wounded and no tank losses.[3] The purpose of this chapter is to explain how it was that lessons first taught in Africa three years earlier had to be taught all over again when the British Army landed in Normandy.

Ironically, given that the British had invented it, the tank was largely an unknown quantity to the typical British soldier in the early years of the Second World War. The German successes in 1939 and 1940 with liberal quantities of armour did nothing to diminish what British generals recognised as 'tank terror' among British infantrymen stationed at home after Dunkirk. Put bluntly, the British infantryman viewed the tank as a virtually invincible monster, whose friendly presence on the battlefield assured him of success. The tank's inherent weaknesses scarcely featured in his thinking. Naturally, he preferred such awesome creatures to advance in front of him where they could do most of the killing and shrug off most of the punishment the enemy could throw at them. As the Halfaya Pass incident suggests, in the first two years of the war official doctrine reflected this ignorant estimation.

Tank crewmen, whose working environment was a good deal less well protected and whose fighting power was rather less awesome than allowed in the average foot-soldier's philosophy, saw things rather differently. For one thing, as we have seen, the tank crew could see very little. Not only could the tanks alone not be relied upon to locate and clear every enemy machine-gun post, but the tanks themselves would be hard put to defend themselves against the large quantity of anti-tank artillery inevitable in any strongly defended enemy position. They needed infantry help in both tasks.

These facts were well known to the writers of British doctrine well before D-Day, although one could not conclude as much from the tactics used in the first attack on Cristot. The British Army had learned the painful lessons of BATTLEAXE, although perhaps not as quickly as it should have done. Subsequent operations in the Western Desert and in Tunisia prompted the publication of new doctrine in May 1943, which should have ensured that tanks and infantry never became designedly separated in the attack in the way that they did on 11 June 1944. It took the troops in Britain preparing for OVERLORD some months to apply the new doctrine in their training but, prompted by a vigorous young staff officer fresh from commanding an armoured regiment in the North African battle, by the beginning of 1944 training was at last beginning to reflect the lessons of experience. None the less, the discredited doctrine that produced the tactics used at Cristot re-appeared before OVERLORD. As will be shown, this extraordinary development, which condemned British troops to the painful relearning of elementary lessons, resulted entirely from the military vanity of General Sir Bernard Montgomery.

DOCTRINE AND TRAINING, 1939–43

In September 1939 the War Office published a new pamphlet on infantry tank operations, outlining the tactical methods by which a combined tank and infantry assault should be conducted. As with all setpiece attacks, an artillery barrage formed the framework upon which the other arms arranged their operations. This, and artillery fire called down by forward observation officers accompanying the tanks, represented the tanks' main redress against enemy anti-tank artillery. There were to be two echelons of tanks with an echelon of infantry advancing behind the first and in front of the second. The task of the first tank echelon was two-fold. Its leading tanks were to 'fall upon' and suppress the enemy defences before they could recover from the effects of the artillery barrage. The following tanks of the first echelon were to regulate their speed to the pace of the following infantry. Their task was to neutralise small-arms fire from enemy who had survived the barrage and the passage of the leading tanks. The following infantry were to keep as close as possible behind the tanks. The closer they were, the better their chances of preventing the re-activation of enemy machine-guns after the passage of the barrage, and the more help they could be to the tanks against hostile anti-tank guns. Additional support for the infantry came from the second echelon of tanks which normally was to move behind the foot soldiers but was to be ready to go forward or to a flank immediately if necessary to deal with troublesome short-range small-arms fire.[4]

It is important to note not only that the tanks led the attack, but that the leading wave of the first echelon was expected to advance independently of the infantry. At least one officer of the Royal Tank Regiment doubted the wisdom of this. Major (later General) H.E. Pyman, an instructor at the Indian Army Staff College until February 1941, taught his students that only if the defence was weakening would it be prudent to push tanks far forward of the infantry. Against a properly prepared and intact enemy position, Pyman maintained that the first echelon should comprise both tanks and infantry in a formation no more than 100 yards deep, moving behind a barrage at infantry speed. He reserved the tanks-only first wave of the first echelon for use only against an enemy that had already cracked.[5] This contrasted starkly with War Office teaching that only when attacking a weak enemy position or when the ground was unsuitable for tanks should the infantry lead.[6]

Pyman's views are of particular interest since he was the staff officer who later helped to correct, temporarily, the bad tactical habits prevailing among tanks and infantry in 21 Army Group before D-Day. Meanwhile, however, operational experience seemed to prove the wisdom of War Office doctrine. During the BEF's campaign in France and Belgium, the imperviousness of the Marks I and II infantry tank to the German 37-mm anti-tank gun was noted by British and Germans alike. But the British remained largely unaware of the anti-tank capability of the 88-mm anti-aircraft gun. In particular, they did not realise the crucial role that weapon had played in defeating the Arras counterstroke, the only substantial offensive experience British armour gained against the Germans before the middle of 1941.[7]

The 7th Royal Tank Regiment, one of the units engaged at Arras, later moved out to the Middle East with Mark II 'Matilda' infantry tanks. The battalion's training in the desert between September and December 1940 strongly emphasised the *MTP* No. 22 pattern of attack: the first (tank-only) wave arriving on the objective between ten and 20 minutes before the second (combined) wave.[8] Such training would serve them well in the forthcoming operations against the Italians as part of Lieutenant-General R.N. O'Connor's Western Desert Force. Although they needed infantry and engineer assistance to clear mines and breach obstacles, the Matildas proved impenetrable to Italian anti-tank artillery. At Sidi Barrani in particular, once the futility of anti-tank fire became apparent, the panic-stricken Italian infantry retreated underground with, as the War Office put it, 'a thick blanket over the head', offering no resistance to the attacking infantry.[9] Such success prompted new emphasis on the bold use of tanks well in advance of supporting infantry, which received official blessing in *ATI* No. 2, *The Employment of Army Tanks in Co-operation with Infantry* (published in March 1941).

The new manual postulated a main German defensive line of about 1,000 yards in depth. At the forward edge of this system, relatively weakly held trench-lines would hold up the attacking force, rendering them vulnerable to anti-tank guns and machine-guns located in defilade towards the rear. To prevail, the attacking force needed to overcome the powerful deep defences, difficult to observe and engage from afar on account of their cunning siting. The solution was for infantry tanks to advance under the cover of artillery fire to engage the deep defensive localities at close quarters. This first echelon of tanks would not pause to deal with the weaker defences at the forward edge of the German system. They would be dealt with by a second echelon of tanks, which would begin its advance as the first echelon began to engage the deep defences. The first infantry in the attack would follow the second echelon of tanks. A local reserve of both arms would follow.[10] *ATI* No. 2 claimed merely to amplify the 1939 doctrine. Indeed, in the sequence 'tanks–tanks–infantry', the new doctrine replicated its predecessor. However, whereas in 1939 the first two items of the sequence had been two waves of the first tank echelon, in 1941 they were two separate echelons. This terminological distinction underlined the independence of the leading tanks.

Having judged that the German defences would be deep, the writers of the new doctrine adopted the principle that the defences must be engaged simultaneously throughout their depth. This reasoning was perfectly sensible but the practical details were dangerous. The task of engaging the defences throughout their depth fell entirely to the two echelons of tanks, the leading one of which would also have artillery support while it advanced to the vicinity of the deepest defences. Up to 1,000 yards would separate these leading tanks from the nearest friendly infantry, who would in consequence be unable to provide any practical support. Their crews able only with difficulty to search the landscape through their vision slits and periscopes for enemy weapons, tanks thrust that far ahead of foot-soldiers were highly vulnerable. As with any artillery-based plan, timing was crucial. The doctrine depended upon everything going perfectly to plan. The first echelon of tanks was to move directly to its objective 'at fair tank speed'.[11] Any delay (perhaps the result of an awkward ditch or some soft ground) would deprive the tanks of the benefit of the artillery fire. It might also cause the second echelon to start its advance before the first echelon could engage the deeper enemy positions. Too much could go wrong. The doctrine relied far too heavily on a naïve notion that the tanks were invincible. They were left little scope to exploit any cover afforded by the ground or to use fire-and-movement techniques. Only in the period between Dunkirk and the failure of operation BATTLEAXE in June 1941 could such tactical guidance have been published. On 20 May 1940 the War Office had asserted that the tank was a vulnerable weapon that could achieve little if not closely followed by infantry.[12] Events over the following ten days, compounded by O'Connor's victories, persuaded the War Office otherwise. Only thus can the 1941 doctrine be explained.

Notwithstanding the War Office's confidence in the invincibility of British tanks, the infantry in the field army were told that they could defeat German tanks with their own weapons. In a book completed in July 1940, the left-wing journalist Tom Wintringham stressed that tanks were especially vulnerable to brave men at short range: 'The most dangerous distance away from a tank is two hundred yards: the safest distance is six inches.'[13] Drawing upon his experience as a battalion commander with the International Brigade in Spain, he described improvised explosive devices with which infantry, Home Guard and even civilians could knock out enemy tanks.[14] A great many such weapons were cobbled together for use by the Home Guard, most of which were at least as dangerous to the user as to the target.[15] The Army seems to have taken up few of these fantastic improvisations, but with the shortage of anti-tank guns senior commanders were at pains to discourage 'tank terror' among the infantry. Troops were encouraged to believe that they could hit back at enemy tanks both with purpose-designed weapons such as rifle-launched anti-tank grenades and, failing that, with normal small-arms fire directed at apertures in the tank's armour. Soon after *ATI* No. 2's publication, Lieutenant-General E.C.A. Schreiber, GOC V Corps, implicitly praised the Home Guard's attitude to anti-tank warfare, pointing out that with its resort to Spanish Civil War improvisations it led the Army.[16] During this period, many infantry battalions concentrated their man-versus-tank expertise in tank-hunting platoons.[17]

In the desperate 12 months following Dunkirk, senior British commanders had little alternative but to take seriously the tank-killing potential of infantry, however unsuitable their weapons for the job. But the contrast between what the infantry were being told they could accomplish against unsupported tanks and what tanks were being told they could accomplish in unsupported attacks is stark. The Germans, on the other hand, equipped with powerful anti-tank guns, had no need to resort to the improvisations promoted by Wintringham and Schreiber, at least not in 1941. Although the British did not learn the lessons of BATTLEAXE straight away,[18] in early lessons from operation CRUSADER, published in March 1942, the War Office proclaimed that the 88-mm gun had ended the infantry tank's former immunity to anti-tank gun fire.[19] Two months later, after further digestion of CRUSADER's lessons, the War Office pronounced the falsification of 'the legend of its [the infantry tank's] invulnerability' – a legend the War Office itself had not been idle in promoting. Only with careful planning and intimate all-arms co-operation, the War Office now maintained, would infantry tanks succeed in future.[20]

At no stage did the War Office admit in as many words that, together with a large number of British tanks, the 88-mm gun had shot to pieces the teaching of *ATI* No. 2 (1941). It would be May 1943 before any replacement was issued. It remained, therefore, as the chief printed source of doctrine for infantry tank units training at home. We have seen that it failed in battle in June 1941. Its flaws were evident even in training. Troops taking part in XII Corps exercise GREATBINGE in November 1941 saw for themselves the perils of allowing infantry tanks to operate beyond the assistance of other arms.[21] Yet three months later the press reported a showcase exercise in which the teaching of the 1941 doctrine was applied.[22] Later in 1942, however, tank units training in Britain adopted more appropriate tactics. Indeed, instructions issued by Major-General G.I. Thomas of 43rd Division, for interbrigade exercise WOOLF in April 1942 reflected proper appreciation of the need for interarm support. WOOLF involved an attack by 130th Brigade with 11th RTR (25th Tank Brigade) on positions held by 129th Brigade. The latter were instructed to 'take every opportunity to attack tanks which become separated from attacking inf'.[23]

Training in practice left doctrine far behind during 1942. This can be seen in the record of 34th Tank Brigade, one of three such formations on the strength of 21 Army Group for OVERLORD. Formed from the former 226th Infantry Brigade in December 1941, two of the new brigade's three tank units, 147th and 153rd RAC, were freshly converted infantry battalions. The third, North Irish Horse, an established tank unit, transferred to 25th Tank Brigade in September 1942, to be replaced by 151st RAC, another former infantry battalion converted on 1 January 1942. It was not until late August 1942, when the brigade was a component of 1st Division, that 147th and 153rd RAC first did any training actually with infantry.[24] A few days later the brigade exchanged places with 25th Tank Brigade in 43rd Division.

The 34th Tank Brigade arrived in its new formation to find that a divisional battle drill for tank–infantry attacks already existed. A demonstration of it had been held in mid-August.[25] However, virtually unpractised in infantry co-operation work as they were, it was late November before 147th and 153rd RAC took part in their first unit-level exercises with infantry. Although no document defining the divisional tank–infantry battle drill has survived, the evidence of these exercises and reference to other documents allows a substantial picture of that drill to be elaborated. It differed substantially from the official doctrine of 1939 and 1941.

All three tank regiments underwent the same exercise separately. After the first two, COs attended a conference to discuss lessons learned. They heard a number of criticisms concerning the execution of the attack. The first tank echelon, they were told, should not have paused on the intermediate objective any longer than necessary for the infantry and the second tank echelon to catch up. The infantry should not have waited there long either and should have kept within 400 yards of the first echelon of tanks.[26] Thus, whereas *ATI* No. 2 1941 ordained that both tank echelons should precede the infantry, in 43rd Division the infantry moved between the two echelons. Whereas in the official doctrine, the first tank echelon might be as far as 1,000 yards ahead of the nearest infantry, in the 43rd Division drill 400 yards was the maximum allowed between the two arms. These were substantial variances from the official doctrine.

Further divergence is evident in the instructions issued to umpires for the third and final exercise. Umpires were enjoined to watch the way tank troops were controlled, the way they used the technique of bounding (one or two tanks of a troop moving from one tactical position to another covered by the fire of the others), the movement of the second echelon of tanks and the infantry, and the efficacy of the mutual fire-support they afforded one another. The tank-versus-anti-tank gunfight was to be watched. Umpires were advised to award a hit to any anti-tank gun if it was well concealed and held its fire until its target was within 500 yards' range, but penalise anti-tank guns if they failed to conceal themselves well. The vulnerability of anti-tank guns if engaged from more than one direction at a time was pointed out, as was the vulnerability of the tanks if they entered a gun's field of fire individually rather than together. However, tank commanders were to be penalised with casualties if they went into battle opened up with their head outside the turret for ease of observation. The advantage thus gained was deemed unrealistic.[27] The clear implication was that purposeful manœuvre was needed by the tanks, both within each troop, by the troops within a squadron and in relation to the infantry. The notion that tanks might move directly to their objective without such manœuvre, implicit in the 1939 doctrine and accentuated in the 1941 doctrine, was absent in the tactical thought of 43rd Division. Conversely, the idea that the infantry might support the tanks with fire clearly featured in 43rd Division's philosophy. In *ATI* No. 2, only if friendly tanks were counterattacked by enemy armour were infantry to provide fire-support.[28] (Quite how useful such support could have been against armour is unclear, whereas LMG fire against unarmoured anti-tank gun positions would be highly effective.)

The practice favoured in 43rd Division of putting the infantry into the attack between rather than behind the two echelons of tanks became known as the 'sandwich' method.[29] What were its attractions over the scheme suggested in the 1941 doctrine? The 43rd Division did emphasise the rapid relief by infantry of the first echelon of tanks at the objective. This was easier if the infantry kept within 400 yards of the leading tanks than if an interval of up to 1,000 yards occurred. In that sense the sandwich method was simply a refinement of the methods proposed in *ATI* No. 2 and indeed in the earlier 1939 doctrine; by compressing the depth of the attacking forces better interarm co-operation at the objective was assured. However, it is likely that other advantages in the sandwich method occurred to 43rd Division: advantages that could be realised during the advance to the objective. *ATI* No. 2 (1941) made little allowance for the visual and aural handicaps under which tank crews operated. Stephen Dyson, who served as a loader/operator in 107th RAC (34th Tank Brigade) in North-West Europe, recalled his tank commander swivelling his periscope in search of potential targets during his first action in Normandy. His tank was later hit by an armour-piercing round that failed to penetrate. The tank commander 'rapidly twiddled his periscope, then suddenly shouted across to me that he had seen the flash of an 88 and ordered the gunner to traverse left'.[30] There can never be any certainty that a man will see all there is to be seen, but it is clear that there was a high chance of even the most attentive tank commander missing important battlefield occurrences that the most neglectful infantryman would see out of the corner of his eye. Peripheral vision, denied to the tank crew, was available to the infantry, along with unimpaired hearing. One Sherman commander in North-West Europe related an incident in his memoirs in which halted, head out of turret, he could not hear machine-gun fire aimed in his direction until the engine was switched off. Dismounted troops a few feet away heard it immediately.[31] In 1943 and 1944 several official reports and battle-experienced commentators drew attention to the relative sensory incapacity of tank crews. Improved interarm communication was the solution, and one means of achieving this was for the infantry to lead the tanks. That way, the tanks could see what was happening to the infantry and the latter could indicate easily to the former the approximate locations of enemy weapons.[32]

Thus, under the 43rd Division drill, the infantry could expect better support from the second echelon of tanks behind them than if those tanks had been ahead. One might add that the tanks themselves would benefit from the infantry-first arrangement. In front, the infantry were better placed to locate and engage enemy anti-tank guns than if they followed the tanks. Moreover, the leading echelon of tanks, up to 400 yards ahead of the infantry and theoretically protected by covering artillery fire from enemy interference, might also expect a little infantry small-arms fire-support, whereas none could be expected from infantry up to 1,000 yards behind.

BATTLE LESSONS AND DOCTRINE, 1943–44

May 1943 saw the publication of a completely revised version of *ATI* No. 2. In view of the clear evidence that the War Office understood the shortcomings of the 1941 edition as early as May 1942, it is hard to acquit those responsible for the preparation of doctrinal guidance of dilatoriness. It did not matter to 34th Tank Brigade which saw no action before July 1944. It did matter to 21st and 25th Tank Brigades which fought in Tunisia. In his despatch following the conclusion of the Tunisian campaign, the commander of First Army, Lieutenant-General K.A.N. Anderson, remarked that 25th Tank Brigade's 'tactical handling in close co-operation with infantry was at times at fault'.[33] Explaining their initial tactical methods in a joint report on the Tunisian campaign's lessons, the commanders of 21st and 25th Tank Brigades described a rather less compact sandwich pattern than that practised in 34th Tank Brigade. In their version, the first tank echelon proceeded at 'best tank pace'. This allowed a rather greater gap to open up between it and the infantry than the maximum 400 yards allowable in 43rd Division. Although not identical to the 43rd Division sandwich, the 21st and 25th Brigade pattern was very different to that ordained in the 1941 doctrine. None the less, the two commanders contended that their inflated sandwich pattern 'never squarely faced' the question of anti-tank mines. Unless the path of an attack was known to be free of such devices, and unless topographical obstacles to tank movement, such as nullahs (which had proved a particular problem in Tunisia), were known not to exist, it was inadvisable to use a first echelon of tanks. Experience taught that if the first echelon became held up by a natural or artificial obstacle the delay would precipitate the attack's failure. Stalled in their advance the tanks would lose the benefit of the artillery support, which latter would advance according to the planned timetable, thus freeing enemy weapons covering the minefield to engage the attacking tanks. Even if the prompt use of smoke and on-call artillery support saved the first echelon of tanks from the attentions of enemy weapons, the attack plan would be irretrievably disrupted.[34]

The 21st and 25th Tank Brigades found that in practice the available means of reconnaissance could not provide a sure enough picture of potential obstacles across the path of a projected attack. Even if a first echelon reached the objective, the second-echelon infantry usually found themselves delayed by enemy small-arms fire, with the result that the first-echelon tanks were forced into a lengthy unsupported occupation of the objective. Therefore 21st and 25th Tank Brigades preferred to dispense with a first echelon of tanks altogether and instead attack with the infantry first and the tanks following closely behind, perhaps going forward of the infantry or to a flank to deal with hostile weapons troubling the foot-soldiers. This was the inflated sandwich pattern without the first echelon and therefore at a pace to suit infantry speed.[35]

The pattern of attack found most effective in Tunisia did not, of course, obviate the problem of mines and topographical obstacles to progress. But it meant that where such impediments arose the tanks would not be alone. They could depend upon infantry assistance, perhaps in the form of advance warning of the obstacle's existence and certainly of counteraction against anti-tank guns opening fire on the tanks.[36] According to the teaching of one battle-experienced tank brigade commander, an anti-tank minefield, although delaying the tanks, was not to delay the infantry. The latter were to continue the advance, benefiting from the protection of the barrage. Meanwhile, the tanks would seek a way around the minefield, or wait while sappers gapped it, giving the infantry such support as they could by fire.[37] Both this teaching and the joint report from 21st and 25th Tank Brigades stressed that the tanks did not need to be in close physical proximity to the infantry in order to deliver effective support. Provided they had observation of the infantry's advance, and were within range, they could support the foot soldiers with fire from hull-down positions hundreds of yards away. By manoeuvring from one hull-down position to another they would limit their vulnerability to anti-tank gunfire. Indeed, although the minefield problem was cited as the chief reason for dropping the first tank echelon doctrine, it is plain that the anti-tank gun problem figured just as prominently in tank crews' fears and in their senior commanders' tactical thought. Indeed, for First Army HQ, the Tunisian campaign had taught that the infantry should deal with anti-tank guns.[38]

Freedom of manoeuvre, desired by the tank men as a countermeasure against enemy anti-tank guns, was not consistent with previous teaching which had envisaged the tanks as either tied to the coat-tails of the infantry, tied to the progress of a barrage, or with the infantry tied to their coat-tails. After Tunisia they wanted the freedom, hitherto seen as the preserve of armoured units, to manoeuvre by troops and squadrons. 'There has been a tendency in the past', wrote the unidentified tank brigadier cited above,

> to look upon the crushing power of the tank, rather than its fire power, as its chief weapon. This is a fallacy. It is the fire power of the tank that kills and subdues the enemy. Therefore, great as the moral effect of the crusher may be, the object of tank manoeuvre when helping infantry must be to get the tanks where they can make the best use of their fire power.[39]

Although this teaching affirmed the object of helping the infantry, the latter clearly did not entirely trust their tank colleagues. Their morale benefited by the close physical presence of friendly tanks and they found it hard to credit the apparent reserve of tank crews who preferred to stay well away from the infantry. Responding to a questionnaire on the lessons of the Tunisian campaign, 1st Division (which fought the campaign as an infantry division although it had earlier been a mixed formation) asserted that no change in official doctrine was needed: except for mine-gapping phases the tanks should lead, accepting whatever casualties they suffered to get the infantry on to their objective. The 1st Division complained that tanks had been very reluctant to lead the infantry over crests, insisting that the infantry go first to deal with any lurking 88-mm guns. Indeed, 1st Division held that 'the A.Tk mine and h[eavy]y A.Tk gun has [*sic*] "seen off" the tk to a great extent'.[40]

The 1st Division's attitude shows poor understanding of the tanks' problems and capabilities. Tank brigades themselves clearly felt that they could still earn their rations. What they did not want was a doctrine that demanded that they always precede the infantry, even if it made an exception where minefields were to be breached. They wanted the freedom to go ahead of the infantry, or fall behind, or go to a flank as the circumstances demanded.

ATI No. 2 (May 1943) promoted a far more sophisticated and mature approach to the combined tank and infantry attack than the 1941 version. Great stress was laid upon the need for thorough understanding between the two arms so that each appreciated the other's problems and how it could help overcome them, for no arm could win battles without the co-operation of others.[41] The limitations of the tank were far more clearly comprehended in the new doctrine. Minefields – hardly mentioned in *ATI* No. 2 (1941) – and other tank obstacles so hampered the operation of tanks that they must be gapped before the tanks could conduct an assault. The tank-suitability of the ground in the rearward areas of the enemy position needed to be assessed. Tanks were best used in concentrated mass on a narrow front. The assignment of objectives needed to recognise the acute problems of observation from within the tank and ideally objectives should be visible from the start-line.[42]

Whereas the 1941 doctrine had made a clear distinction between the assault upon a well-organised enemy position and that on hastily organised defences, *ATI* No. 2 (1943) specified only the former. Such an attack, which would require detailed information on the enemy's dispositions, acquired through both air and ground reconnaissance, would usually have three phases: (1) initial penetration; (2) assault on rearward areas where minefields would be less of a hindrance; and (3) fluid warfare, the product of the general disintegration of the enemy's defensive efforts. Although there was no general rule as to which arm – tanks or infantry – should lead the assault, the doctrine was quite specific that in the first phase tanks in the assault echelon (the new term for first echelon, numerical designations having been discontinued) would be of little value. Initial penetration was likely to involve the gapping of minefields and other obstacles, a task best left to specialist infantry and engineers. For the first phase, therefore, tanks were to be confined to the support echelon (formerly known as the second echelon) giving the assault echelon fire-support. Whichever arm led, it was imperative that the other get forward to join the leading arm on the objective (in the case of the first phase, a bridgehead beyond the belt of mines or other obstacles) as early as possible. As for the second phase, it was generally preferred that the assault echelon comprise both tanks and infantry. This afforded benefits to both arms. The tanks gained the considerable protection of the infantry against enemy anti-tank guns and concealed infantry with close-quarters weapons who had survived the supporting artillery fire. They were also assured of the early presence of the infantry when they reached the objective. The infantry profited by the artillery fire plan, which was directed to the support of the leading edge of the assault, and had the intimate support of the tanks against any troublesome surviving enemy.[43]

Although minefields would still be encountered during the second phase of the attack, they were unlikely to be continuous, so the use of tanks in both waves of the assault echelon was deemed sound provided mine-clearing troops and infantry moved with them. The task of the leading wave would be to close with the objective and subdue it by fire. The second wave would engage defiladed anti-tank guns that disclosed themselves. Both waves of tanks would tack to and fro across the ground, presumably in an effort to confound the aim of hostile anti-tank gunners. The foot-soldiers would move behind or among the tanks using 'all available cover and the fieldcraft in which they have been trained'. If cover was sparse, the infantry could use the cover afforded by the tanks themselves. Their principal task was to help the tanks negotiate minefields and other obstacles. Engaging enemy anti-tank weapons with small-arms fire was the job of infantry mounted in carriers. It was felt that they would be better able to do the job than closed-down tanks. Where the objective was a long distance from the start-line, it was suggested that the foot infantry infiltrate forward of the start-line under cover of smoke or darkness to covered positions ahead of zero hour and there await the arrival of the tanks as the attack proper got under way.[44]

The function of the support echelon during the second phase was to help mop up and consolidate the objective ready for the next move forward. It would cross the start-line as soon as the fire of the assault echelon was beginning to subdue the defending enemy and would deal with any enemy posts still active after the passage of the assault echelon. The support echelon would include both infantry and tanks. Tank commanders would keep their heads out of their turrets to facilitate good observation and communication with the infantry.[45]

In the third, fluid, phase the attack assumed some of the characteristics of mobile warfare, demanding quick decision-making and action rather than the deliberate moves of the earlier phases. In such action the behaviour of the tank brigade, regiment or squadron needed to emulate that of its armoured counterpart. The infantry tanks' task was to ensure that the momentum of the attack was maintained while the mobile forces of the armoured division moved up to exploit. Provided the area was thought to be free of minefields the assault echelon would comprise tanks only. It would advance quickly to subdue the objective, at which time the support echelon of infantry and tanks, waiting in the area of the start-line, would go forward to complete the victory.[46] The doctrine did not actually say so, but it would appear that in this fluid phase the tank brigade was to act as a provisional armoured brigade.

The implicit assumption of the 1941 doctrine was that the tanks required little support because their armour limited their vulnerability. In 1943, by contrast, this flavour of armoured omnipotence was heavily diluted. Firstly, the likelihood of minefields and other obstacles blocking the armour's path was recognised. So, the first phase of an operation must clear a path through the mines – a task in which tanks could be of little use. Even when the minefields had been breached, tanks required the intimate support of other arms if they were not to suffer badly. Although they might lead the assault after the initial penetration, the infantry must form part of the assault echelon both to provide fire-support against enemy positions and to help the tanks to cross obstacles. The attack-in-depth philosophy of 1941 had not disappeared. There were still two echelons, the second of which was not to start its task of clearing the battlefield of enemy until the first was heavily engaging the defences in depth. But the need for the leading edge of the attack to have intimate support against enemy defences during its advance had been acknowledged. This was the purpose of the infantry and the second wave of tanks in the assault echelon.

The one area in which the new doctrine failed to anticipate the lessons from Tunisia was in the matter of the tanks' insistence that they need not move alongside the infantry to deliver effective support. *ATI* No. 2 (1943) did not allow that possibility at all. It was not until an article published in *Current Reports from Overseas* (*CRO*) in July 1943 that this notion was raised by the War Office, although a foreword cautioned that the piece 'should be read as illustrating but in no way modifying' the teaching of *ATI* No. 2 (1943).[47] By incorporating that article in the official lessons on tank and infantry co-operation in Tunisia,[48] the War Office later gave its blessing to the practice. Even so, *MTP* No. 63, *The Co-operation of Tanks with Infantry Divisions* (published in May 1944) made no mention of the possibility of remote support by the tanks for the infantry, and implied close physical proximity of the two arms.[49]

It would of course have been contradictory and confusing for the War Office in one breath to recommend that tanks and infantry should advance in close proximity to one another for the better security of both arms, and in the next to license the tank arm to move away from the infantry in order to exploit natural cover. Perhaps it was for that reason that neither the 1943 edition of *ATI* No. 2 nor *MTP* No. 63 incorporated the remote support idea. Another probable reason was the armament carried by Churchill tanks. At this time most Churchills mounted the six-pounder. Those mounting the two-pounder were being converted to the larger gun. But neither gun fired a satisfactory high explosive (HE) round, leaving the machine-guns as the main weapon against unarmoured targets, with all the limitations of range and trajectory that implied. The six-pounder's inadequacy is illustrated by the fact that the army in North Africa went to considerable lengths to design a local modification for the Churchill by which to fit 75-mm guns salvaged from disabled Shermans.[50] Apparently alluding to this, one tank brigadier argued that the introduction of an HE-firing gun for all tanks only reinforced his axiom that it was the tanks' fire-support for the infantry and not their close physical presence that mattered.[51]

In any case, tank brigades training in Britain did not feel bound by the new *ATI* No. 2. Another of the tank brigades that took the field in Normandy in the summer of 1944 was 6th Guards Tank Brigade, which had converted from an armoured brigade in January 1943. Combined tank and infantry attack exercises carried out with the infantry of 15th Division in the summer of 1943 show that the doctrine published in May had not been fully absorbed. Divisional exercise CATTERICK at the beginning of August, for example, involved an attack by 44th Brigade supported by 6th Guards Tank Brigade. Two tank battalions were to form the assault echelon. Two infantry battalions each with a tank squadron in support (presumably moving behind) were to form the support echelon. They were to cross the start-line a full 35 minutes after the assault echelon. The battle plans show that the latter was to negotiate no man's land, a distance of about one mile, and closely engage the enemy before the support echelon moved.[52]

The same pattern of attack is evident in other exercises at battalion level, for examples exercise BOLTON on 15–16 June[53] and exercise HEATHER two months later.[54] None of these exercises involved the actual breaching of minefields, but the attacks in BOLTON and HEATHER were both from a bridgehead created after the imaginary gapping of a minefield by other troops and so demanded that the attackers carry out the necessary approaches to the forming-up place through mine-free lanes. It appears that the officers of 6th Guards Tank Brigade failed to read *ATI* No. 2 (1943) until after BOLTON in June 1943; at least in that exercise the numerical echelon designations were used in the exercise operation orders, whereas in later exercises the terms ordained in the new doctrine appeared instead. One can thus conclude that the minefield problem was well understood by this formation before *ATI* No. 2 (1943). Clearly, the new doctrine stimulated no change whatsoever in tactical practice. Use of an all-tank assault echelon similarly continued in 27th Armoured Brigade (an independent formation equipped with amphibious Shermans, whose role once ashore was as infantry support rather than 'armoured').[55]

As has been shown, the extensive use of minefields was one of the factors that confounded the tactics outlined in the 1941 doctrine. There is no doubt that the mine problem impressed itself upon tank units training in Britain well before *ATI* No. 2 (1943). In view of the deep minefields through which Eighth Army had to break at El Alamein it would be surprising if it had not. In fact, in a perverse sense it appears to have embedded itself too deeply in the consciousness of unblooded troops and in doing so displaced the older problem of anti-tank guns. The training of 6th Guards Tank Brigade in the summer of 1943 suggests that the Guards felt that once the main minefields were gapped they were collectively unstoppable. This was simply wrong. In action, extraneous fire-support rarely managed to destroy so many anti-tank guns that when it lifted the tanks would not still have formidable defences to overcome. This was enough of a problem for the School of Infantry to suggest that Churchill tanks might actually advance within the area being pounded by the artillery barrage. This would enable them to destroy enemy anti-tank guns at close range while the latter were still subject to the neutralising effects of the artillery. In the summer of 1943 trials were carried out at the School of Artillery, Larkhill, to determine the survivability of Churchill tanks under a 25-pounder HE barrage. 'While direct hits from 25pdrs may disable Churchills', the report argued, 'the losses from the enemy are likely to be very much fewer if his anti-tank gunners are being vigorously shelled.'[56] The War Office later endorsed the practice of sending Churchills into the barrage area.[57]

Some idea of the scale of the anti-tank gun problem can be gained from the Larkhill trials' findings as to the probable number of casualties that would be suffered in a barrage zone. Thirty-six Churchills (i.e. two squadrons) in an area of 600 yards by 200 yards covered by 32 guns (four batteries) firing five rounds per minute would suffer seven casualties. If the number of guns was doubled, the casualties would rise to 13. The trials showed that 25-pounder HE would rarely penetrate the tank. Only one incident of personal casualty was mentioned, caused by a direct hit that blew a periscope back into the tank. For the most part the casualties took the form of immobilising damage to track and suspension components, easily repaired once the vehicle was recovered after a successful battle. None the less, the results and the War Office's endorsement of them show that 20–35 per cent of assault-echelon tanks put out of action by friendly fire was deemed a worthwhile price to pay for the avoidance of casualties from enemy anti-tank guns.

The import of these results is not that the casualties from enemy anti-tank guns invariably exceeded the scales incurred from a friendly barrage. Instead the report suggested that by sending assault-echelon Churchill tanks into the barrage a commander could be sure that they would suffer no casualties to anti-tank guns and predict fairly accurately the losses from friendly HE fire. The implication was that no such prediction could reliably be made of losses to anti-tank gun fire if the tanks did not enter the barrage zone. They might be zero: they might be 100 per cent. For the present purpose it is merely necessary to know that the artillery could not be relied upon to put a tank-only assault echelon on the objective with tolerable casualties. For tank brigades to assume otherwise in their training was wrong.

It is significant that the idea behind the Larkhill trials came from the School of Infantry. The principal infantry training manual of the time, which had been written at the school, favoured the sandwich pattern for tank–infantry attacks.[58] Experimental work carried out with the school's attached Churchill squadron and infantry battalion led to a shift in favour of a mixed-assault echelon with tanks supporting the infantry with fire from hull-down positions.[59] None the less, at a meeting of senior staff of the school on 16 July 1943, Colonel I.M. Stewart (the Assistant Commandant) contended that, notwithstanding the lessons from North Africa, the moral value (to the infantry) of the tanks leading in the attack presented a strong case for such tactics.[60] Stewart seems not to have been aware then of the results from Larkhill, the report of which had been issued a week earlier. Clearly he did not overlook the perils tank crews faced if they ventured well ahead of the infantry: the trials were intended to see whether the risks could be minimised. But equally clearly, there existed in infantry circles a demand that they be accepted. Major-General D.C. Bullen-Smith debated the subject with his subordinate commanders in 51st Division during a model exercise held in September 1943 shortly after he assumed command of the division in Sicily. Bullen-Smith, formerly the commander of 15th Division in Britain, insisted that the sandwich pattern of attack was the correct method. Lieutenant-General O.W.H. Leese, the corps commander, agreed. But the COs and brigadiers of 51st Division, speaking with the authority of recent battle experience (which Bullen-Smith lacked), demurred. In Sicily, 51st Division had the support of an armoured regiment equipped with Shermans. Bullen-Smith, who must have learned informally of the outcome of the Larkhill trials, pointed out that Churchill tanks could operate within the barrage area. Even this apparently failed to shift the consensus of opinion, which was that tanks should support the infantry by fire from hull-down positions rather than lead them on to the objective.[61] Incidentally, no instance of Churchill tanks designedly operating within an artillery barrage in battle has been discovered by the author. One tank CO informed his men that he disagreed with the War Office's advice that they could do so.[62]

As for 34th Tank Brigade, it would appear that 43rd Division preferred to continue with the sandwich pattern of attack. However, the brigade and division parted company in September 1943 and changes in tactical teaching followed swiftly. It no doubt helped that for the remainder of 1943 the brigade was affiliated for training purposes to 59th Division, whose troops had negligible training in co-operation with tanks.[63] The brigade's new commander, Brigadier W.S. Clarke (appointed on 3 July), was free to determine the training agenda.

In a training memorandum issued on 6 September 1943 brigade HQ set out the pattern of attack to be practised with 59th Division. Simplicity was to be the keynote of all combined tactics, so the directive ran. From the infantryman's point of view, all that mattered was the three tank troops assigned to co-operate closely with each attacking company: one troop per platoon. These would cross the start-line behind the infantry and would take whatever action was necessary against any enemy whose action held the infantry up. The association between each of these three tank troops and the infantry platoon it was supporting was inviolable. The other two troops of their squadron would usually cross the start-line behind the tank and infantry echelon formed partly by the three troops and would support the progress of the combined attack in front of them with their fire. If conditions allowed, these two troops might catch up with the tank and infantry echelon or go forward or to a flank of it, the better to deliver fire-support. It appears that the criterion most affecting the freedom of action of the two 'spare' troops was the suspected presence or otherwise of enemy minefields. If minefields were known not to exist then the two troops could overtake the tank and infantry echelon, in which case the attack would assume the sandwich pattern. The sandwich pattern would be adopted only in the absence of minefields. The 34th Tank Brigade had learned from 25th Tank Brigade that in battle it was unusual for tanks to lead in an attack, so units of the former brigade were enjoined to make co-operating infantry understand that they would not often have tanks in front of them.[64]

The 1943 doctrine undoubtedly influenced 34th Tank Brigade's new teaching, both on the question of enemy minefields and in the composition of echelons. Even if conditions allowed the two 'spare' troops to lead, squadron commanders were to maintain a tight control over them to prevent their straying beyond the effective support of the following tanks.[65] What was quite absent was any reference to the possible existence of more than one attacking echelon. In effect, the ensemble of three infantry platoons, each closely attended by a tank troop, with two tank troops working to a roving brief, amounted to one echelon containing two waves of tanks. *ATI* No. 2 (1943) recommended two such echelons, the first of which was to proceed under artillery cover directly to seize the objective whereupon the second echelon crossed the start-line and mopped up the intervening area. At the minor tactical level, the variance from doctrine has little importance, for the action of the tanks and infantry comprising the single-echelon-type attack adopted by 34th Tank Brigade would be equally good practice for the action of either the assault or support echelons in the officially recommended pattern of attack. However, the official doctrine was designed to realise the concept of the attack in depth just as its 1941 predecessor had been. So at the level of higher tactics, the neglect of the official doctrine was rather dubious.

The neglect of the multi-echeloned pattern of attack was the main reason brigade HQ could proclaim the new teaching to be simple. This was a thoroughly disingenuous claim. Although the existence of only one echelon simplified the planning and arrangement of the attack, for the infantry and tanks actually involved in the single echelon the attack was rather more complicated than it had been in the sandwich pattern. In the latter, the relative positions of the tanks and infantry remained constant. In 34th Tank Brigade's new tactics two troops in each squadron were, subject to local conditions, free to move in whatever relation to the rest of the force offered the best prospects. This obliged squadron and troop commanders to make decisions as to where the 'spare' troops should go and to keep those decisions under constant review as the tactical situation evolved. In November 1943 brigade HQ acknowledged complaints by 'NCOs and ORs (and probably, in fact, junior offrs also)' that the constant changes in attack formation confused them. This caused bewilderment at brigade HQ, which could only repeat the canard that the new tactics should be easier to master than the 43rd Division sandwich pattern.[66]

The two 'spare' troops, whose flexible role seems to have caused so much difficulty, gave the 34th Tank Brigade pattern of attack a character that approached that discernible in the battle experience reports. That is to say, a substantial proportion of the tank force taking part in an attack were not directly tied to the infantry. Their freedom of manoeuvre was constrained by the requirement not to stray beyond supporting range of the rest of the squadron, whose progress was governed by that of the infantry, but then the battle experience descriptions did require the tanks to keep the infantry in sight. The teaching of 34th Tank Brigade compromised between the demands of the infantry for the close physical presence of tanks (a demand honoured in official doctrine) and the findings of battle experience that such close proximity was not needed and made the tanks' task more dangerous than necessary. One effect of allowing the tanks, or a proportion of them in the case of 34th Tank Brigade, this independence was to make possible far more sophisticated minor tactics by the tanks. Liberated from the infantry, they could make full use of their mobility, provided of course that they did not neglect their task which was to support the other arm. Infantry tank minor tactics thus took on the resemblance of cruiser tank minor tactics. Indeed it is noteworthy that Major-General M.B. Burrows of 11th Armoured Division directed units of 29th Armoured Brigade to pay particular attention to the article in *CRO* that set out the teaching of a tank brigade in North Africa.[67]

By this time, 34th Tank Brigade formed part of Second Army, 21 Army Group, designated for the invasion of North-West Europe. Lieutenant-General K.A.N. Anderson, the commander of Second Army, felt that tank brigades should be prepared to perform the functions of armoured brigades. Accordingly 34th Tank Brigade carried out some training in the armoured role in the autumn of 1943. Clarke was not discouraged by the results of this training, but found that 'more attention must be paid to taking up hull and turret down posns, and frequent practice must be given to Sqn and Tp Ldrs in the drill of constantly changing posns behind a crest'. Like Burrows, Clarke directed attention to the *CRO* article.[68] If tank crews were not fully up to the mark in cruiser tank tactics, then neither were they fully trained for infantry tank tactics. Clearly recognition was growing that at the minor tactical level there was little difference between the two. The problem of the anti-tank gun was the unifying factor.

In November 1943, 21 Army Group published a pamphlet entitled *The Co-operation of Tanks with Infantry Divisions in Offensive Operations.* Prepared by a committee of highly experienced officers of field and general rank led by Pyman, now BGS (Training) with 21 Army Group,[69] the pamphlet drew heavily on *ATI* No. 2 1943. In some respects it provided greater detail than the War Office manual, particularly in a series of diagrams showing various alternative constructions of the assault and support echelons, but there was nothing fundamentally new. Pyman contended that circumstances favouring the use of an all-tank assault echelon would be rare. Not one of the nine diagrams showing alternative patterns for the composition of echelons showed such a thing.[70]

Pyman's pamphlet emphasised that the Sherman tanks with which armoured regiments were equipped were not suitable for work that involved closing with enemy positions strong in anti-tank guns. Their armour was too light and they would suffer heavy casualties. If assigned to co-operate with infantry in the attack, therefore, their role would be to remain well to the rear in hull-down or turret-down positions and engage the enemy's defences with HE from their 75-mm guns. This would be a lengthy process, but until the enemy's anti-tank defences were largely destroyed the Shermans should not go forward.[71]

In his careful delimitation of the Sherman's possible functions, Pyman conformed perfectly to official policy. As the War Office reiterated in January 1944, it was impossible to combine in one tank the agility required in the armoured role and the heavy armour required in the infantry support role. There was, therefore, no general-purpose tank in the British Army.[72] For both tactical and organisational reasons, this policy was becoming impossible to sustain. As seen above, so far as minor tactics were concerned there was little to distinguish the actions of the two types of tank. In any case, when Paget asked for the repatriation from the Middle East of two tank brigades for inclusion in 21 Army Group he was instead sent two Sherman-equipped armoured brigades. Some debate took place with 21 Army Group HQ over what was to be done with these brigades. Major-General C.W.M. Norrie, the RAC adviser, argued forcefully the War Office line that Shermans were unsuited for infantry tank work. He adduced Pyman, who had commanded a Sherman regiment in Eighth Army, in his support. On 6 November 1943, however, Lieutenant-General W.D. Morgan, Paget's Chief of General Staff, ruled that the doctrine should be adjusted to allow Shermans to function as infantry tanks.[73] It is possible that the sections in Pyman's pamphlet on the employment of Shermans in infantry co-operation were last-minute additions made as the outcome of these transactions. If so, the additions were half-hearted and pleased no one, least of all General Montgomery who was to take over as Commander-in-Chief within weeks. It is equally possible, though, that Pyman

147

included the passages as a guide to the substantial numbers of amphibious Shermans scheduled to support the initial landings. Their idleness simply on the grounds of theoretical unsuitability for participation in setpiece attacks could not be tolerated in the critical first hours of the invasion. In that case Pyman's pamphlet did not correspond with the training activities of 27th Armoured Brigade and, with Morgan's ruling on 6 November, was out of date even before its issue.

In his memoirs, Pyman claimed that his pamphlet failed to gain Paget's approval and so was never published. He was mistaken. The pamphlet was distributed on 30 December 1943.[74] However, although it enjoyed only a brief currency, it was Montgomery, not Paget, who did for it. The lessons Montgomery's Eighth Army drew from tank–infantry co-operation in the desert varied significantly from those reported by First Army in Tunisia. Where there were no minefields, Eighth Army taught that the sandwich pattern was perfectly suitable.[75] When the DMT, Major-General J.A.C. Whitaker, visited Eighth Army HQ in October 1943 he was told that the 1943 doctrine overstressed the danger of mines and that tanks should normally form the assault echelon. He got a different story from lower formations, however. One corps commander told Whitaker that tanks should never lead infantry in the attack. In 7th Armoured Division (no longer under Eighth Army command), Whitaker learned, the infantry brigade always led.[76]

Eighth Army published its own pamphlet on tank–infantry co-operation in November 1943. This manual promoted the line Whitaker had been given at Army HQ that tanks should lead the attack once enemy minefields had been breached. Reflecting experience in the Western Desert, Eighth Army ordained the following composition for an attacking force. (The scales were based on a force of one unit each of infantry and tanks, plus two companies of sappers, supported by three field artillery regiments. The pamphlet implied that the same proportions should be observed if the circumstances demanded a larger or smaller total force.) The first echelon comprised one rifle company, one tank squadron, three sections of three infantry carriers each, the infantry mortar platoon (six three-inch mortars) and a sapper company. Its task was to make gaps in the enemy's minefield, and the tank squadron's task was to provide intimate covering fire while the infantry and sappers lifted the mines. Once the gapping was complete, the second echelon, comprising one squadron of tanks only, moved up to lead the attack from the bridgehead established on the enemy side of the minefield. The third echelon comprised two rifle companies, the third tank squadron and two artillery forward observation officers; the rifle companies led. The fourth echelon consisted of the infantry and tank unit HQs with the fourth rifle company and the second sapper company, to be joined by the tank squadron of the first echelon, held as a reserve. Thus, Eighth Army doctrine ordained that, once the minefield had been gapped, the attack should assume the sandwich pattern.[77]

On 8 January 1944, in conference with his COs, Brigadier Clarke of 34th

Tank Brigade discussed the Eighth Army tank–infantry attack doctrine 'and pointed out that certain recent important events made it at least possible that we would be ordered to adopt this very different procedure in future'.[78] The appointment of the commander of Eighth Army to succeed Paget as Commander-in-Chief of 21 Army Group was undoubtedly the 'important event' Clarke had in mind. Some weeks earlier Montgomery saw a copy of Pyman's 21 Army Group pamphlet. He did not like it at all. He objected to Pyman's distinction between infantry tanks and cruiser tanks, and so saw no need for the separate section on Sherman tank tactics. Among a host of other detailed criticisms, he objected to the inclusion of the series of diagrams showing alternative patterns of formation for a tank–infantry force. Montgomery felt that these diagrams were positively harmful since they made no provision for the inclusion of other arms. He preferred just one general diagram 'to act as a guide for staff officers writing orders for the forming up of the attacking force'.[79]

On 7 December Montgomery complained to Nye about Pyman's pamphlet. Nye responded a fortnight later refuting Montgomery's spurious claims that no one had consulted Eighth Army about 21 Army Group's doctrine and rejecting his arrogation of unique doctrinal authority.[80] This was water off a duck's back to Montgomery. Undoubtedly on his orders, in February 1944, 21 Army Group published a new pamphlet entitled, like the Eighth Army pamphlet, *Notes on the Employment of Tanks in Support of Infantry in Battle*, and word for word almost exactly the same.[81] Thus within the space of two months 21 Army Group published two quite different and mutually contradictory sets of doctrine for tank–infantry co-operation.

In its brief life before supersession by Montgomery's doctrine, Pyman's pamphlet did bring about improvements in the tactical habits of 6th Guards Tank Brigade. In co-operation training with infantry in February 1944, 3rd Tank Scots Guards covered assault-echelon work, whereas in similar training four months earlier co-operative training had been confined to the support echelon.[82] As will be seen, when they first went into action in Normandy, the Scots Guards neglected Pyman's teaching, with mixed results. As for 34th Tank Brigade, that formation got early warning of the imposition of the Eighth Army doctrine, which the brigadier clearly realised was quite different from the customised version of *ATI* No. 2 1943 that had formed brigade HQ's teaching since the previous September. Following publication of the Eighth Army doctrine under 21 Army Group's imprimatur, Clarke ordered that it should form the basis for tank–infantry training,[83] and the brigade's Standing Operation Instructions issued in May incorporated the essential elements of that teaching.[84]

Thus, it became the doctrine of 21 Army Group that in combined tank and infantry attacks the tanks should lead and the infantry should follow. Three years of experience had taught everyone, except apparently Montgomery and his lieutenants, that such tactics were ruinous. Montgomery's intervention ensured that the lessons of BATTLEAXE would have to be learned all over again in Normandy.

CONCLUSION

The central query over tactics for the co-operation of tanks and infantry as revealed above concerns the extent to which such tactics needed to be truly co-operative. That the tanks were there to support the infantry was never in doubt: that the infantry also needed to support the tanks was. It might seem almost facile to focus so much attention on the relative positions of the two arms in a combined force formed up for the attack. On that factor, however, the ability of each arm to support the other depended. At the start of the war the British Army's doctrine was by no means perfectly judged. It envisaged part of the tank component going well forward of the nearest infantry. Pyman's interpretation of how an attack should be carried out shows that at least some officers realised that the official thinking was too confident in the powers of unsupported armour. It was unfortunate that the successes of Matilda tanks against the Italians in the winter of 1940–41 emboldened the War Office to strengthen the emphasis on the unsupported action of tanks in the attack. In an attack on a well-organised enemy position manned by well-trained troops in good morale, such tactics were dubious. Even if the enemy had no anti-tank guns, bold infantry could knock out tanks using grenades. No tank could easily defend itself against close-range attack and a proportion of British infantry were trained to exploit that very weakness. In the desert a separation of the leading tanks from the infantry of up to 1,000 yards, sanctioned in *ATI* No. 2 (1941), brought nothing but failure when the British Army faced the Wehrmacht, which was armed with some of the most powerful anti-tank guns of the war.

The folly of such tactics was manifest even in the artificial circumstances of training exercises in Britain. The battle experience reports published by the War Office in the spring of 1942 only confirmed what many tank officers training in Britain had already worked out. It is deplorable that the War Office neglected to publish any replacement doctrine before May 1943. Knowing that *ATI* No. 2 (1941) was discredited, tank brigades and the infantry divisions of which they became components in the summer of 1942 were left to decide for themselves the teaching by which they would train. Some variation on the sandwich-pattern theme seems to have been adopted by most. Battle experience in Tunisia showed the virtues of a spatially close relationship between the tanks and the infantry. It was this quality that Brigadier Clarke of 34th Tank Brigade chose to accentuate when released from the evidently conservative direction of 43rd Division in September 1943. No effort had been made in 43rd Division to adopt the doctrine set out in *ATI* No. 2 (1943). Upon leaving the division, Clarke chose to adopt only the minor tactical aspects of the new official teaching and to neglect the depth of battle inherent in the official tactics. But Clarke went rather further towards the full application of the new doctrine than other formations, which persisted with the sandwich method – a tactic that 21st and 25th Tank Brigades had found to be defective.

As if it were not bad enough that the War Office effectively left field units without a doctrine by which to train for a year or more before the issue of *ATI* No. 2 (1943), it is truly extraordinary that a proper doctrine having been published, one that comprehended lessons learned in battle, no mechanism seems to have existed independently of the command structure to enforce it in all units and formations. The very nature of infantry tank formations' work demanded that all infantry units and all tank units observe a common doctrine. If not, infantry and tanks, meeting for the first time shortly before they were to go into battle together, might have quite different conceptions as to how they should co-operate. Every War Office pamphlet on infantry and tank co-operation stressed the need for a doctrine common to both arms. Yet not one of the infantry tank formations whose records have been examined here actually applied the doctrine that the War Office ordained. Before *ATI* No. 2 (1943) appeared this failure was excusable on the grounds that the War Office doctrine was wrong. No such justification existed from May 1943. That tank brigades continued to plough their own separate furrows reflects credit on nobody.

The first effort to impose a common doctrine was Montgomery's importation of the Eighth Army doctrine. It is a revealing sidelight on the awe in which Montgomery was held that Brigadier Clarke hastened to introduce the imported doctrine in 34th Tank Brigade even though he knew it to be misguided. He had not paid similar heed to War Office doctrine. Undoubtedly, he feared the consequences if caught in disobedience of the new C-in-C. Ironically, Eighth Army's doctrine was wrong. Subordinate formations were by no means unanimous in endorsement of a tank-first pattern of attack even during Montgomery's tenure. By the summer of 1944 Eighth Army had shaken off the dubious doctrine Montgomery enforced in 21 Army Group and taught that in combined tank and infantry attacks the infantry should normally lead.[85]

Pyman was by no means *persona non grata* with Montgomery. Appointed CO of 3rd RTR in Eighth Army shortly before Montgomery took over, he held that command until February 1943. Promoted brigadier and sent back to Britain, he joined Paget's staff as BGS (Training). Although Montgomery abolished that post in January 1944, he secured for Pyman the post of BGS XXX Corps, where he stayed for a year before becoming Dempsey's Chief of Staff in Second Army.[86] Had Pyman not been his protégé, Montgomery's conceit, arrogance and vanity, his supreme faith in his own qualities and tendency to deny merit in those who were not of his circle might explain his rejection of Pyman's pamphlet. As it was, notwithstanding Montgomery's numerous detailed criticisms, the Eighth Army-derived pamphlet that replaced Pyman's work was a good deal less detailed in minor tactical guidance. In general, Montgomery felt Pyman's pamphlet to be too long and too detailed, hence his objection to the nine diagrams Pyman included to show alternative patterns of combined tank–infantry attack.[87] It is probable that in his enthusiasm to delete detail Montgomery never paused to consider its precise meaning, instinctively believing such matters to be beneath the notice of an Army Group HQ and more properly the concern of divisional and brigade staffs and regimental officers. This made for simple and brief doctrine, which suited Montgomery's predilections. Though perhaps not important to Montgomery, the details were important to the officers and men who would have to apply the doctrine. Although few of them had any active experience, they had picked up from battle-experience reports that the pattern of attack was important. They were right to have done so, as the two attacks on Cristot show. Montgomery's airy neglect of the details and his apparent imposition of a spurious teaching made quite the wrong impression on officers who noticed these things because their lives depended on them.

9

Armour in North-West Europe

For at least 18 months before D-Day Montgomery and the War Office had disagreed over tank policy. Montgomery rejected the War Office's distinction between infantry tanks and cruiser tanks. Instead he insisted that all fighting tanks should be capable of performing both roles. The rights and wrongs of the dispute need not detain us here, but the disagreement itself had very serious consequences in Normandy. Historians of the Normandy campaign have rightly emphasised the unusual nature of the Norman topography. The sunken lanes and thick hedgerows bounding small fields hindered cross-country movement and gave the defending Germans the great advantage of easy concealment. It is universally accepted, and not disputed here, that the topography helped the Germans to mount a very strong defence.

According to War Office teaching, as we have seen, armoured divisions were not suitable instruments for attacking strong enemy defences. It was a task best left to infantry formations supported by infantry tanks. Although Montgomery rejected the cruiser tank/infantry tank distinction it is not clear to what extent he had fully considered the organisational implications of his capital tank philosophy as it affected armoured divisions. In pursuance of War Office policy the armoured division was structured to preclude intimate co-operation between armoured regiments and infantry battalions. Most of the infantry were held in the infantry brigade and most of the armour was held in the armoured brigade. For the two arms to co-operate at the minor tactical sub-unit level demanded a different organisation. As it was, an attack by an armoured division was either an armoured brigade task in which the armour attacked with a certain amount of mopping up support by the motor battalion, or an infantry brigade task in which the armour had no part at all. Both Guards and 11th Armoured Divisions carried out the vast majority of their training in England according to those principles. They spent only a very short time, measurable in days rather than weeks, in the autumn of 1943 and the spring of 1944, in training armoured regiments with infantry battalions.[1]

Thus, as this chapter will show, Britain's armoured divisions were neither trained nor organised for the kind of battles they would have to fight in Normandy. Although the tank brigades and independent armoured brigades were intended for that kind of battle, thanks partly to bad doctrine and partly

153

to doctrinal indiscipline, their training was misconceived. Moreover, unsteady though progress towards a well-founded tactical method was before 1944, the process degenerated into a shambles when Montgomery began to throw his weight about 21 Army Group. This chapter will show the battlefield consequences of the sorry story that was tank–infantry co-operation training in Britain before D-Day. On a happier note, the British Army was not incapable of meeting the demands of battle. Once experience in Normandy showed the way, British armour and infantry proved more than up to the task. This merely underlines the pity of the incompetent direction those troops received during their training.

The 7th Armoured Division was the first British armoured division to see action in Normandy. On 10 June the division started the advance southwards from Bayeux that was to end in the bloody and humiliating reverse at Villers Bocage three days later. On the first day the armoured brigade led the advance with the infantry brigade some miles in the rear. After a rapid advance of about six miles the armour neared Bucéels where small enemy infantry detachments using grenades and anti-tank weapons, and backed up by small numbers of 88-mm guns exploited the close bocage country to stem the advance. Brigadier James Hargest, the New Zealander accompanying XXX Corps as an observer, realised that the armour needed the support of the infantry brigade but the GOC, Major-General G.W.E.J. Erskine, demurred. For operations the next day, however, the division was reorganised as two brigade groups, each consisting of infantry, armour and artillery. Hargest somehow overlooked this reorganisation when he sneered at the division's hardly glorious progress on 11 June.[2] By that time German resistance was hardening and, as we shall see, the details of the armour–infantry co-operation practised that day left much to be desired. But divisional HQ felt that its new organisation gave the formation the wherewithal to achieve 'a slow but steady advance with the minimum of casualties'.[3] This was not what higher commanders had in mind and the division was ordered to mount the right-hook movement that culminated in the Villers Bocage fiasco.[4]

It is curious that Erskine should have been so reluctant to send his infantry forward on 10 June. He had commanded 7th Armoured Division since January 1943, guiding the Desert Rats from the Libyan sands through Tunisia and thence up the west coast of Italy from Salerno. The close country of the latter theatre demanded a similar change in organisation to that found necessary on 11 June 1944 in Normandy. The infantry of the armoured brigade's motor battalion were not sufficient for the tasks of overcoming enemy-held woods and villages and protecting the armour, which the abundance of tank obstacles generally confined to the road. Conditions in Italy had been foreseen and armoured regiments had trained in co-operation with the lorried infantry battalions beforehand.[5] Had the same foresight been shown in the case of Normandy, 10 June might have gone differently for 7th Armoured Division.

Both Guards and 11th Armoured Divisions, especially the latter, might also have benefited from such foresight. On 17 June Lieutenant-Colonel J.R. Bowring, the official battle observer with XXX Corps, issued a report entitled 'Impressions on Fighting in NORMANDY'. His passage on tank tactics is worth quoting in full since it succinctly summarises the experience of 11 days fighting.

> It is quite clear from even a short experience of fighting in this type of country that the tanks require a great deal more infantry with them than is provided by the Motor Battalion. The Motor Battalion is only sufficient to clear a limited number of localities and protect them at night. In this country where pockets of resistance such as snipers and machine gunners lie and allow the tanks to by-pass them, opening up after the tanks have passed them, it is necessary to have working with the tanks sufficient infantry to flush, capture or kill the enemy who adopts these tactics. The armoured division organisation provides enough infantry for this to be done, and I am satisfied that it is only a matter of evolving correct tactics to tie together the infantry and tanks so that both can work together on perhaps slightly new lines of tactics to achieve what we desire. It is most noticeable that tanks on the move through enemy territory now complain frequently that enemy infantry are infiltrating between their various troops and squadrons. In the past they complained of anti-tank guns at long range, but in this country they are much more nervous of infantry at close range, partly because of the sniping which they know they will receive when they have by-passed the infantry and partly because of the feeling of nervousness which they get from passing continuously through close country unsearched for concealed short-range anti-tank weapons and infantry.[6]

Both 21 Army Group and the War Office endorsed Bowring's remarks.[7] However, it would be the end of July before armoured divisions acted on them in battle.

One point from Bowring's analysis is worth elaborating upon. His mention of 'short-range anti-tank weapons' referred to the Panzerfaust, a hand-held recoil-less gun that fired a hollow-charge rocket-propelled grenade that could penetrate 200 mm of armour. First used in Russia in the summer of 1943, early versions of the weapon had a range of only about 30 metres, but a new model introduced in the summer of 1944 had a range of 80 metres and later models could achieve a 100-metre throw. Panzerfaust's short range limited it to a close-quarters role. Indeed, inaccuracy severely curtailed its effectiveness at ranges greater than 40 yards.[8] However, given plenty of cover and a stout-hearted firer it made an excellent anti-tank weapon.

Although British troops had encountered German hand-thrown and hand-placed hollow-charge anti-tank grenades before, they seem not to have encountered the infinitely more dangerous rocket-propelled devices until

May 1944 during the push up the Liri Valley in Italy. On 10 June, acting on the basis of a signal sent on 26 May, the War Office published a brief account in *Current Reports from Overseas*, a notably prompt response and an indication that the new weapons had caused alarm. The article described specially trained enemy detachments, which exploited standing crops and other cover to attack tanks 'at point-blank range with magnetic hollow charges, smoke and anti-tank rocket launchers'. Reporting high tank casualties in the assault echelon, the War Office counselled that infantry should move close enough to the tanks to eliminate the German tank-hunters before they could do their work.[9] This merely underlined the wisdom of official doctrine for tank and infantry co-operation and the folly of the Eighth Army doctrine Montgomery had imposed on 21 Army Group. Unfortunately it came too late to influence the doctrine that tank and armoured units of the latter formation took into their first Norman battles.

The 11th Armoured Division arrived in Normandy in the middle of June. Its first battle was operation EPSOM, west of Caen, which started on 26 June. Whereas the plan for 7th Armoured Division's first Norman battle two weeks earlier had put the armoured division in the forefront of the attack, the plan for EPSOM envisaged that 15th Division would break through the enemy's main defences, seize crossings over the River Odon and then allow 11th Armoured Division to sweep through to seize bridges across the River Orne about five miles to the south-east. The 15th Division failed to make the expected progress. The 11th Armoured Division was launched anyway, from the village of Cheux to try to reach the Odon about three miles away, only to be similarly baulked. Further efforts by 15th Division the following day secured a bridge across the Odon at Tourmauville, but 11th Armoured Division's efforts to exploit towards the Orne were stemmed before Hill 112, which was as far as the British advanced during EPSOM.[10] After EPSOM, Roberts reached the same conclusion as 7th Armoured Division concerning the need for tank–infantry co-operation within the armoured division. His desire to secure this, however, was frustrated by the fact that his lorried infantry brigade was taken from his command to continue the struggle for Hill 112.[11]

Meanwhile, Guards Armoured Division assembled in Normandy at the beginning of July. The War Diaries of units show that during its second week in France the division carried out training in tank and infantry co-operation, infantry battalions with armoured battalions, 'in anticipation of possible fighting in the Bocage area'.[12] However, the Guards' first operation was not in the bocage but in the 'good tank country' to the east of the Orne, in operation GOODWOOD.

The story of GOODWOOD is a complex one involving campaign strategy, British manpower reserves, tank strengths and Anglo-American military relations. There is no need to rehearse fully the controversy surrounding the operation, for our concerns here are purely tactical. GOODWOOD envisaged a great armoured drive southwards from the bridgehead east of the Orne below Caen held by 51st Division. The job was assigned to VIII Corps, commanded by Lieutenant-General R.N. O'Connor, with all three British armoured divisions, Guards, 7th and 11th, under command. Because the bridgehead was of constricted dimensions, and in a vain effort to deny the Germans any intelligence of the impending attack, none of the armoured divisions was allowed to cross the river until the night before the attack started. It proved impossible to pass all their components into the bridgehead in good time. Dempsey, commander of Second Army, ordered O'Connor to concentrate on getting armoured brigades over, leaving everything else for later.[13] As if this problem were not enough, 51st Division had laid a deep minefield to protect its position. This could not be lifted and so the attacking forces had to funnel into the attack through a small number of cleared lanes. These bottlenecks caused great traffic congestion which prevented the timely reinforcement of 11th Armoured Division, which was leading, when it ran into heavy opposition.

However, for the first five miles or so of the advance the opposition was light and well within the capacity of armoured brigades to handle. In this early stage of the battle the armour profited by both an artillery barrage, behind which they advanced, and the lingering effects of a tremendous aerial bombardment delivered before zero hour. Subsequent investigation found that the bombing had destroyed few enemy anti-tank guns, but it had temporarily incapacitated their crews.[14] As the advance continued, the artillery support ceased. Left behind the Orne as they were, the guns lacked the necessary range.[15] The enemy, meanwhile, recovering from the incapacitating effect of the bombing, began to resist strongly. As early as 15 July, three days before the attack, German intelligence had predicted a strong British offensive east of the Orne. D'Este has described the defences the British armoured divisions bumped into on the first day of GOODWOOD as 'perhaps the best defensive structure they [the Germans] had yet been able to prepare in Normandy'.[16] The artillery barrage and the air bombing carried the British armour deep into those defences, but not right through them. In the village of Cagny and on the Bourguébus ridge remained formidable static defences, in rear of which a mobile reserve of Panther and Tiger tanks lay quite untouched by the firepower with which the British prepared their attack. The ground south of the Caen–Vimont railway sloped gently upwards to the Bourguébus ridge: it presented few obstacles to mechanised movement, but equally few areas in which tanks could take cover from German fire. It was in this area that 11th Armoured Division on 18 July and 7th Armoured Division the following day suffered the heaviest casualties. All told, the three armoured divisions suffered more than 400 tank casualties before the operation was abandoned on 20 July – more than 40 per cent of their tank strength.[17]

GOODWOOD was not a defeat for the British. It expanded the Allied bridgehead southwards by about seven miles and, in conjunction with the II

Canadian Corps operation ATLANTIC on the right, finally cleared the Germans out of Caen. At the strategic level, GOODWOOD served Montgomery's purpose admirably since it 'wrote down' powerful German forces that might otherwise have been used to hinder the American breakout in the west. At the tactical level, though, it was a failure. Second Army's initial orders to VIII Corps on 13 July specified Bretteville-sur-Laize, Vimont, Argences and Falaise as the objectives. Two days later, on Montgomery's instructions, Falaise and Argences were dropped.[18] In the event, VIII Corps reached no further south than Bourguébus, failing entirely to gain the high ground between that place and Bretteville about six miles further south. Dempsey had hoped that the German defences would crumble away, allowing exploitation as far south as Argentan, 30 miles south of Bourguébus.[19]

Why did GOODWOOD fail? Certainly all three armoured divisions were badly impeded by the congestion in the Orne bridgehead which prevented tanks of 7th Armoured Division reinforcing the depleted armour of 11th Armoured Division in the south until the afternoon of the first day. The same congestion prevented 32nd Guards Brigade from following up 5th Guards Armoured Brigade at the speed they might otherwise have done. The 11th Armoured Division's infantry brigade, held back to clear the villages of Cuverville and Demouville in the north on orders from O'Connor, was not available to Roberts when he might have used it during the morning of 18 July. Divisional artillery power was caught up in the bridgehead traffic and so could not support the armour. Yet how might these wasted resources have influenced the battle? Only by taking part in setpiece attacks at strengthening enemy defences on Bourguébus ridge and to the east of Cagny. Hastings has put his finger on the reason for the failure of GOODWOOD: '. . . Second Army sought to attack powerful and skilfully-directed German defences. Major changes of British tactics would have been necessary to bring about a different outcome.'[20] British armoured divisions were neither designed nor trained for the kind of attack the German defences demanded.

In one sense GOODWOOD shows British tactical doctrine for armoured divisions to have been wholly inadequate. One might well ask why British armoured divisions were incapable of such an attack. But viewing British doctrine in its own terms, GOODWOOD bloodily vindicated the doctrinal precept that armoured divisions were not suitable instruments for attacking well-organised enemy defences. Interviewed many years afterwards, Roberts averred that GOODWOOD was a justified misuse of armour, the justification being that Montgomery could afford to lose tanks (VIII Corps' tank losses in GOODWOOD were made good within two days) but was desperately short of infantry replacements.[21] Be that as it may, although the circumstances of operation EPSOM varied enormously from those of GOODWOOD the same basic misuse of armour occurred, albeit on a smaller scale, when 11th Armoured Division was launched against an unbroken enemy defence. GOODWOOD was no aberration, made necessary by the shallow pool of remaining British manpower. It fitted the pattern of how British armoured divisions had been employed in Normandy hitherto. Their employment disregarded the doctrine in which they had been trained. No wonder that few successes came their way.

After GOODWOOD 11th Armoured Division's next battle was the so-called British breakout from Caumont at the end of July, operation BLUECOAT. Guards Armoured Division also took part in BLUECOAT, but in the meantime was slated to lie in the rear of the Canadian operation SPRING, waiting to exploit a breakthrough that never came. So BLUECOAT was the Guards' next action too. Between GOODWOOD and BLUECOAT Roberts reorganised 11th Armoured Division into two brigade groups, each comprising two armoured regiments (the divisional armoured reconnaissance regiment, 2nd Northamptonshire Yeomanry, being treated as an armoured regiment) and two infantry battalions. Adair carried out a similar reorganisation in Guards Armoured Division, although apparently with little forethought and in some haste.[22] BLUECOAT, and the drive southwards during the first half of August against an enemy who was still resisting strongly, saw both 11th and Guards Armoured Divisions advancing by means of tank and infantry co-operation. Even when German resistance turned to flight 11th Armoured Division retained the mixed brigade group organisation for the rapid advance to the Seine in the last two weeks of August.[23]

In his memoirs Field Marshal Carver (who commanded 1st RTR in 7th Armoured Division from April 1943 until promoted to command 4th Armoured Brigade in Normandy in July 1944) recalled that before D-Day the idea of reorganising the armoured division to facilitate greater armour–infantry co-operation was extensively mooted, but rejected on the grounds that Montgomery foresaw only a short period of fighting in the bocage.[24] In fact, although 11th Armoured Division returned to the standard armoured divisional organisation for the dash from the Seine to Antwerp, Roberts restored the mixed-group pattern thereafter[25] and Adair maintained Guards Armoured Division in mixed groups throughout the rest of the war. 'Adopting this organisation', he wrote, 'was the best thing I ever did.'[26] In his memoirs, Roberts wrote that the organisation and tactics of armoured divisions evolved continually during the war, and that it was only with BLUECOAT that the correct solution was struck.[27] The picture that emerges from the Normandy campaign, however, is that as a result of Montgomery's rejection of War Office policy the problem had changed. In his address to officers upon taking command of 11th Armoured Division in 1943, Roberts spoke from his experience as the commander of 26th Armoured Brigade with First Army in Tunisia, rather than as an armoured regimental and brigade commander with Eighth Army in the desert, on the grounds that topographically Tunisia bore the greater resemblance to North-West Europe.[28] He said nothing to suggest any need for close armour–infantry co-operation within the armoured division. But then he expected armoured divisions to be used to exploit gaps in enemy defences created by infantry divisions, in accordance with doctrine.[29] Their use for other tasks in Normandy confounded him and necessitated the change of organisation. The introduction of short-range anti-tank weapons such as the Panzerfaust compounded the problem, ensuring that tanks could never again overrun an infantry position with any confidence as to their invulnerability.

As it happens, only 6 per cent of tank losses in Normandy were from Panzerfäuste. The figure rose to 9 per cent in Belgium and Holland, fell back to 7 per cent in Germany west of the Rhine, and leapt to 34 per cent east of the Rhine – a jump probably explained by Germany's shortage of anti-tank artillery and the terrain's suitability for Panzerfaust action. However, the effect of the weapon on tank operations exceeded its casualty toll, for the mere possibility of Panzerfäuste delayed tanks while infantry support was summoned.[30] The new weapon rendered the offensive methods British armoured divisions had previously trained in and applied highly dangerous. Hitherto, tanks had little to fear from enemy infantry. Small-arms fire could be evaded by the simple, if inconvenient, expedient of closing down. Hand-placed hollow charges could be little more than an irritant, fatal for some tank crews but often suicidal for the individuals using them because they exposed themselves to the retribution of neighbouring tanks. Panzerfaust enabled an infantryman to destroy a tank from cover. While speculative fire at likely Panzerfaust hides offered a partial solution to the problem, against dug-in enemy the only complete solution was a thorough search by infantry.[31] Against relatively large and immobile towed anti-tank guns, medium-range machine-gun fire and long-range HE fire could neutralise and destroy, allowing the armour to advance, leaving following infantry to mop up survivors. If those survivors were armed with Panzerfäuste the advancing armour risked heavy casualties unless the affiliated infantry accompanied rather than followed. The effect was to blur the distinction between the tactics of infantry tanks and those of cruiser tanks, but many tanks and lives would be lost before this became clear.

In Normandy sustained progress by armour was possible only when infantry co-operated closely. This was not simply a function of the bocage. It was primarily a function of the strength of the defences. The bocage helped the Germans to mount a strong defence but, as GOODWOOD proved, it was an aid the Germans could manage without when necessary. Battle experience before Normandy proved that tank support was not, as had been thought, a panacea that ensured an easy infantry advance. It brought its own tactical problems, chief of which was that of ensuring the tanks' security against weapons that could destroy them but were relatively harmless to infantry. While tanks could handle machine-guns, the chief local obstacle to infantry movement (artillery and mortars, being long-range, high-trajectory weapons and thus able to conceal themselves absolutely, were best left to friendly artillery), they could not do so unless arrangements were made against tank killers. For reasons connected with the relative insensibility of closed-down tank crews, dismounted infantry proved the best remedy. Even if the destruction of an enemy anti-tank gun was accomplished with an HE shell fired by a tank, establishing the location of such threats was much easier for the infantry. Thus tank-and-infantry attack tactics became not so much one arm supporting the other as each arm supporting the other, co-operation in its true mutual sense. By the end of 1943, infantry-tank units training in Britain were beginning to understand this. When the cruiser tanks of armoured regiments found that they could not get on in Normandy without infantry support, the solution was to adopt infantry-tank tactics. The fact that in the artificial world of doctrine cruiser tanks were a principal arm whereas infantry tanks were a support arm was quite irrelevant. So what became of infantry-tank tactics in Normandy?

As we have already seen in the two attacks on Cristot in June 1944, attacking with a first echelon composed only of tanks proved no more advisable in Normandy than it had in Tunisia or in operation BATTLEAXE in 1941. It did not always result in failure, as it did at Cristot, but if the enemy's defences were strong failure was the likely outcome. The methods proposed in the Eighth Army doctrine were quite inferior to those outlined in Pyman's pamphlet that the former superseded in 21 Army Group. Norman topography and German Panzerfäuste exacerbated this inadequacy. Between 6 and 16 July, 1st/5th Queen's Royal Regiment of 7th Armoured Division's 131st Infantry Brigade practised a new technique for overcoming bocage defences with the division's armour, which involved the methodical clearing of each field.

> First the infantry would creep down the hedges, covered by the tanks. They would then clear the far hedge, look through it to spot any hidden German anti-tank guns. When things looked alright [sic] the tanks were called up + the process repeated. If an enemy anti-tank gun were spotted, the infantry were to stalk it or tell the tanks who would do the stalking.[32]

Such a technique in an unidentified Norman battle was reported on very favourably to the War Office by an officer recovering from wounds. The attack concerned was by an infantry battalion supported by a squadron of Shermans, which was split up among the two leading companies. Before the infantry advanced, the tanks machine-gunned the hedges to the flanks and front. The infantry then advanced to the first hedgerow and dealt with any anti-tank guns beyond it before the tanks came up. If the infantry spotted an enemy machine-gun post they fired a green Verey flare in its direction to alert the tanks which would then engage it. The process was repeated for each field until the objective was reached. There were no tank casualties. The infantry suffered eight killed and 40 wounded. The enemy lost more than 300, of which 292 were taken prisoner. They also lost one 75-mm anti-tank gun and two MG 34s.[33]

It is instructive to compare this method with that practised in 7th Armoured

Division during its unsuccessful attempt to capture Tilly-sur-Seulles in June. The 1st/5th Queen's had a squadron of tanks under command and an artillery battery in support. 'Infantry got held up by machine-gun fire + call up the tanks to help. When the tanks come up they get shot at by the concealed enemy tanks behind.'[34] It must at once be conceded that the problem here was rather more severe than that envisaged by 1st/5th Queen's in July or experienced in battle by the wounded officer cited above, in that in June tanks rather than merely anti-tank guns confronted the British armour. A tank was more difficult for infantry to deal with and if unseen was hard for a British tank to engage even if penetrable by its ammunition. None the less, by speculative shooting of the hedgerows the tanks could materially help the infantry forward and when forward the infantry could assess the form beyond the hedgerow. Since later in the campaign the infantry proved capable of locating anti-tank guns they must surely have been capable of locating concealed tanks. Once the nature of the problem was known then attention could be turned to how to overcome or circumvent it. Before Tilly in June, 1st/5th Queen's and their armoured colleagues seem never to have known the nature of the problem until it was too late and not to have used tactics that might have enabled them to have found out.

As a general rule, then, tank–infantry attacks were best made with the most intimate battlefield co-operation between the two arms, meaning that each should support the other in the leading echelon. It is worthwhile briefly examining instances that appear to confound that rule.

The first battle of 6th Guards Tank Brigade was operation BLUECOAT on 30 July, in which the brigade supported 15th Division. In the initial phase of the operation 2nd Gordon Highlanders and 9th Cameronians attacked the Lutain Wood and Septs Vents area about a mile south of Caumont, supported by 4th Tank Grenadier Guards. The 2nd Argyll and Sutherland Highlanders were then to pass through to mount an attack on the Les Loges ridge, about two miles further south, with 3rd Tank Scots Guards in support. However, resistance in the Lutain Wood and Sept Vents area was strong, and the Argylls and Scots Guards had to fight their way forward. This delay threatened to prevent the tanks arriving on the start-line for the Les Loges attack in time to benefit from the planned barrage. So the Scots Guards CO ordered his tanks to go forward as fast as they could, leaving the infantry behind. The country south of Caumont was particularly thick bocage which the Germans, apparently thinking it impenetrable to tanks, had neglected to defend with anti-tank guns. The Churchill's exceptional gradient-climbing ability confounded the Germans on this point and enabled the Scots Guards to advance and cross their start-line without the infantry who were still held up behind. By 2.30 p.m. a tank squadron was on the ridge, to be joined shortly afterwards by a second.[35]

Circumstances at Caumont led the 3rd Tank Scots Guards to behave more in the manner of an armoured regiment than the infantry-tank unit it was. It is an obvious conclusion, but none the less worth stating, that it was not so much the bocage country that prevented the execution of the armoured role in Normandy as the defences the Germans installed there. Where, as at Caumont, those defences had little anti-tank strength, armour had a relatively easy time. Provided the enemy defences did not include anti-tank weapons the Eighth Army method of tank–infantry co-operation worked perfectly well. Another example occurred on 11 August when an infantry battalion with two Sherman squadrons under command attacked a ridge near the village of La Villette, about four miles north of Condé-sur-Noireau. The attack was delivered into the enemy's flank when he was probably expecting any attack to be frontal, which probably accounts for the lack of anti-tank fire. One squadron of Shermans led the attack behind a barrage timed at their speed. They seized their objectives without casualty, although the accompanying infantry carrier platoon suffered heavily from small-arms, artillery and mortar fire aimed harmlessly at the tanks. The infantry following up had no protection from the barrage and suffered casualties from enemy fire from the flanks until a hastily organised smokescreen was laid. Had they been up with the tanks they would have suffered in the same way as the carriers. There would, however, have been more opportunity for liaison between the foot-soldiers and the tanks to direct the latter's fire on to troublesome enemy weapons.[36]

These examples of the Eighth Army doctrine of tank–infantry co-operation working do not, therefore, disprove the rule against it. Indeed, there was a nasty sequel to the Scots Guards' success at Les Loges ridge. The Argylls, the infantry that the tanks left behind, later made a relatively easy advance to Les Loges village, a few hundred yards north-west of the ridge. However, they were reluctant to move on to the exposed ridge itself with their anti-tank guns. This left the Scots Guards' tanks in sole occupation of the objective. A subsequent counterattack by three Jagdpanthers, delivered from a wood to the north-east that lay in an area supposed to have been cleared by the flanking 43rd Division, claimed very heavy casualties among the tanks on the ridge. The position none the less held, and after self-propelled artillery was brought up the Scots Guards were allowed to withdraw at 10 p.m. Had those Jagdpanthers entered the odds earlier in the day it is probable that they could have prevented the British tanks ever getting on to the ridge and the story would have been one of failure rather than success with heavy casualties.

All this is not to say that the tactics outlined in Pyman's 21 Army Group pamphlet guaranteed success. There were occasions when the defences were just too strong. On 6 August, for example, a squadron of 3rd Tank Scots Guards supported 10th Highland Light Infantry (HLI) in an attempt to seize the village of Estry (about four miles north of Vassy). The enemy in the village had already repulsed one attack that day. The HLI's attempt started at 7.15 p.m. The attack went in on a two-company front, each company supported by two tank troops. The company on the right reached the objective. On the left, however, the attack had to pass through the same bocage and orchard terrain in which the earlier attack had stalled and an intense fire fight took place in which the tanks, directed by the infantry, managed to silence all the machine-guns holding up the advance. Further progress was then halted by a Panther which knocked out the leading troop commander's tank. Although self-propelled artillery, guided by the now dismounted troop commander, shortly destroyed the Panther, renewed anti-personnel resistance prevented further advance. Both tanks and infantry spent the night in close leaguer, remaining there throughout the next morning under heavy machine-gun and mortar fire until ordered to withdraw. Estry proved to be held as a strongpoint by 9th SS Panzer Division and would resist further, stronger, attacks before the German retreat began.[37]

The HLI assault on Estry was supposed to have opened with a medium artillery concentration on the village, but this did not materialise. Whether the issue would have been any different had the artillery offensive taken place cannot be known, but may be doubted in view of the limited lethality of artillery on dug-in troops and the fact that it was to be in the form of a brief concentration rather than a barrage. What seems clear, though, is that the tactics of tank–infantry co-operation used had been right. Although the tanks could presumably have advanced with impunity against the machine-gun fire the infantry would have had to remain behind and seek to overcome that fire alone. The tanks meanwhile would have been easy prey to enemy armour which could then have proceeded to destroy the infantry further back. Estry held because the Germans were strong in tank-killing defences there rather than through deficiencies in the tactics used to attack the place.

It would be unfair to blame Montgomery entirely for the tactical errors into which tank–infantry co-operation fell. While Montgomery's intervention made the situation worse, it was already bad. Pyman's pamphlet can be seen in retrospect to have been about to improve matters markedly, but it is questionable that it would have gained universal acceptance within 21 Army Group had Montgomery not vetoed it. The problem facing 21 Army Group was not merely a matter of bad doctrine; it was also a matter of doctrinal indiscipline. Regardless of what Whitehall said, units and formations pleased themselves when it came to tank–infantry co-operation tactics. The variety of different methods and the variety of the results they achieved is illustrated by the record of 1st East Riding Yeomanry (ERY) in Normandy.

The regiment landed on D-Day as part of 27th Armoured Brigade supporting 3rd Division. On 7 June 'A' and 'B' squadrons took part in an unsuccessful attack on Cambes, supporting 2nd Royal Ulster Rifles (RUR) from the right and left flanks respectively. This was clearly a mobile operation, for one troop penetrated the village and destroyed two PzKw Mark IV tanks, one half-track and three lorries. Two days later 'A' squadron again supporting 2nd RUR attacked the same place, but instead of actually accompanying the infantry the tanks stood off and 'shot the RUR successfully into the village'. This was not a completely safe procedure: the squadron lost two tanks and one officer killed to enemy anti-tank guns. On 28 June 'C' squadron, attached to 2nd RUR, attacked the village of La Bijude, by now a strongpoint in the German defences north of Caen. The plan was for the squadron to advance with two troops up behind artillery concentrations down the slope into the village and occupy it. If successful, an infantry company was to follow up. It was not successful. 'C' squadron tried twice, each time coming under heavy machine-gun and anti-tank fire. By the time the attack was called off seven tank casualties had been suffered, three men were dead and six wounded.[38]

During operation CHARNWOOD, in which Caen north of the Orne was finally captured, 1st ERY supported battalions of 59th Division in successive attacks on the villages of Galmanche, Malon and St Contest. For these operations, the idea of the tanks actually moving in the attack was dropped. Instead they were to support the infantry by fire from static positions, much as they had done on 9 June. The 1st ERY's conduct in CHARNWOOD is not to be equated with the battle lessons reported from Tunisia which, for all that they stressed that the tanks need not physically accompany the infantry, did none the less emphasise the constant need for forward movement by the tanks and the maintenance of visual contact between the two arms. Instead, 1st ERY fought CHARNWOOD in a self-propelled artillery role. A deplorably low level of co-operation with the infantry is evinced by the facts that the tanks provided no fire-support for the infantry's attack on the first objective, Galmanche, because of lingering mist and smoke from the artillery barrage, and that when they moved forward to that village in order to support another battalion's attack on the next objective they found the place still occupied by the enemy.[39] The self-propelled artillery mode of operating may well have been prompted by the regiment's unhappy experience ten days earlier, but it was not standard practice throughout 27th Armoured Brigade. The 13th/18th Hussars' 'B' squadron's experience on 8 July was quite different. They spent the day in support of 6th North Staffordshire Regiment, whose objective was La Bijude, and seem to have operated in close proximity to the infantry throughout the day. Indeed, if the regiment's War Diarist is to be believed, the armoured troops did their best, without success, to persuade the reluctant infantry to tackle the main residuary enemy resistance outside the village after the latter had been captured.[40]

Historians have criticised the low standard of tank and infantry co-operation in the British Army in Normandy. It was not only in retrospect that such judgements could be made. One battalion commander, in a paper circulated within 21 Army Group HQ in September 1944, claimed that he had rarely experienced satisfactory co-operation with tanks. Among the reasons he outlined for this were that his battalion had never been allotted the same co-operating tank regiment or squadron more than once, that some of them were trained for infantry co-operation and others for cruiser-tank work, that tactics varied from squadron to squadron and that some squadron commanders failed to understand that they were the supporting arm.[41] His remarks angered the RAC Branch, which, wishfully claiming that the man's experience was not representative, vetoed the paper's external distribution. A clearly frustrated Lieutenant-Colonel R.G. Lewthwaite, the Operations Branch officer dealing with the matter, noted that the battalion commander's comments were the 'exact counterpart of account of Inf by OC Staffs Yeo'.[42]

In view of the tactical pluralism tolerated in tank–infantry co-operation before Montgomery took over 21 Army Group, the flaws in the doctrine he imposed when he assumed command and the negligible attention to the subject within armoured divisions, such evidence of interarm misunderstanding is no surprise. The varying approaches to the problem attempted within 27th Armoured Brigade in Normandy reflect the failure to achieve a well-founded consensus on the matter before D-Day. Criticism of poor tank–infantry co-operation within armoured divisions, while not invalid, is unfair. The Normandy battles were not what the British armoured divisions had trained for because such battles were not the task assigned to them in doctrine. It was all very well for Montgomery to reject that doctrine, but the consequence was that the armoured divisions were set to do work for which they were neither trained nor organised. Whether one blames the War Office for the inflexibility inherent in doctrine, or Montgomery for failing to grasp the limitations the training and organisation of his armoured divisions placed upon the tasks they could reasonably be expected to accomplish, is a matter of personal taste. The armoured divisions themselves were not to blame.

What armoured divisions in appropriate organisation and with appropriate tactics could achieve they showed in operations after GOODWOOD. On 10 September, for example, a battle group comprising 1st Herefordshire Regiment, 2nd Fife and Forfar Yeomanry (FFY) in Shermans and a battery of field guns (all from 11th Armoured Division) fought what the War Office described as 'a model encounter battle' on the Helchteren–Hechtel road in Belgium. The enemy held a wood and some broken ground before it. His armament included an 81-mm mortar battery and a number of infantry anti-tank weapons, either Panzerfäuste or the similar Panzerschrecke. The actual assault, which was launched from a flank, was a company/squadron operation with another company/squadron group providing frontal fire-support to supplement that delivered by the artillery battery and the battalion's three-inch mortars. The 2nd FFY's tank squadrons were under strength at the time, with about ten tanks apiece. The attacking troops were organised as an assault echelon comprising two platoons and two troops (probably each of four tanks), and a reserve echelon of one platoon and two tanks. Tanks and infantry moved together, fire and movement being practised on a tank–infantry section basis. The attack succeeded, with at least 30 enemy killed and 400 prisoners taken, at a cost of four dead and 11 wounded. There were no tank casualties.

But the operation had not been incident-free. The moment it started, machine-gun fire from the initial objectives threatened to bring it to a premature halt. Once that opposition had been overcome, further machine-gun fire from previously unlocated positions once again checked the attack. In both cases, tank machine-gun fire retrieved the situation. Then one platoon commander, his sergeant and his corporals fell to enemy mortar fire. Machine-gun fire from yet more unlocated positions temporarily halted the attack while the reserve platoon and the two reserve tanks were sent up. When they attempted to resume the attack the tanks came under anti-tank fire which was overcome by one of the infantry sections with a bayonet charge.[43] This operation was clearly no pushover. Its success illustrates what could be achieved when armour and infantry practised truly mutual and intimate co-operation in battle. Before the end of July 1944, interarm co-operation of that quality was not common and tactical failures were correspondingly frequent. The reasons for this can be traced to doctrinal error, consequent training error and the incompatibility of Montgomery's methods with official doctrine.

10

Conclusion

At the beginning of this book we noted Murray's hypothesis that the British Army's leadership during the Second World War failed to establish and enforce a coherent and effective tactical doctrine. The evidence surveyed in this study bears that hypothesis out. Doctrine was in many cases wrong. In any case, right or wrong, troops in training frequently ignored it. The British Army's performance was not hopeless. Much good work was done between Dunkirk and D-Day. But somehow the Army never managed to collect the good together and eliminate the bad.

So far as the infantry arm is concerned, the great promise of battle drill to improve the minor tactical skills of junior officers and their men was not fully realised. Some of the blame for this is due to the very nature of battle drill – its imposition of a drill on what ideally was a matter for individual decision-making in individual circumstances. Battle drill represented off-the-peg tactics when what was wanted was bespoke. However, a suit that does not fit perfectly is of more use than one that would fit like a glove but is never made. The critics of battle drill offered no better alternative. Without battle drill the minor tactical skills of most British infantrymen would have been of little more immediate use than a tailor's paper patterns are to his client. They would have gone into battle naked.

But battle drill was not the main cause of infantry minor tactical weakness. An off-the-peg suit can, after all, be adjusted. No one ever suggested that the off-the-peg tactics of battle drill would not need adjustment in action. Where infantry training went awry was in the growing tendency to suppose that minor tactics were unnecessary in attacks that were based tactically around an artillery barrage. Infantry minor tactics came to be regarded as an alternative to artillery-based tactics rather than as a set of complementary techniques to be applied when the blunt artillery instrument was no longer suitable. The notion that the two types of fighting might be necessary in the same battle passed away. It left the expectation that an infantry setpiece attack behind artillery support required little if any actual infantry fighting. When in battle that expectation was falsified, too few infantrymen knew what to do.

Until *Army Training Memorandum* No. 51 of November 1944 the dichotomy of artillery-dominated tactics on the one hand and battle drill minor tactics on the other did not feature in any War Office publication. On the contrary, doctrine noted the need for minor tactics to fill the gaps that the gunners could not. The failure, therefore, was not a matter of War Office doctrine. It was one of training and is most readily apparent in the neglect of the 'closing with the enemy' stage of battle in 'full-sail' exercises. Indeed, the War Office criticised this common omission in its manual on umpiring published in February 1944. Battle drill minor tactics came to be seen as a special technique to be used only in discrete single-arm infantry actions.

It is ironic that the battle school movement, which did so much to invigorate the infantry with tactical self-confidence, fell in with the barrage-laden ethos just enough to accept that the simple section and platoon battle drills with which it started could not profitably be applied in setpiece artillery-led attacks. Instead, battle schools taught the unworkably complex lane method. The application of simple battle drill tactics in situations that could not be foreseen, situations created by the imperfect development of artillery-based plans, was in consequence little practised in training. To the extent that the expression in the *Army Training Memorandum* of the spurious dichotomy of minor tactics and artillery-based tactics represented a shift in doctrine, it was a case of doctrine adjusting to conform not to battle experience but to unrealistic training habits, the origins of which predated battle drill.

If doctrine demanded the practice of infantry minor tactics even in attacks in which an artillery fire-plan dominated tactical planning, why were field formations allowed to neglect that aspect of tactics in their training? Did no one monitor infantry training habits with a view to identifying such basic flaws? There was an Inspector-General of Training at the War Office, a post filled by Lieutenant-General C.G. Liddell (formerly Adjutant-General), but the appointment was abolished in October 1942 and there is no evidence that Liddell took any interest in doctrinal enforcement.[1] Regular systematic inspection of training for doctrinal conformity independently of the chain of command seems not to have taken place. It would have required a dedicated team of inspectors observing training in units over extended periods. Had it been considered, such a luxury would probably have been rejected as both too costly and inconsistent with commanders' responsibility for their troops' training.

Senior commanders were not necessarily interested in the task of doctrinal enforcement. Montgomery, for example, was famously free with his axe when he judged subordinate officers to be inadequate. His judgements, though, appear to have been based not upon any narrow analysis of what the victim was and was not training his troops to do but upon a more general impression of the manner in which he discharged his multifarious responsibilities. Indeed, he maintained that when observing exercises general officers should concentrate on the performance of unit, brigade and divisional commanders, leaving any observation of minor tactics to staff officers.[2] Fitness for command, quite properly, was Montgomery's criterion. However, it would appear

that an officer could be fit for his appointment without necessarily conforming to doctrine in the training of his troops. His ignorant intervention in the
field of tank–infantry co-operation puts Montgomery himself in this category.

That an efficient means of doctrinal enforcement would have eliminated
the weakness in infantry training identified in this study must in any case be
doubted. The reasons for the neglect of minor tactics in large-scale exercises
were fully explored in Chapter 3. In retrospect, one can see that such neglect
had serious consequences. Had they existed, however, teams of training
inspectors would probably have overlooked the omission provided that minor
tactics were properly covered in section, platoon and company training. The
marriage of all aspects of military operations in a single exercise is probably
impossible even if one exempts casualties and material damage. Dangerous
consequences from the separation of minor tactics and artillery-based tactics
would probably not have been obvious, especially if the inspectors were not
themselves battle-experienced. Battle experience, of course, was in short
supply among the troops training at home.

A further doubt as to the probable efficacy of any system of doctrinal
enforcement in this area arises from the possibility that, irrespective of War
Office doctrine, senior commanders from Montgomery downwards really did
regard artillery-dominated tactics as a complete substitute for infantry minor
tactical skills. That is implied in one recent study of the operational technique
of 21 Army Group.[3] Another forthcoming work promises to trace the origins
of this thinking back into the 1920s.[4] None the less, official doctrine during
the Second World War took a realistic line on the need to integrate infantry
minor tactics into those based on artillery fire-power. That was a sound
doctrine and it is the contention of this study that infantry training betrayed
it.

What makes that failure inexcusable is that infantry tactics had barely
changed since 1918. Neither had basic weaponry – rifle and light machine-
gun – undergone any radical change. If the British infantry of 1918 could train
itself in modern tactics there was no excuse for its successor of 25 years later
not to. That the battle drill movement initially encountered such resistance
from the regulars reflects poorly upon the latter. That, despite the massive
boost supplied by Wigram and his disciples, infantry tactics ultimately
advanced little from the standards of 1916 is disgraceful.

The armoured arm wallowed in a rather different boat. The slowest British
tank to see service in the Second World War, the Infantry Tank Mark I (withdrawn from field units soon after Dunkirk), was as fast as its most lively
predecessor of the Great War, the Medium A. No British tank of the earlier
conflict even had a revolving turret. The interwar years offered no opportunity
to test the rapidly improving technology of armoured warfare, or the tactical
and strategic theories for its use, in battle conditions. There were no *Notes
from Theatres of War* or *Current Reports from Overseas* for the Royal Tank
Corps. It is no matter for astonishment that some wrong turnings were taken.

It is true that the German Army, in stressing interarm co-operation, came far closer to the optimum shape and methods for an armoured division before the outbreak of war than did the British. None the less it is often overlooked that major reorganisation followed its successes in 1939 and 1940.[5] The Wehrmacht's blitzkrieg victories were to a great extent made possible by the material, psychological and intellectual unpreparedness of their opponents.[6] The Germans did not allow the glories thus won to obscure the many flaws revealed by their experience. Moreover, the war in 1939 and 1940 was staccato in development and left the Germans in possession of the battlefields, so allowing the leisure and the facilities to study the lessons of experience.

Contrast the German situation with the British. The only substantial experience British armour gained against the Wehrmacht before the middle of 1941 was the Arras counterstroke in May 1940: a magnificent effort whose failure, and that of the campaign of which it was a part, prevented the British from learning its lessons. In particular, the British remained largely unaware that it was the 88-mm gun that had stopped the attack.[7] The Bartholomew report on the lessons of the BEF's experience did not even allude to Arras.[8] Empirically founded tactical precepts, clearly among the fruits that the Germans plucked from their battle victories, were far more difficult for the British to harvest from their defeats. It is no coincidence that the first editions of *Notes from Theatres of War* dealt not with the failed BATTLEAXE offensive of June 1941 but with the successful, albeit flawed, operation CRUSADER launched five months later. Even so, for most of 1942 the desert war was confused, indecisive and at times disastrous. The British enjoyed no period of respite comparable to the Phoney War period enjoyed by the Germans in which to study recent operations and apply lessons. So although the lessons drawn from that pell-mell were by no means entirely discreditable, and allowed a start to be made in 1942 to the job of making armoured formations at home doctrinally fit for war, it was not until the strategic initiative lay firmly with the Allies that the process could gather pace.

It was a process bedevilled by confusion over the tactical implications of the HE-firing tank gun – a major blot upon the War Office's record in doctrinal dissemination. But two parallel developments eclipsed that failure: Montgomery's refusal to honour War Office thinking on the separate roles of infantry tanks and cruiser tanks; and the introduction of the Panzerfaust. The latter should have been anticipated because the British infantry had deployed a similar weapon, the PIAT, since early 1943. It is not at all surprising that the Germans should have developed their own short-range hollow-charge launcher. Be that as it may, just as 11th Armoured Division, courtesy of Roberts, its new GOC, embraced tactics that corresponded to best practice in North Africa, the Germans put up a weapon that confounded those tactics. Guards Armoured Division, lacking the stimulus of suitably experienced leadership, lagged behind even the cruelly confounded 11th.

The Panzerfaust only compounded the difficulties caused to armoured divisions by Montgomery's capital tank philosophy and to tank brigades by his rash dismissal of Pyman's tank–infantry co-operation doctrine. The War Office had not distinguished itself in its tardy issue of a sound doctrine on the latter subject. Widespread disregard of that doctrine, when it came, by tank brigades and independent armoured brigades did not help, but Pyman's work appears to have set matters right, only to be blown apart by his patron Montgomery. Tactical conditions in Normandy prompted commanders to drop the Eighth Army doctrine and by the time armoured divisions reorganised themselves for tank–infantry co-operation the need for infantry to accompany the leading tanks was well understood. Undoubtedly, though, lives and battles were unnecessarily lost before matters were put right. That such expenses were not avoided was Montgomery's fault.

A much clearer, but still unplayed, role for doctrinal enforcement is apparent in the armoured arm than in the infantry. Several examples of unquestionable failure to observe doctrine were discussed in Chapters 7 and 8. However, the inability of War Office doctrine to keep pace with tactical and weaponry developments would have caused inspectors, had they existed, to do as much harm as good. In RAC HQ the armoured arm potentially had a more responsive and flexible instrument of doctrinal enforcement than the War Office could have offered but, as discussed in Chapter 6, RAC HQ seems to have been toothless in everything but technical administration. Toothless is not a word that describes Montgomery. His arrival brought enforcement because no one dared defy him. But Montgomery had time neither for official doctrine, nor to ensure that what he put in its place was wise and that the troops were properly organised and trained to apply it.

The four years of preparation before the British Army went to Normandy were not wasted. Had 21 Army Group been prepared by the doctrine and training practices of 1941, it would have failed. Yet things could have been better. In a number of crucial respects the opportunity of four years of training informed by the experiences of friendly troops actively engaged overseas had not been fully exploited. This book has revealed the detailed reasons for that. In these closing paragraphs it is perhaps appropriate to discuss wider and more general phenomena.

The way the European war unfolded presented the British Army with a rare opportunity. While a proportion of the troops available engaged the enemy in what proved to be the subsidiary theatres of the Mediterranean, the bulk of the British Army remained at home, uncommitted. There, free of the immediate distractions of battle, it prepared for the critical campaign in North-West Europe. Unlike most armies before most wars, this was not a case of an army forced to prepare for war on theoretical precepts, on prognostications of what it would take to defeat the enemy armed forces. Collectively the British Army knew how to take on the Germans successfully because part of it was actually doing so. The problem lay in spreading that understanding from the 'empiricists' in the Mediterranean to the 'theorists' who would need it in

North-West Europe. Large-scale rotation of troops, preferably on an individual basis rather than by whole units or even sub-units, out of Home Forces and the War Office and into those active theatres, and vice versa, would have been the ideal solution. It was not possible, however. Operational and morale considerations argued against the removal of successful troops from the front line and their replacement with novices. In any case, lack of shipping made it impracticable.

Instead, the British Army attempted a bureaucratic solution. Instead of moving experience into and out of the front line, the Army moved paper. Staff officers sitting at desks gathered and interpreted reports from the front and brewed them up to produce the doctrine by which to train the unblooded troops at home. Given that few of the officers involved at the British end had direct experience, it is hardly surprising that inconsistencies, errors and omissions crept into the literature they produced. In the field Army at home, for whose benefit this material was published, few of the officers could interpret what they read with an experienced eye. Few, it seems, had the time to study doctrinal material properly anyway. Further errors in applying doctrine in training are thus unsurprising. But at the bureaucratic level, the system worked tolerably well. The various pamphlets were produced and distributed, and much of what they contained was good. There can be no doubt that the British Army at home would have been immeasurably poorer without it. Given that there were plenty of other calls on the energies of the Army in this most total of wars, this counts as a considerable achievement.

Bureaucratic organisation of complex tasks was one of the British Army's strong suits. Doctrinal dissemination, a worthy avenue for that talent, pales into insignificance beside some of the other bureaucratic achievements of British arms in this period. The organisation of operation OVERLORD, for example, surely figures as one of the marvels of modern military history. Although the material that the bureaucratic system of doctrinal dissemination put out was by no means perfect, it would be naïve to expect perfection given the constraints that prevailed. No matter how well conducted, bureaucratic activity – staff work to call it by its military name – is not in itself enough. The British Army excelled at planning for foreseeable eventualities. It was the unforeseeable, or rather unpredictable, eventualities that caused the problems.

There is here a general truth to be drawn about the British Army during this period. We have been concerned in this study mainly with minor tactics. This was a province in which the staff officer's powers were largely ineffective. Staff officers could not tell subalterns from which direction they would first come under fire, who would be the first casualties and whose wireless sets would be rendered useless by accidental immersion in a stream that was not marked on anyone's map. Staff officers could not tell subalterns, NCOs and other ranks what they should do in such circumstances or in any other unpredictable situation. It was unpredictable, minor events on the ground that collectively deprived British troops of many a victory in Normandy. Failure to prepare all ranks to function effectively when events defied the plan was the greatest flaw in the British Army's training programmes between Dunkirk and D-Day.

Instead the British Army hoped to win its battles through thorough planning and preparation for those features of a battle that were amenable to such planning and preparation. We can see this in the extensive attention properly given to artillery tactics and the improper neglect of the last 200 yards problem (when artillery could not be used) in the infantry attack. The drift towards setpiece attacks in the armoured divisions is part of the same failing. Even the idea of calculating the scale of casualties likely to be suffered by infantry tanks operating within the barrage betrays this strong urge to know exactly what would happen in an attack and so minimise the need for low-level initiative and decision after the starting whistle sounded. It was a natural urge and a healthy one, until it worked to exclude preparation for the possibility of deviation. In the conduct of training and operations in the British Army, preparing for the expected and the theoretically sound took priority over expecting the unexpected. What could not be made comprehensible on a planning desk remained uncomprehended. What could not be tidily put across on the printed page of a training manual remained beyond the scope of practical training. Neat system smothered all that was chaotic and unpredictable, except of course on the battlefield, where such things remained abundant and fecund.

None the less, the Allied Expeditionary Force of which 21 Army Group formed a component prevailed. Germany was vanquished and Montgomery's men played a substantial part in the victory. Did it matter that they were unskilled in minor tactics? One recent historian of the campaign thinks not. Where 21 Army Group was strong was in artillery fire-power and in the organisational and technological means of making that fire-power tell. It was fire-power that unlocked the German defences in North-West Europe, not tactical skill on the part of the front-line infantry and armour. Fire-power made tactical skill unnecessary. Assault troops, hobbled by their tactical unfitness, used the artillery as a crutch. Had they not done so, had they deployed the tactical skills necessary to fight their way forward with their own weapons, they would have suffered heavier casualties than they did and their morale would have suffered accordingly. Montgomery could afford neither. The artillery-dominated tactics he favoured, a preference shared by his army and corps commanders, were the only practicable ones given the fragility of morale and the dwindling reserves of manpower.[9]

That analysis is primarily applicable to the inadequacy of infantry tactics. However, in so far as it implies a conscious decision by Montgomery, it might also explain the misuse of armoured divisions and Montgomery's horribly misguided tank–infantry tactics. But it repeats the British Army's mistake in its divorce of minor tactics from artillery-based tactics. In most barrage-led attacks a point came when the leading troops faced a choice between attempting to fight forward with their own weapons and not going forward at all.

Bidwell, a leading authority on British artillery tactics, derides the use of artillery as a tactical crutch for incompetent infantry. Artillery-dominated tactics were the British Army's staple for the first three years of the Great War. In Bidwell's words, 'fundamentally they were a failure'.[10] It would be stretching the truth to claim that 21 Army Group's operations were such a thing, but tactically they were not a startling success. Not one of the three great British offensives before the American breakout – EPSOM, CHARNWOOD and GOODWOOD – carried its objectives. And, if artillery-dominated tactics were meant to preserve infantry manpower they failed: casualties in Normandy exceeded even the most pessimistic forecasts.[11]

Of course it mattered that British troops lacked minor tactical skill. It would, in any case, be crass to suppose that all of them were so afflicted. The British Army in North-West Europe was not innocent of the kind of qualities for which Montgomery's approach appears to have had no need. This is the place to pay tribute to the enterprise and initiative demonstrated by thousands of British soldiers from the rank of private upwards. But these qualities emerged despite, rather than because of, the training system.

Notes

1: Introduction

1. Carlo D'Este, *Decision in Normandy: The Unwritten Story of Montgomery and the Allied Campaign* (London: Pan, 1984), Ch. 16 and especially, p. 297.
2. Max Hastings, *OVERLORD: D-Day and the Battle for Normandy* (London: Pan, 1985), pp. 146 and 172–80.
3. Richard H. Kohn (ed.), 'The Scholarship on World War II: Its Present Condition and Future Possibilities', *Journal of Military History*, 55, 3 (July 1991), pp. 378–9.
4. D'Este, *Decision in Normandy*, pp. 293–5; Hastings, *OVERLORD*, p. 174.
5. Hastings, *OVERLORD*, pp. 220–31.
6. D'Este, *Decision in Normandy*, pp. 271–2.
7. Williamson Murray, 'British Military Effectiveness in the Second World War', Williamson Murray and A.R. Millet, *Military Effectiveness*, Vol. III (Boston, MA: Allen & Unwin, 1988), p. 125.
8. Kohn (ed.), 'Scholarship on World War II', pp. 378–9.
9. Shelford Bidwell, *Gunners at War: A Tactical Study of the Royal Artillery in the Twentieth Century* (London: Arms & Armour Press, 1970), p. 223.
10. John Ellis, *Brute Force: Allied Strategy and Tactics in the Second World War* (London: André Deutsch, 1990).
11. Murray, 'British Military Effectiveness', p. 129.
12. 'Reports on State of Training of Field Force Formations', 22 April 1942, WO 205/1C.
13. Shelford Bidwell and Dominick Graham, *Fire-Power: British Army Weapons and Theories of War 1904–1945* (Boston, MA: Allen & Unwin, 1985).
14. See Murray, 'British Military Effectiveness', pp. 119 and 124.
15. See C.H. Boucher, 'Infantry Tactics', *Army Quarterly*, July 1948, p. 246.
16. See *MTP* No. 23, *Operations*, Part IX, *The Infantry Division in the Attack* (21 July 1941), Section 8, paras 1 and 6; *MTP* No. 2, *The Offensive* (June 1943), Part 1, Ch. 3, Section 18.
17. Michael D. Doubler, *Closing with the Enemy: How GIs Fought the War in Europe 1944–1945* (Kansas: University Press of Kansas, 1994).
18. Chris Ellis and Peter Chamberlain (eds), *Handbook on the British Army 1943* (Military Book Society, 1974), pp. 7–11; John D. Cantwell, *The Second World War: A Guide to the Documents in the Public Record Office* (London: HMSO, 1993), pp. 178–91; R. Macleod and D. Kelly (eds), *The Ironside Diaries 1937–1940* (London: Constable, 1962), pp. 341 and 378.
19. Nigel Hamilton, *Monty: Master of the Battlefield* (London: Hamish Hamilton, 1983), pp. 502–3 and 527–9. See also H.E. Pyman, *Call to Arms* (London: Leo Cooper, 1971), pp. 65–6.

2: The dissemination of doctrine

1. See for example *MTP* No. 22, *Tactical Handling of Army Tank Battalions*, Part II, *Battle Drill and Manœuvre* (August 1939) and Part III, *Employment* (September 1939), contents page and 'Prefatory Note' respectively.
2. *The Distribution of General Staff Publications* (January 1942), para. 6 (superseding a May 1941 publication of the same title).
3. J.W. Gibb, 'The Second World War: 1939–1945: Army: Training in the Army', unpublished War Office monograph *c.* 1946, WO 277/36, p. 351; *ATM* No. 24 (18 September 1939), Part II, para. 14.
4. *MTP* No. 23, *Operations*, Part II, *The Infantry Division in Defence* (23 March 1942). See Maj.-Gen. C.C. Malden's minute to VCIGS, 6 November 1940, WO 32/9834.
5. J.L. Brind, 'The Sword and a Piano: The Recollections of a Retired Officer' (unpublished memoir), pp. 73–4 and 82.
6. See *ATM* No. 24 (18 September 1939), Appendix IV.
7. J.P. Vivian, 'A History of the School of Infantry' (unpublished memoir), WMWTC; interview with Maj. R.M.T. Kerr, 22 March 1995; Wigram, letter to his wife, 18 October 1942, private collection.
8. *ATM* No. 45 (29 May 1943), Part IV, para. 43.
9. Gibb, 'Training in the Army', WO 277/36, p 353.
10. See the papers of the Bartholomew Committee, WO 32/9581.
11. *ATM* No. 33 (June 1940), Part II, para. 20. See J.A. English, *The Canadian Army and the Normandy Campaign: A Study of Failure in High Command* (New York: Praeger, 1991), pp. 160–1.
12. *ATM* No. 33, Part II, para. 19 and *ATM* No. 34 (31 July 1940), para. 23.
13. 'Letter to a Platoon Commander in England', Allfrey Papers, 2/8, LHCMA; *ATM* No. 45 (29 May 1943), Appendix A. On Lt-Col Bryan, see D. Forman, *To Reason Why* (London: André Deutsch, 1991), p. 80.
14. *ATM* No. 50 (August 1944), para. 18 and Appendix C.
15. *MTP* No. 33, *Training in Fieldcraft and Elementary Tactics* (March 1940), Ch. 2, Section 22.
16. Maj.-Gen. J.L.I. Hawksworth, DMT, Minutes of Southern Command Army Commander's Conference, 1 February 1941, item 8, WO 199/1650.
17. *ATI* No. 1, *Notes on Tactics as Affected by the Reorganisation of the Infantry Division* (21 January 1941).
18. G. Le Q. Martel, *Our Armoured Forces* (London: Faber & Faber, 1945), pp. 101–4.
19. Malden, minute to VCIGS, 6 November 1940, WO 32/9834.
20. Hawksworth, Minutes of Southern Command Army Commander's Conference, 1 February 1941, item 8, WO 199/1650.
21. See *CRO* No. 1 (September 1942), p. 2.
22. MT1 minute 20 August 1943 to Research Secretariat, WO 231/10, and other papers in that file.
23. For example, *CRO* No. 24 (20 November 1943) which dealt with 7th Armoured Division's advance to the River Volturno in Italy; and *CRO* No. 35 (29 April 1944) which dealt with 56th Division and the battles for Mount Camino in November and December 1943.
24. *CRO* No. 48 (29 July 1944), Section 1. Other examples are *CRO* No. 49 (5 August 1944), Section 1, and *CRO* No 51 (19 August 1944), Section 2.
25. *CRO* No. 74 (31 January 1945), Section 3.
26. *CRO* No. 8 (24 July 1943), Section 2, and *NTW* No. 16 (October 1943), Part III, Section 11.
27. Montgomery, letter 25 June 1944, WO 205/756.
28. 'IMMEDIATE REPORT IN 24', 19 June 1944, WO 205/404.

29. S. Dyson, *Twins in Tanks: East End Brothers in Arms: 1943–1945* (London: Leo Cooper, 1994), pp. 46–7.
30. Letter to Chief of Staff 21 Army Group, 19 July, and Chief of Staff's letter, 22 July 1944, WO 205/756.
31. Letter from War Office (MT16) to Supreme Commanders and Commanders-in-Chief, 30 July 1944, WO 205/756.
32. See *ATM* No. 25 (13 October 1939), Part III, para. 4.
33. *A Drill for the Assault on a Highly Defended Locality (Provisional)* (June 1943).
34. *The Co-operation of Tanks with Infantry Divisions in Offensive Operations* (November 1943), *Notes on the Employment of Tanks in Support of Infantry in Battle* (February 1944), *Some Notes on the Conduct of War and the Infantry Division in Battle* (date not known but before December 1944), *Some Notes on the Use of Air Power in Support of Land Operations and Direct Air Support* (date not known but before December 1944) and *The Armoured Division in Battle* (December 1944).
35. *I Corps Tactical Notes* (October 1940).
36. Lt-Col Wigram, *Battle School* (July 1942). Published without attribution by Northern Command.
37. See for example the doctrinal quibbles raised in the War Office Directorate of Research over the Home Forces pamphlet, *A Drill for the Assault on a Highly Defended Locality (Provisional)* (June 1943) – minutes dated 2 and 3 August 1943, WO 231/51.
38. *Battle Training in Word and Picture* (London: George Newnes), No. 1, p. 3, and see *ATM* Nos 26 (13 November 1939), Part I, para. 10, and 27 (16 December 1939).
39. For example, Brig. Hanbury Pawle, *Notes on the Framing of Tactical Exercises for Officers of the Territorial Army* (1939); Maj. A.W. Valentine, *More Sand Table Exercises* (8th edn, 1941); *Street Fighting for Junior Officers* (1941); Lt-Col G.M. Gamble, *Simplified Tactical Instruction* (4th edn, 1941); Maj. C.R. Ward, *Section Training Exercises* (4th edn, 1941).
40. Gibb, 'Training in the Army', WO 277/36, p. 354.
41. Southern Command letter to GHQ Home Forces, 24 October 1941, and Anderson letter to HQ Southern Command, 20 October 1941, WO 199/1654.
42. Gibb, 'Training in the Army', WO 277/36, p. 356–7.
43. Michael Joseph, *The Sword in the Scabbard* (London: Michael Joseph, 1942), p. 218.
44. See for example the journal of Lt H.T. Bone, IWM 87/31/1, 24 January 1941.
45. Lt H.J. Belsey, letter to his wife, 16 December 1943, IWM 92/11/2. (Emphasis in original.)
46. *ATM* No. 39 (17 April 1941), Part II, para. 4.

3: 'Full-sail' exercises

1. D. Niven, *Niven* (London: Hamish Hamilton, 1984), p. 74. See also J.L. Brind, 'The Sword and a Piano: The Recollections of a Retired Officer' (unpublished memoir), p. 48.
2. See Brind, 'The Sword and a Piano', p. 48; Diary of Major-General G.W. Symes, 16 and 17 December 1940, IWM 82/15/1; War Diary of 4th Wiltshire Regiment, 31 May 1942, WO 166/9016; Len Waller, 'How Ever Did We Win? A Common Soldier's Account of World War Two' (unpublished memoir), IWM 87/42/1, p. 21; 'SOUTH EASTERN COMMAND EXERCISE "TIGER"', paper of 11 May 1942 addressed to subordinate corps commanders by Lt-Gen. B.L. Montgomery, at Appendix C to War Diary of G Branch, 11th Armoured Division, May 1942, WO 166/6519; E.A. Codling, unpublished and untitled memoir, IWM 88/4/1, pp. 6, 11–13.
3. See Brian Bond, *British Military Policy between the Two World Wars* (Oxford: Clarendon Press, 1980), pp. 37 and 328–9.

4. *GHQ Exercise "BUMPER" 27 Sep – 3 Oct 1941: Narrative of Events* (October 1941), papers of Lt-Gen. W.H. Stratton, IWM 71/5/1; J.W. Gibb, 'The Second World War: 1939–1945: Army: Training in the Army' (unpublished War Office monograph), WO 277/36, p. 191; Appendix A to letter from C-in-C Home Forces, 22 February 1943, in 'Umpires – Instructions & Correspondence' file, WO 199/817.

5. '5 Corps Training Report, October 1940 – March 1941', 21 February 1941, at annexure A to War Diary of G Branch, V Corps, February 1941, WO 166/249/4.

6. Carl von Clausewitz, *On War* (Harmondsworth: Penguin, 1982), pp. 133, 344.

7. *MTP* No. 61, *Umpiring* (February 1944), Section 2.

8. Ibid., Section 4.

9. Ibid.

10. Ibid., Sections 2 and 3.

11. Ibid., Section 2, and *ATM* No. 36 (September 1940), Appendix A.

12. *MTP* No. 37, *The Training of an Infantry Battalion* (June 1940), Ch. VIII, Section 36.

13. See T. Harrison Place, 'Tactical Doctrine and Training in the Infantry and Armoured Arms of the British Home Army, 1940–1944' (University of Leeds, PhD thesis, 1997), pp. 40–1 for details.

14. *MTP* No. 61 (February 1944), Section 2.

15. *GHQ Home Forces Standing Orders and Instructions for Exercises* (1943), Appendix B, para. 2 and Appendix C, paras 5, 8 and 13.

16. '5 Corps, Standing Orders for Corps Exercises', 15 March 1941, at appendix F to War Diary of G Branch, V Corps, March 1941, WO 166/249/4.

17. For example, see 'Notes on Visit to 56 London Division 12/13 December', 16 December 1940, WO 199/282.

18. Symes Diary, 7 December 1941, IWM ref. 82/15/1.

19. *MTP* No. 61 (February 1944), Section 2.

20. '5 Wilts Exercise CUCKOO GENERAL INSTRUCTIONS', 17 August 1943, appended to War Diary of 5th Wiltshire Regiment, June 1943, WO 166/12774.

21. '43 Div Trg Exercise No. 9 "VULCAN" GENERAL INSTRUCTIONS', 5 December 1943, at appendix B to War Diary of G Branch, 43rd Division, December 1943, WO 166/10562.

22. '43 Div Trg Exercise No. 8 "MARS" Exercise Instructions', 20 October 1943, at appendix F to War Diary of G Branch, 43rd Division, October 1943, WO 166/10562.

23. Diary of G Branch, 43rd Division, 16–19 January 1943 and '43 Div Training Directive – Period to 31 Dec 43', 25 September 1943, at appendix A to the September 1943 War Diary, WO 166/10562.

24. '11 Armd Div Exercise "CHRIS" 15/17 Sep 41', 12 September 1941, at appendix A to War Diary of HQ 29th Armoured Brigade, September 1941, WO 166/1119; 'Notes on Conduct of Exercise' at appendix D to War Diary of G Branch, 11th Armoured Division, September 1941, WO 166/860; '5 GDS ARMD BDE EXERCISE NORMANDY, General Instruction No. 1', 11 October 1942, appended to War Diary of HQ 5th Guards Armoured Brigade, October 1942, WO 166/6655.

25. '11 Corps District Exercise "BULL"', 10 September 1942, appendix B, at appendix A to War Diary of G Branch, 11th Armoured Division, September 1942, WO 166/6519.

26. 'PROVISION OF UMPIRES', among papers for exercise BLACKCOCK at appendix A to War Diary of G Branch, Guards Armoured Division, September 1943, WO 166/10452.

27. *MTP* No. 61 (February 1944), Section 4, para. 67.

28. 'SOUTH EASTERN COMMAND EXERCISE "TIGER"', paper of 11 May 1942 addressed to subordinate corps commanders by Lt-Gen. B.L. Montgomery, at appendix C to War Diary of G Branch, 11th Armoured Division, May 1942, WO 166/6519.

29. War Diary of 4th Wiltshire Regiment, 30 September 1941, WO 166/4738.

30. '3 Tk SG Diary of Exercise "BLACKCOCK"', 19 October 1943, appended to War Diary of 3rd Tank Scots Guards, September 1943, WO 166/12470.
31. War Diary of 1st Motor Grenadier Guards, 2 October 1943, WO 166/12464.
32. '3 Tk SG Diary of Exercise "BLACKCOCK"', 19 October 1943, appended to War Diary of 3rd Tank Scots Guards, September 1943, WO 166/12470.
33. 'Operations in Woldavia', among papers for exercise BLACKCOCK at appendix A to War Diary of HQ 6th Guards Tank Brigade, October 1943, WO 166/10741.
34. '11 Armd Div Intelligence Summary No. 5. Period 2100 hrs 17 Feb – 2100 hrs 18 Feb', included in exercise papers at appendix C to War Diary of G Branch, 11th Armoured Division, February 1944, WO 171/456. See also War Diary of 159th Brigade, 13–24 February 1944, WO 171/691.
35. '11 Armd Div Intelligence Summary No. 9. For period 2100 hrs 21 Feb to 2100 hrs 22 Feb', included in exercise papers at appendix C to War Diary of G Branch, 11th Armoured Division, February 1944, WO 171/456.
36. 'Exercise "EAGLE" GENERAL INSTRUCTION', at appendix C to War Diary of 2nd Fife and Forfar Yeomanry, February 1944, WO 171/853.
37. War Diary of 2nd Armoured Irish Guards, 30 September 1943, WO 166/12468.
38. War Diary of 4th Wiltshire Regiment, 25–28 January 1943, WO 166/12773.
39. War Diary of 153rd RAC, 25 January 1943, WO 166/11117.
40. R.I. Higgins, 'A Few Memories' (unpublished memoir), IWM Ref. 86/49/1, p. 123.
41. *MTP* No. 37, *The Training of an Infantry Battalion* (June 1940), Ch. VII, Section 31.
42. Exercise papers at appendix E to War Diary of 5th Wiltshire Regiment, October 1942, WO 166/9017.
43. War Diary of G Branch, 43rd Division, 12–14 August 1942, WO 166/6249; War Diary of HQ 129th Brigade, 1 September 1942, and '129 Inf Bde Trg Instruction No. 3 Sep 42–Feb 43', 6 September 1942, at appendix A to September 1942 War Diary, WO 166/6594.
44. *NTW* No. 16, *North Africa, November 1942–May 1943* (October 1943), Part III, Section 9, para. 3.
45. *MTP* No. 23, *Operations*, Part IX, *The Infantry Division in the Attack* (21 July 1941), Section 8, para. 1.
46. *NTW* No. 16 (October 1943), Part III, Section 10, para. 4.
47. Responses by Battle School and First Army to British Military Training Directorate (North Africa) BNAF, Infantry Questionnaire, question 2, WO 231/10.
48. *NTW* No. 13, *North Africa – Algeria and Tunisia, November 1942–March 1943* (May 1943), Section 13.
49. War Diary of G Branch, 43rd Division, 29 August 1943, and '43 Div Training Directive – Period to 31 Dec 43', 25 September 1943, at appendix A to War Diary, September 1943, WO 166/10562.
50. See '5 Wilts Exercise ARSEWAZE GENERAL INSTRUCTION', at appendix D to War Diary of 5th Wiltshire Regiment, November 1943, WO 166/12774; also, 'Exercise "1087"', 10 March 1944, at appendix F to the battalion's March 1944, WO 171/1395. An earlier series of platoon exercises went by the codename 1066. Presumably, the interest in Norman affairs manifest in such codenames was entirely coincidental.
51. Quoted in M. Hastings, *OVERLORD: D-Day and the Battle for Normandy* (London: Pan, 1985), p. 170.
52. '43 Div Trg Exercise No. 8 "MARS" Exercise Instructions', 20 October 1943, index 1, among exercise papers at appendix F to War Diary of G Branch, 43rd Division, October 1943, WO 166/10562.
53. '43 Div Exercise MARS General Idea', index 2, and 'Special Idea', index 3, among exercise papers at appendix F to War Diary of G Branch, 43rd Division, October 1943, WO 166/10562.

54. 'Exercise MARS Narrative of Events 214 Inf Bde', index IVA, ibid.
55. Ibid.
56. 'Exercise VULCAN NARRATIVE OF EVENTS', at appendix D to War Diary of G Branch, 43rd Division, December 1943, WO 166/10562.
57. '43 Div Trg Exercise No. 9 "VULCAN" GENERAL INSTRUCTIONS', 5 December 1943, at appendix B to War Diary G Branch, 43rd Division, December 1943, WO 166/10562.
58. 'Phase I DIRECTIVE TO COMD EASTLAND (OC 8 BN RIFLE BRIGADE)' and 'Phase II Directive to Comd WESTLAND (Comd 159 Inf Bde)', among papers for exercise BRIDLINGTON at appendix C to War Diary of G Branch, 11th Armoured Division, August 1943, WO 166/10521.
59. *MTP* No. 37 (June 1940), Ch. VII, Section 34.
60. Guards Armoured Division letter 30 December 1942, among papers for exercise BLACKMORE, at appendix A to War Diary of G Branch, Guards Armoured Division, February 1943, WO 166/10542.
61. See 'DO'S [*sic*] and DONT'S [*sic*] FOR ALL RANKS ENGAGED IN TRG', in 'Brigade Orders by Brigadier J.G. Sandie, DSO, MC, Commander of 159 Infantry Brigade, Part I', appended to April 1943 War Diary of HQ 159th Brigade, WO 166/10792. The official film of inter-army exercise SPARTAN, which took place in March 1943, showed a hayrick accidentally set on fire through troops' carelessness – *Exercise Spartan* (1943), IWM Film No. WOY 110.
62. '5 Corps Exercise No. 5. Final Conference – 31 March 41. Remarks by the Corps Commander', at appendix A to War Diary of G Branch, V Corps, April 1941, WO 166/249/4.
63. War Diary of 2nd Armoured Irish Guards, 30 September 1943, WO 166/12468, and see above.
64. War Diary of HQ 159 Infantry Brigade, 13–24 February 1944, WO 171/691, and see above.
65. War Diary of 3rd Irish Guards, 13–24 February 1944, WO 171/1257.
66. 'Oxford and Buckinghamshire Light Infantry. World War II History Notes', National Army Museum.
67. AORG Memorandum No. 37, 'Exercise SPARTAN', 16 March 1943, WO 291/392.
68. *ATM* No. 45 (29 May 1943), Part III, para. 36.
69. *MTP* No. 61 (February 1944), Section 4.
70. C.T. Framp, 'The Littlest Victory' (unpublished memoir), IWM Ref. 85/18/1, pp. 27–8.
71. D. Anderson, *Three Cheers for the Next Man to Die* (London: Robert Hale, 1983), p. 47.
72. 'SOUTH-EASTERN COMMAND EXERCISE "TIGER"', paper of 11 May 1942 addressed to subordinate corps commanders by Lt-Gen. B.L. Montgomery, at appendix C to War Diary of G Branch, 11th Armoured Division, May 1942, WO 166/6519.
73. Hastings, *OVERLORD*, p. 56.
74. B.L. Montgomery, *The Memoirs of Field Marshal the Viscount Montgomery of Alamein K.G.* (London: Collins, 1958), p. 33.
75. For examples see *ATM* No. 46 (16 October 1943), Part II, para. 19 and *NTW* No. 16 (October 1943), Part III, Section 10, para. 7. See also 'Notes by Col. T.N. Grazebrook, lately comd 6 Inisks [*sic*] in N. Africa, Sicily and Italy', 3 January 1944, WO 231/14.
76. *CRO* No. 36 (6 May 1944), Section 2, para. 33.
77. Anderson, *Three Cheers*, p. 14.
78. *MTP* No. 61 (February 1944), Section 4, paras 58 and 60.
79. *Exercise Spartan* (1943), IWM Film No. WOY 110.
80. Higgins, 'Memories', p. 142.
81. For example, *The Instructors' Handbook on Fieldcraft and Battle Drill* (October 1942), Ch. II, Section 25, para. 1.

82. '4 LINCOLNS OO No. 1 COUNTER ATTACK CORSICA', dated 3 November 1943, among exercise papers at appendix A to War Diary of 4th Lincolnshire Regiment, November 1943, WO 166/12672.

83. 'Exercise "CATTERICK" 31 Jul/1 Aug', dated 31 July 1943, among exercise papers at appendix B to War Diary of HQ 6th Guards Tank Brigade, July 1943, WO 166/10741.

84. '214 Inf Bde Bn Schemes with Div Arty Sp', dated 25 September 1943, at appendix B to War Diary of G Branch, 43rd Division, September 1943, WO 166/10562.

85. *MTP* No. 23, *Operations, Part IX, The Infantry Division in the Attack* (21 July 1941), Section 8, para. 5, and *MTP* No. 2, *The Offensive* (June 1943), Part 1, Ch. 3, Section 18.

86. *MTP* No. 61 (February 1944), Section 4.

87. *CRO* No. 15 (11 September 1943), Section 3, para. 45.

88. *MTP* No. 61 (February 1944), Section 4.

4: *Infantry and battle drill*

1. See S. Bidwell and D. Graham, *Fire-Power: British Army Weapons and Theories of War 1904–1945* (Boston, MA: George Allen & Unwin, 1985), Book II, especially pp. 83–5; S. Bidwell, *Gunners at War: A Tactical Study of the Royal Artillery in the Twentieth Century* (London: Arms & Armour Press, 1970), pp. 35–6; Paddy Griffith, *Battle Tactics of the Western Front: The British Army's Art of Attack 1916–1918* (New Haven, CT, and London: Yale University Press, 1994), Part 2. Also see J.M. Bourne, 'British Generals in the First World War', in G.D. Sheffield (ed.), *Leadership and Command: The Anglo-American Military Experience Since 1861* (London: Brassey's, 1997), especially pp. 110–12.

2. *Infantry Training*, Vol. II, *War* (November 1921), Ch. III.

3. Chris Ellis and Peter Chamberlain (eds), *Handbook on the British Army, 1943* (Military Book Society, 1975), pp. 24–5 and Fig. 9; *ATM* No. 32 (20 May 1940), Part IV, para. 14, as corrected in *ATM* No. 33 (2 July 1940); Frederick Myatt, *The British Infantry 1660–1945: The Evolution of a Fighting Force* (Poole, Dorset: Blandford Press, 1983), pp. 198–202.

4. See diary of Maj.-Gen. G.W. Symes, end-of-year summary, 1940, IWM; War Diaries of 141st Brigade, 26 August 1941, WO 166/1004 and 129th Brigade, 27 August 1941, WO 166/979; 'Notes on Visit to Western Command 2–4 Dec', 5 December 1940, by Lt-Col A.J.H. Dove, GHQ Staff Officer, WO 199/282; Maj.-Gen. J.E. Utterson-Kelso's paper 'The Training of Infantry', c. November 1941, WO 199/725

5. W.S. Churchill, *The Second World War*, Vol. III (London: Reprint Society, 1952), p. 658; Minutes of meeting, 9 September 1941, on the Home Army's winter activities, items 9 and 19, WO 163/154.

6. 'Reports on State of Training of Field Force Formations', 22 April 1942, WO 205/1C.

7. War Diaries of North Irish Horse, 51st RTR and 142nd RAC, WO 166/6899, WO 166/6925 and WO 166/6975.

8. Minutes of meeting, 9 September 1941, on the Home Army's winter activities, items 9 and 19, WO 163/154.

9. 'The Training of Infantry', paper by Utterson-Kelso, WO 199/725.

10. Ibid.

11. Michael Joseph, *The Sword in the Scabbard* (London: Michael Joseph, 1942), pp. 195, 199, 204.

12. See file 'Drill – Simplification of. 1941–1942', WO 32/9838.

13. '141 (LON) INF BDE TRAINING INSTRUCTION NO. 11', 24 April 1941, appended to War Diary of HQ 141st Brigade, April 1941, WO 166/1004.

14. A.H.S. Adair, *A Guards' General: The Memoirs of Major-General Sir Allan Adair* (London: Hamish Hamilton, 1986), p. 100.
15. See B. Bond (ed.), *Chief of Staff: The Diaries of Lieutenant-General Sir Henry Pownall*, Vol. 1 (London: Leo Cooper, 1972), pp. 248–9; War Diary of 1st Coldstream Guards, September 1939 – May 1940, WO 167/698; extracts from a letter written by Maj. F.W. Priestley, second-in-command of 5th Glosters in France during the Phoney War, and '1939/45 War in France: Short Account by Lt. Col. Reeve Tucker, from joining the Regiment until just before capture' (concerning 2nd Glosters), both in archive of the Gloucestershire Regiment, Black File No. G14, Regiments of Gloucestershire Museum, Gloucester; and, for a description of the activities of the territorial component of the BEF, K.J. Drewienkiewicz, 'Examine the Build-Up, Early Training and Employment of the Territorial Army in the Lead-Up to, and the Early Days of, the Second World War' (Royal College of Defence Studies, thesis, 1992), especially pp. 34 and 44.
16. '5 Corps Training Report, October 1940–March 1941', 21 February 1941, at annexure A to War Diary of G Branch, V Corps, February 1941, WO 166/249/4.
17. Montgomery's personal memoranda for commanders, 16 May and 27 August 1941, papers of Lt-Gen. C.W. Allfrey, 1/2 and 1/6 respectively, LHCMA.
18. *Infantry Training, Training and War, 1937* (August 1937), Ch. XI, Section 67.
19. *Infantry Section Leading* (1938), Ch. IX, Section 56.
20. *MTP* No. 33, *Training in Fieldcraft and Elementary Tactics* (March 1940), Ch. 2, Section 7.
21. Ibid., Ch. 3, Section 30, and Ch. 4, Section 37.
22. *Infantry Training, Training and War, 1937* (August 1937), Ch. VII, Section 33.
23. *MTP* No. 33 (March 1940), Ch. 2, Section 19.
24. Joseph, *The Sword in the Scabbard*, p. 210; J.P. Vivian, 'A History of the School of Infantry' (unpublished memoir), WMWTC, and interview 9 August 1995.
25. H. Buckle, 'Recollections from Yesteryear' (unpublished memoir), IWM 81/10/1, p. 11.
26. 'Extracts from Minutes of the Commander-in-Chief's Conference Held at GHQ, 14th May 1942', item 23(h), WO 199/1656.
27. 'The Army: Memorandum on the Training of Prospective Officers', 4 January 1941, WO 216/61; Richard Spender, 'The Officer Cadet', *The Collected Poems* (London: Sidgwick & Jackson, 1944), pp. 6–8. Spender attended 163 OCTU, January–April 1941 and died in action in 1943.
28. See J.E. Edney, 'One Three One Over Eight' (unpublished memoir), IWM ref. 85/6/1, p. 3. Also see the following for evidence of training at Officer Training Units to which officers commissioned during the Great War who had returned for service after 1939 were sent for refresher training: Joseph, *Scabbard*, pp. 97–100; papers of Lt H.P. Hunt, IWM 81/16/1.
29. Montgomery's personal memorandum for commanders, 27 August 1941, papers of Lt-Gen. C.W. Allfrey, 1/6, LHCMA.
30. Field Marshal Viscount Alanbrooke, 'Notes on My Life', Vol. II, p. 85, Alanbrooke Papers, 3/A/II, LHCMA. See also David Fraser, *Alanbrooke* (London: Collins, 1982), p. 108.
31. Lt H.T. Bone, Journal, 7 May and 15 June 1940, IWM 87/31/1.
32. Ibid., 27 June 1940.
33. J.W. Gibb, 'The Second World War: 1939–1945: Army: Training in the Army' (unpublished War Office monograph), WO 277/36, p. 108; appendix A to GHQ Home Forces, letter 29 April 1942, WO 32/10466.
34. Montgomery's personal memoranda for commanders, 27 August 1941, papers of Lt-Gen. C.W. Allfrey, 1/6, LHCMA.
35. '5 Corps School', WO 32/10466.
36. '12 Corps School. Tactical Wing', WO 32/10466.

37. Interview, 22 March 1995, with Maj. R.M.T. Kerr, who attended the IX Corps Platoon Commanders' course.
38. 'Bde Training Programme', 3 July 1941, at Appendix A to War Diary of HQ 129th Brigade, July 1941, WO 166/979.
39. Norman Craig, *The Broken Plume: A Platoon Commander's Story, 1940–45* (London: IWM, 1982), p. 33.
40. Minutes of meeting, 29 January 1941, WO 216/61.
41. Griffith, *Battle Tactics*, pp. 99–100.
42. Nigel Nicolson, *Alex: The Life of Field Marshal Earl Alexander of Tunis* (London: Weidenfeld & Nicolson, 1973), pp. 45, 58, 85, 88.
43. '1st Corps, Corps Commander's Conference, 7 Aug 40, Minutes', item 1, appended to War Diary of G Branch, I Corps, August 1940, WO 166/169.
44. W. Morgan, 'The Revival of Battle Drill in World War 2', *Army Quarterly and Defence Journal*, 104, 1 (October 1973), pp. 57–60; 'Minutes of Conference on Winter Training Held at HQ 1st Corps, 12 Oct '40', item 3, appended to War Diary of G Branch, I Corps, October 1940, WO 166/169; *I Corps Tactical Notes* (October 1940).
45. 'I Corps Platoon Commanders School. Syllabus and Programme', appended to War Diary of 1st Duke of Wellington's Regiment, October 1940, WO 166/4236.
46. Nicolson, *Alex*, pp. 118–19; Appendix to '2 Coldm Gds Training Instruction No. 1. Winter 1940/41', at Appendix 2 to War Diary of 2nd Coldstream Guards, October 1940, WO 166/4092; War Diary of 1st King's Shropshire Light Infantry, 7 November 1940, WO 166/4400; and 2nd Hampshire Regiment, see '2 Hamps Winter Training Instruction No. 1 – General', appended to September 1940 War Diary, WO 166/4324.
47. Nicolson, *Alex*, passim.
48. '131st Infantry Brigade. Notes on Training', 21 November 1939, and '131st Infantry Brigade, Training Instruction No. 1', 29 November 1939, at Appendices 6 and 8 respectively to War Diary of HQ 131st Brigade, November 1939, WO 166/982; J.A. English, *The Canadian Army and the Normandy Campaign: A Study of Failure in High Command* (New York: Praeger, 1991), p. 110.
49. 'Minutes of a Meeting held at GHQ Home Forces at 1415 Hrs 12 December 1941', item 20, WO 199/244.
50. Vivian, 'School of Infantry', WMWTC; Mrs Olga Wigram in interview, 5 April 1995; Brig. J.L. Brind, letter to WMWTC, 1 August 1988. See Lt-Col Wigram, *Battle School* (July 1942), pp. 17–18, for account of the Chelwood Gate school's conception.
51. *Battle School*, p. 21; Vivian, 'School of Infantry', WMWTC.
52. 'THE SCHOOL OF BATTLE DRILL. TRAINING PROGRAMME', 9 July 1941, at appendix B to War Diary of HQ 141st Brigade (47th Division), July 1941, WO 166/1004; Vivian, 'School of Infantry', WMWTC.
53. *Battle School*, pp. 62–5 and 160–1; *The Instructors' Handbook on Fieldcraft and Battle Drill* (October 1942), Ch. II, Section 30.
54. War Diary of 11th Royal Fusiliers, August 1941, WO 166/4536.
55. Ibid., 21 June 1941.
56. Roy Farran, *The History of the Calgary Highlanders, 1921–1954* (Calgary: Bryant Press, 1954), pp. 97–8. See English, *Canadian Army*, Ch. 5, for a comprehensive account of battle drill in the Canadian Army.
57. *The Glen* (regimental journal of the Calgary Highlanders), III, 13 (November 1941).
58. *ATM* No. 22 (April 1939), Part II, para. 3.
59. *ATM* No. 41 (8 October 1941), Part IV, para. 22. For Dill's visit see War Diary of 17th Royal Fusiliers, 26 September 1941, WO 166/4542.
60. J.L. Brind, 'The Sword and a Piano: The Recollections of a Retired Officer' (unpublished memoir), p. 76. See also C.H. Boucher, 'Infantry Tactics', *Army Quarterly*, July 1948, pp. 246–55, especially p. 247.

61. *Battle School*, pp. 23–4.
62. Alexander's introduction to his *I Corps Tactical Notes*, reproduced in Morgan, 'Revival', pp. 57–60, and in *Battle School*, p. 22.
63. *Battle School*, p. 23. *The Instructors' Handbook . . .* (October 1942), Introduction. *Infantry Training*, Part VIII, *Fieldcraft, Battle Drill, Section and Platoon Tactics* (4 March 1944), Ch. 4, Section 21.
64. *Battle School*, pp. 24 and 27–8.
65. *Infantry Training, 1937*, Supplement No. 1, *Tactical Notes for Platoon Commanders* (first published February 1941. The copy seen is an amended reprint of 3 October 1941).
66. *Battle School*, p. 25.
67. *MTP* No. 33, *Training in Fieldcraft and Elementary Tactics* (March 1940), Ch. 3, Section 26.
68. Denis Forman, *To Reason Why* (London: André Deutsch, 1991), pp. 31–2, 42.
69. Ibid., pp. 21–4 and 29–30.
70. J.G.E. Hickson, 'Battle School', *Blackwood's Magazine*, 253 (March 1943), p. 213.
71. Ibid., pp. 205–7; hand-written memoir by Dr A.S. Wallace, privately supplied to the author, May 1996; Forman, *To Reason Why*, pp. 40–1; interview with Mrs Olga Wigram, 15 April 1995; Richard Hargreaves, 'Some Recollections on the Battle School Movement', handwritten memoir, privately supplied to the author, May 1996.
72. 'Minutes of 1st Battle School Conference Held at the Horse Guards on 17 and 18 Jun 42', item 3a, National Archives of Canada, Ottawa, RG 24 9764.
73. *The Instructors' Handbook . . .* (October 1942), Appendix B.
74. See Vivian, 'School of Infantry', WMWTC; War Diary of 70th Durham Light Infantry, 13 July 1943; Brind, 'The Sword and a Piano', p. 79; Forman, *Reason*, pp. 50–61; Wallace, memoir; War Diary of 1st Herefordshire Regiment, 16 April 1943 and 25 May 1943, WO 166/12568. Additional information from Maj. R.M.T. Kerr in conversation, 22 March 1995.
75. Gammell, letter to his subordinate commanders, 30 July 1940, Papers of Lt-Gen. J.A.H. Gammell, IWM 73/14/1.
76. Brind, 'The Sword and a Piano', pp. 73–4.
77. Forman, *To Reason Why*, pp. 42–3.
78. Quoted in C. Northcote Parkinson, *Always a Fusilier: The War History of the Royal Fusiliers (City of London Regiment) 1939–1945* (London: Sampson Low, 1949), p. 53.
79. *The Times*, 25 November 1941, p. 5.
80. *The Times*, 27 April 1942, p. 2.
81. '"DAVID" CONFERENCE – THIRD PERIOD', an address by Allfrey, 1942, Allfrey Papers Ref. 2/2, LHCMA; 'MEMORANDUM ON BATTLE DRILL', stated to be by Montgomery, appended to 'Lessons from Trg Camps and Adv Gd Exercises', 2 October 1942, by Brig. B.B. Rackham, commander of 7th Brigade, in 'Bde Comds Personal File – Training – 44 Inf Bde', papers of Brig. H.D.K. Money, IWM 72/14/1; R.H. Ahrenfeldt, *Psychiatry in the British Army in the Second World War* (London: Routledge & Kegan Paul, 1958), pp. 198–201.
82. J.A. English and B.I. Gudmundsson, *On Infantry* (Westport, CT: Praeger, 1994), p. 105.
83. Ahrenfeldt, *Psychiatry in the British Army*, pp. 201–4, and *Battle School*, p. 94.
84. 'MEMORANDUM ON BATTLE DRILL', stated to be by Montgomery, papers of Brig. H.D.K. Money, IWM Ref. 72/14/1.
85. *ATM* No. 35 (30 August 1940), Part III, para. 12. See Griffith, *Battle Tactics*, pp. 71–2, on the similar methods of Maj. R.B. Campbell, Assistant Inspector of Physical and Bayonet Training at GHQ in France during the Great War.
86. Carlo D'Este, *Decision in Normandy: The Unwritten Story of Montgomery and the Allied Campaign* (London: Pan, 1984), pp. 283–4.

87. 'Notes on visit by BGS (Ops) to SCOTTISH COMMAND 8th–11th January 1942', by Brig. P.S. Gregson-Ellis, BGS (Ops), GHQ Home Forces, 12 January 1942, WO 199/279.
88. Lt-Gen. H.C. Loyd, Chief of Staff, Home Forces, letter 9 February 1942, WO 199/725. Paget seems never to have learned that Southern Command had the same plan as Montgomery – see Appendix A to 'Agenda to Army Commanders [sic] Conference – 22 Jan 42', WO 199/1655.
89. War Office Morale Committee report for February to May 1942, Part I, Section 3, WO 163/51, Ref. AC/G(42)20.
90. War Office Morale Committee report for August to October 1942, 28 December 1942, WO 163/51, Ref. AC/G(42)41.
91. Captain 'X' (pseudonym of W.G.C. Shebbeare), A Soldier Looks Ahead (London: George Routledge, 1944), p. 12.
92. Wallace, memoir.
93. See, for example, 'Corps Commander's Personal Memorandum No. 3', 4 April 1942, by Lt-Gen. J.A.H. Gammell, GOC XII Corps, Gammell Papers, IWM 73/14/1; and '"DAVID" CONFERENCE – THIRD PERIOD', Allfrey Papers, 2/2, LHCMA.
94. 'MEMORANDUM ON BATTLE DRILL', stated to be by Montgomery, papers of Brig. H.D.K. Money, IWM 72/14/1.
95. 'Minutes of 1st Battle School Conference Held at the Horse Guards on 17 and 18 Jun 42', closing address by Maj.-Gen. (Infantry) GHQ, National Archives of Canada, Ottawa, RG 24 9764.
96. Arthur Bryant, The Turn of the Tide 1939–1943: A Study Based on the Diaries and Autobiographical Notes of Field Marshal The Viscount Alanbrooke, KG, OM (London: The Reprint Society, 1958), p. 196; Fraser, Alanbrooke, p. 271; John Kennedy, The Business of War (London, Hutchinson, 1957), p. 198.
97. Wigram, letter to his wife, ? February 1942, private collection.
98. ATM No. 44 (22 October 1942), Part III, para. 25.
99. Brind, 'The Sword and a Piano', pp. 73–4, and interview 25 January 1995.
100. Infantry Training, Part VIII, Fieldcraft, Battle Drill, Section and Platoon Tactics (4 March 1944), Ch. 4, Sections 27 and 30. Parade ground battle drills had featured in MTP No. 41, The Tactical Handling of the Armoured Division and its Components, Part 3, The Motor Battalion (June 1943), Appendix D.
101. Gibb, 'Training in the Army', WO 277/36, pp. 4, 354.
102. 'Report of Joint Committee on Instruction of Officers and Schools', 17 May 1942, WO 216/82.
103. Brind, 'The Sword and a Piano', p. 76.
104. Alanbrooke, 'Notes on My Life', Vol. II, p. 85, Alanbrooke Papers, 3/A/II, LHCMA; Fraser, Alanbrooke, pp. 108–9.
105. Brooke, minute to Nye (VCIGS), 28 May; Nye, minutes to Whitaker (DMT), 2 and 9 June 1942, WO 216/82.
106. Wigram, letter to his wife, 26 July 1942; Mrs Olga Wigram, letter to Wigram, 27 July 1942, private collection.
107. Brig. J.L. Brind, interview 25 January 1995; Maj. R.M.T. Kerr, interview 22 March 1995; Maj. J.P. Vivian, interview 9 August 1995; Wigram, letters to his wife, 31 August and 9 September 1942 (by which latter date Wilson had returned to duty), private collection.
108. Journal of the Royal United Service Institution, 89, 553 (February 1944), pp. 1–9.
109. D. Fraser, And We Shall Shock Them (London: Hodder & Stoughton, 1983), pp. 105, 107; 'War Office Morale Committee Report for May to July 1942', 23 September 1942, para. 3(b), WO 163/51, AC/G(42)32.
110. 'The Army Council. Minutes of the Fourteenth Meeting held in Room 204, The War Office on Tuesday 11th August 1942', item 11, WO 163/51; John Ferris, '"Worthy of Some Better Enemy?": The British Estimate of the Imperial Japanese Army 1919–41,

and the Fall of Singapore', *Canadian Journal of History*, XXVIII (August 1993), pp. 247 and 252; Wigram, letter to his wife, 11 October 1942, private collection.

111. Maj. J.L. Brind, School of Infantry, letter to Mr D.Y. Mason of the BBC, 10 November 1942, WMWTC.

5: The failure of infantry

1. J.A. English, *The Canadian Army and the Normandy Campaign: A Study of Failure in High Command* (New York: Praeger, 1991), pp. 107, 116 and 122, note 46.

2. J.A. English and B.I. Gudmundsson, *On Infantry* (Westport, CT: Praeger, 1994), p. 105, and B.H. Liddell Hart (ed.), *The Rommel Papers* (London: Collins, 1953), p. 184.

3. *NTW* No. 11, *Destruction of a German Battery by No. 4 Commando during the Dieppe Raid* (February 1943), para. 1.

4. *NTW* No. 19, *Burma, 1943/44* (May 1945), Section 20, para. 4.

5. 'Lessons of the Tunisian Campaign, 1942–3 (British Forces)', Ch. 4, Section 5, WO 231/10.

6. *CRO* No. 74 (31 January 1945), Section 3, para. 26.

7. *NTW* No. 16, *North Africa, November 1942–May 1943* (October 1943), Part IV, Section 21, para. 2.

8. '"DAVID" CONFERENCE – THIRD PERIOD', an address by Allfrey, 1942, Allfrey Papers, 2/2, LHCMA; 'MEMORANDUM ON BATTLE DRILL', stated to be by Montgomery, appended to 'Lessons from Trg Camps and Adv Gd Exercises', 2 October 1942, by Brig. B.B. Rackham, commander of 7th Brigade, in 'Bde Comds Personal File – Training – 44 Inf Bde', Papers of Brig. H.D.K. Money, IWM 72/14/1.

9. 'Exercise "NONSTOP" Appdx "C" – Notes on Current Training', 14 May 1943, among the papers for exercise NONSTOP at Appendix D to War Diary of 5th Wiltshire Regiment, May 1943, WO 166/12774.

10. Ibid.

11. *The Instructors' Handbook on Fieldcraft and Battle Drill* (October 1942), Ch. II, Section 25.

12. 'Exercise "NONSTOP" Appdx "C" – Notes on Current Training', 14 May 1943, among the papers for exercise NONSTOP at Appendix D to War Diary of 5th Wiltshire Regiment, May 1943, WO 166/12774.

13. 'Notes on Field Firing', appended to War Diary of 4th Somerset Light Infantry, May 1942, WO 166/8964.

14. Battle Drill Film H, *Platoon Flanking Attack* (November 1942), IWM Film No. WOY 299.

15. War Diary of 1st Motor Grenadier Guards, February (appendices A–D) and March (Appendices A, C and two unnumbered) 1942, WO 166/8569.

16. 'The Responsibility of the Unit Commander. Field Force Divisions Only', undated draft briefing prepared in connection with the Homes Forces Brigadiers General Staff Conference, 30–31 March 1942, WO 199/1658; 'Minutes of BsGS Conference 30/31 March 1942', Item 11, WO 199/244. See also Michael Joseph, *The Sword in the Scabbard* (London: Michael Joseph, 1942), pp. 80–1 and 217–18, and Captain 'X' (pseudonym of W.G.C. Shebbeare), *A Soldier Looks Ahead* (London: George Routledge, 1944), p. 69.

17. 'Foreword by Comd The 43 Div', and Kenrick's letter to his subordinate officers, 14 May 1943, among papers for exercise NONSTOP at Appendix D to War Diary of 5th Wiltshire Regiment, May 1943, WO 166/12774.

18. *ATM* No. 51 (November 1944), para. 2.

19. *MTP* No. 23, *Operations*, Part IX, *the Infantry Division in the Attack* (21 July 1941), Section 8, para. 5.
20. *The Instructors' Handbook* . . . (October 1942), Ch. II, Section 35, para. 1.
21. Geoffrey Picot, *Accidental Warrior* (Harmondsworth: Penguin, 1994), pp. 282–3.
22. *CRO* No. 82 (28 March 1945), Section 4.
23. 'Extract from Major North's DO letter dated 11.8.43', WO 231/11.
24. *NTW* No. 16 (October 1943), Part III, Section 10, para. 6.
25. *NTW* No. 14, *Western Desert and Cyrenaica, August/December 1942* (June 1943), Part III, Section 20, para. 5. See also *NTW* No. 2, *Cyrenaica, November/December 1941* (7 March 1942), Part II, Section 6, and *NTW* No. 4, *Cyrenaica, November 1941/January 1942* (May 1942), Part I, Section 3.
26. *NTW* No. 20, *Italy, 1943/1944* (May 1945), Ch. 5, Section 29, para. 7.
27. 'MT Instructional Circular No. 17 – Notes from Sicily' circulated by GHQ Middle East on 18 September 1943, para. 19, WO 231/14, also circulated within 21 Army Group, WO 205/478.
28. 'Discussion on Lessons Learned during the Year of Fighting from El Alamein to Messina', WO 231/16.
29. *The Instructors' Handbook* . . . (October 1942), Ch. IV, Section 56, para. 3.
30. School of Infantry film, *Battle Drill: Frontal Attack (Lane Method)* (April 1943), IWM Film No. WOY 145.
31. 1st Division response to British Military Training Directorate (North Africa) BNAF Infantry Questionnaire, section (a), question 10, WO 231/10.
32. *Battle Drill: Frontal Attack (Lane Method)* (April 1943), IWM Film No. WOY 145.
33. *CRO* No. 68 (20 December 1944), Section 2.
34. *ATM* No. 45 (29 May 1943), Appendix A; 'Letter to a Platoon Commander in England', Allfrey Papers Ref. 2/8, LHCMA.
35. Wigram, letter to Brig. A.G. Kenchington, DMT, BNAF, 16 August 1943, WO 231/14.
36. G. Taylor, *Infantry Colonel* (Upton-on-Severn, Worcestershire: Self-Publishing Association, 1990), pp. 46–7, 54–5 and *passim*.
37. *The Instructors' Handbook* . . . (October 1942), Ch. II, Sections 22, 23; *Infantry Training*, Part VIII, *Fieldcraft, Battle Drill, Section and Platoon Tactics* (4 March 1944), Ch. 4, Section 28.
38. See John Keegan, *Six Armies in Normandy: From D-Day to the Liberation of Paris* (Harmondsworth: Penguin, 1983), pp. 170–1, for 15th Division on the first day of EPSOM. See Patrick Delaforce, *Monty's Ironsides: From the Normandy Beaches to Bremen with the 3rd Division* (Stroud, Gloucestershire: Alan Sutton, 1995), pp. 63–5, for another example from 8th Brigade on 28 June 1944.
39. 'BATTLE NOTES 13–16 June 44', by Brig. James Hargest, CAB 106/1060.
40. 'Oxford and Buckinghamshire Light Infantry World War II History Notes', National Army Museum.
41. Alexander McKee, *Caen: Anvil of Victory* (London: Papermac, 1985), p. 167.
42. *CRO* No. 70 (3 January 1945), Section 1.
43. Norman Craig, *The Broken Plume: A Platoon Commander's Story, 1940–45* (London: IWM, 1982), p. 33.
44. Directorate of Infantry, 'Progress Bulletin (Infantry)', No. 15, 17 October 1944, Part I, Section II, WO 165/94.
45. Extract stated to be from a pamphlet produced by 50th Division after the Sicily campaign, para. 22, IWM, Montgomery Papers, BLM/68.
46. *CRO* No. 71 (10 January 1945), Section 1.
47. Immediate Report IN20, 'Impressions on Fighting in NORMANDY', 17 June 1944, WO 205/422. The transcription is faithful to the original. See also Immediate Report No. 12, CAB 106/963, and *CRO* No. 48 (29 July 1944), Section 2, for refined versions.

48. Papers for exercise INITIATIVE, appended to War Diary of 1st Herefordshire Regiment, May 1944, WO 171/1307.
49. 'Minutes of 1st Battle School Conference Held at the Horse Guards on 17 and 18 Jun 42', item 2, National Archives of Canada, Ottawa, RG 24 9764.
50. *Battle School* (July 1942, but written in October 1941), p. 121.
51. Ibid., pp. 119–31.
52. 'Minutes of 1st Battle School Conference ...', item 10, National Archives of Canada, Ottawa, RG 24 9764.
53. Extract stated to be from a pamphlet produced by 50th Division after the Sicily campaign, para. 10, IWM, Montgomery Papers, BLM/68.
54. *ATM* No. 48 (May 1944), Part II, para. 18.
55. 'THE FIRE-POWER OF THE INFANTRY SECTION', 28 March 1944, among the papers of Michael Swann, a member of Army Operational Research Section No. 6, attached to the School of Infantry.
56. It was listed in the April 1944 *Army List* but not in the July 1944 edition.
57. Directorate of Infantry, 'Progress Bulletin (Infantry)', No. 16, 18 November 1944, Part I, Section I, WO 165/94.
58. J.F. Amsden, 'A Brief Account of the Military Service of John Amsden from January 1943 to September 1947', unpublished memoir, 1987, IWM 87/23/1, p. 11.
59. Diary of David Rooney, 11 June–1 July 1945, transcripts privately supplied to the author.
60. R. St Lawrence, 'A Note on the Battle School Movement', unpublished memoir, 1996, privately supplied to the author.
61. Wigram, letter to Brig. A.G. Kenchington, DMT, BNAF, 16 August 1943, WO 231/14.
62. C.H. Boucher, 'Infantry Tactics', *Army Quarterly*, July 1948, pp. 246–55, especially pp. 251–3.

6: *The armoured arm*

1. War Diary of 2nd Armoured Irish Guards, 31 October 1942, WO 166/8576.
2. For the experiences of a private soldier in RAC Corps training, see the letters of Private Leslie Blackie, July 1944 to February 1945, IWM PP/MCR/178. For those of one marked out as a potential leader, see Captain J.F. Amsden, 'A Brief Account of the Military Service of John Amsden from January 1943 to September 1947' (unpublished memoir, 1987), IWM 87/23/1, pp. 3–4.
3. G.L. Verney, *The Guards Armoured Division: A Short History* (London: Hutchinson, 1955), p. 20.
4. 'Reports on State of Training of Field Force Formations', 22 April 1942, WO 205/1C.
5. War Diary of 2nd Armoured Irish Guards, 16 September 1942, WO 166/8576.
6. Ibid., 1 April 1942.
7. *Home Forces Standing Orders and Instructions for Exercises* (3rd edn, 1943), Appendix C, paras 5 and 13.
8. *MTP* No. 61, *Umpiring* (February 1944), Section 7.
9. Ibid.
10. 'GOC's Remarks at Final Conference on 11 Armoured Div Exercise "BULL". Tank v Tank Battle 21/9/41', at Appendix F to War Diary of G Branch, 11th Armoured Division, September 1941, WO 166/860.
11. J.P. Harris, *Men, Ideas and Tanks: British Military Thought and Armoured Forces, 1903–39* (Manchester and New York: Manchester University Press, 1995), pp. 166–70 and 188. See B. Holden Reid, *Studies in British Military Thought: Debates with Fuller*

and Liddell Hart (Lincoln, NB: University of Nebraska Press, 1998), pp. 49-50 for the riposte of Fuller's principal admirer.

12. For a sympathetic account of this episode in Hobart's career, see Kenneth Macksey, *Armoured Crusader: A Biography of Major-General Sir Percy Hobart* (London: Hutchinson, 1967), pp. 160-72. For a more balanced treatment see J.P. Harris, 'Sir Percy Hobart: Eclipse and Revival of an Armoured Commander, 1939-45', in Brian Bond, *Fallen Stars: Eleven Studies of Twentieth-Century Military Disasters* (London: Brassey's, 1991). See also Harris, *Men, Ideas and Tanks*, pp. 284-5, 297 and 306-7.

13. G. Le Q. Martel, *An Outspoken Soldier: His Views and Memoirs* (London: Sifton Praed, 1949), pp. 164 and 173, and K. Macksey, *A History of the Royal Armoured Corps and its Predecessors, 1914-1975* (Beaminster, Dorset: Newtown, 1983), p. 86.

14. Martel, *An Outspoken Soldier*, pp. 179-80.

15. Letter from Lt-Gen. H.C. Loyd 28 September 1941, at Appendix 1 to War Diary of HQ No. 1 Armoured Group, October 1941, WO 166/1359.

16. 'Minutes of the Commander-in-Chief's Conference Held at GHQ, 6 Nov 41', item 3, WO 205/1C.

17. Martel, *An Outspoken Soldier*, pp. 167-9.

18. Minute by Maj.-Gen. A.W.C. Richardson (Director of Armoured Fighting Vehicles at the War Office), 27 April 1942, commenting upon Martel's ideas for reorganisation of the War Office, WO 216/80.

19. 1942 War Diary of HQ No. 1 Armoured Group, WO 166/6554.

20. B.H. Liddell Hart, *The Tanks: The History of the Royal Tank Regiment and its Predecessors Heavy Branch Machine Gun Corps and Royal Tank Corps* (London: Cassell, 1959), Vol. 1, p. 300.

21. Harris, *Men, Ideas and Tanks*, pp. 241 and 276-9.

22. Montgomery to Brooke, 12 January 1943, Montgomery Papers, BLM 49/14, IWM – letter reproduced in S. Brooks (ed.), *Montgomery and the Eighth Army* (London: Bodley Head, 1991), pp. 114-21.

23. For instance, see R.M. Ogorkiewicz, *Armoured Forces: A History of Armoured Forces and their Vehicles* (London: Arms & Armour Press, 1970), pp. 125-6. Also see Field Marshal Carver's foreword to B. Perrett, *Through Mud and Blood: Infantry/Tank Operations in World War II* (London: Robert Hale, 1975), pp. 11-12.

24. Nye to Montgomery, 7 October 1943, Montgomery Papers, BLM 117/3; 'Future Design of the Capital Tank', 24 October 1944, BLM 129/2, IWM – letter reproduced in Brooks (ed.), *Montgomery*, pp. 299-302; *ATM* No. 47 (15 January 1944), Part II, para. 21.

25. Martel, *An Outspoken Soldier*, p. 205.

26. Montgomery to Nye, 28 August 1943, Montgomery Papers, BLM 117/2, IWM – letter reproduced in Brooks (ed.), *Montgomery*, pp. 273-7.

27. 'Future Design of the Capital Tank', 24 October 1944, Montgomery Papers, BLM 129/2, IWM.

28. 'Memorandum on British Armour', 6 July 1944, Montgomery Papers, BLM 117/14, IWM.

29. 21 Army Group pamphlet, *The Armoured Division in Battle* (December 1944), para. 21.

30. 'Report on the Visit by Lt Gen G.LeQ. Martel to the Middle East, Burma and Tunisia', undated but approximately February 1943, para. 35, WO 193/26. See also Martel's books *Our Armoured Forces* (London: Faber & Faber, 1945), pp. 161-2 and 242, and *An Outspoken Soldier*, p. 188.

31. Note by Brig. G.N. Tuck dated 6 December 1942 on MI3(c) paper, 'Offensive Tactics – Lessons of the War on the Eastern Front', WO 231/7.

32. Montgomery to Brooke, 12 January 1943, Montgomery Papers, BLM 49/14, IWM – letter reproduced in Brooks (ed.), *Montgomery*, pp. 114-21.

7: Armoured divisions

1. B.H. Liddell Hart, *The Tanks: The History of the Royal Tank Regiment and its Predecessors Heavy Branch Machine Gun Corps and Royal Tank Corps* (London: Cassell, 1959), Vol. 1, and *The Memoirs of Captain Liddell Hart*, 2 vols (London: Cassell, 1965).
2. Brian Bond, *British Military Policy between the Two World Wars* (Oxford: Oxford University Press, 1980), Chs 5 and 6; R.H. Larson, *The British Army and the Theory of Armoured Warfare, 1918–1940* (London: Associated University Press, 1984); H.R. Winton, *To Change an Army: General Sir John Burnett-Stuart and British Armoured Doctrine, 1927–1938* (Lawrence, KS: University Press of Kansas, 1988).
3. J.P. Harris, 'British Armour, 1918–1940: Doctrine and Development', in J.P. Harris and F.H. Toase (eds), *Armoured Warfare* (London: Batsford, 1990), p. 29. (For a useful summary of the Liddell Hart paradigm and other historians' work within it, see pp. 27–30 of this work.) Azar Gat's 'Liddell Hart's Theory of Armoured Warfare: Revising the Revisionists', *Journal of Strategic Studies*, 19, 1 (March 1996), especially pp. 5–12, challenges the arguments not only of Harris but also of the toilers in the Liddell Hart paradigm.
4. Harris, 'British Armour'; J.P. Harris, *Men, Ideas and Tanks: British Military Thought and Armoured Forces, 1903–1939* (Manchester and New York: Manchester University Press, 1995), Chs 7 and 8.
5. Larson, *The British Army*, p. 228.
6. M. Carver, *The Apostles of Mobility: The Theory and Practice of Armoured Warfare* (London: Weidenfeld & Nicolson, 1979), pp. 99–100.
7. *MTP* No. 41, *The Armoured Regiment* (July 1940), Ch. VII, Section 23.
8. R.M. Ogorkiewicz, *Armoured Forces: A History of Armoured Forces and their Vehicles* (London: Arms & Armour Press, 1970), p. 60.
9. *ATI* No. 3, *Handling of an Armoured Division* (19 May 1941), Part 1, Section 2.
10. *MTP* No. 51, *Troop Training for Cruiser Tank Troops* (1 September 1941), Section 3.
11. *ATI* No. 3 (19 May 1941), Part I, Section 3; *MTP* No. 41, *The Tactical Handling of the Armoured Division and its Components*, Part 1, *The Tactical Handling of Armoured Divisions* (July 1943), Ch. 2, Section 4; *MTP* No. 41, Part 3, *The Motor Battalion* (June 1943), Ch. 1. See Bart H. Vanderveen, *The Observer's Fighting Vehicles Directory, World War II* (London and New York: Frederick Warne, 1972), pp. 114 and 121, for details of the American armoured trucks and half-tracks in British service.
12. *ATI* No. 3, Part I, Section 3.
13. Ibid., Part II, Sections 8 and 9.
14. See *MTP* No. 41, Part 1 (July 1943), Ch. II, Sections 4, 5 and 7.
15. Ibid., Ch. I, Section 2, para. 5.
16. 'Notes on Conduct of Exercise', 17 September 1941, and 'GOC's Remarks at Final Conference on 11 Armoured Div Exercise "BULL"', at Appendices D and F respectively to War Diary of G Branch, 11th Armoured Division, September 1941, WO 166/860.
17. Visit of the Commander-in-Chief to The Guards Armoured Division, 6 February 1942, item 5, 'Notes of 6 Guards Armoured Brigade Demonstration, Serial No. 6', WO 199/283.
18. War Diary of 2nd Armoured Irish Guards, 1 April and 16 September 1942, WO 166/8576.
19. War Diary of 1st Motor Grenadier Guards, 6 June 1942, WO 166/8569.
20. Ibid., 25 May 1942.
21. *MTP* No. 41, Part 1 (July 1943), Ch. II, Section 5.
22. War Diary of HQ 29th Armoured Brigade, July 1942, WO 166/6665.
23. Harris, *Men, Ideas and Tanks*, pp. 306–7 and 314 note 112; and K. Macksey, *Armoured*

Crusader: A Biography of Major-General Sir Percy Hobart (London: Hutchinson, 1967), p. 103.

24. *MTP* No. 41 (July 1940), Ch. VII, Section 21; *ATI* No. 3 (19 May 1941), Part 2, Section 8; *MTP* No. 34, *Royal Armoured Corps Weapon Training*, Part 6, *Royal Armoured Corps Practices* (November 1942), Section 5.
25. See Liddell Hart, *The Tanks*, Vol. 2, pp. 62 and 111.
26. *ATM* No. 43 (23 May 1942), Part IV, para. 27; *ATM* No. 45 (29 May 1943), Part IV, para. 43.
27. '11 ARMOURED DIVISION TRAINING INSTRUCTION NO. 3 (Troop Training)' and Appendix No. 1, at Appendix L to divisional G Branch War Diary, May 1941, WO 166/860; 'Guards Armoured Division Training Directive No. 1 – Detailed Notes on Individual and Crew Training for Armoured Brigades', 21 August 1941, Appendix C, 'Notes on Tank Fire', at Appendix C to divisional G Branch War Diary, July–October 1941, WO 166/879.
28. Harris, *Men, Ideas and Tanks*, pp. 2, 306–7 and 314 note 112.
29. '11 ARMOURED DIVISION TRAINING INSTRUCTION NO. 3 (Troop Training)' and Appendix, at Appendix L to divisional G Branch War Diary, May 1941, WO 166/860.
30. War Diary of 2nd Armoured Irish Guards, 1 April 1942, WO 166/8576.
31. For evidence see ibid., and War Diary of 22nd Dragoons, 1–3 November 1942, WO 166/6897.
32. See 'Training Directive No. 3', 9 November 1942, at Appendix K to War Diary of 1st Armoured Coldstream Guards, November 1942, WO 166/8564.
33. *MTP* No. 41 (July 1940), Ch. III, Section 10; and *ATI* No. 3 (19 May 1941), Part II, Section 8.
34. *MTP* No. 51 (1 September 1941), Ch. IV, Section 35.
35. 'GOC's Remarks at Final Conference on 11 Armoured Div Exercise "BULL"', at Appendix F to War Diary of G Branch, 11th Armoured Division, September 1941, WO 166/860.
36. Liddell Hart, *The Tanks*, Vol. 1, p. 300. Note that this report has Hobart using stationary fire.
37. Visit of the Commander-in-Chief to The Guards Armoured Division, 6 February 1942, item 5, 'Notes of 6 Guards Armoured Brigade Demonstration, Serial No. 6', WO 199/283.
38. War Diary of 2nd Armoured Battalion, Irish Guards, 22 May, 5–6, 19–20 and 22 June and 9 July 1942, WO 166/8576; A.H.S. Adair, *A Guards' General: The Memoirs of Major-General Sir Allan Adair* (London: Hamish Hamilton, 1986), p. 135.
39. War Diary of 2nd Armoured Irish Guards, 23 July 1942, WO 166/8576.
40. 'GHQ Exercise "BUMPER" 27 Sep–3 Oct 1941. Comments by Commander-in-Chief, Home Forces, October 1941', papers of Lt-Gen. W.H. Stratton, IWM 71/5/1.
41. *MTP* No. 41, Part 2, *The Armoured Regiment* (February 1943), Ch. V, Sections 27 and 28.
42. *NTW* No. 14, *Western Desert and Cyrenaica, August/December 1942* (June 1943), Part III, Section 16, para. 4.
43. See 'Exercise RASPBERRY 22 & 23 Nov' at Appendix A to War Diary of 2nd Fife and Forfar Yeomanry, November 1942, and the entry for 22–23 November, WO 166/6904, and the summary for that month in the War Diary of HQ 29th Armoured Brigade, WO 166/6665. See also summary for the month of May 1943 in War Diary of HQ 29th Armoured Brigade, WO 166/10737. Guards Armoured Division seems not to have practised the lying-up battle.
44. *MTP* No. 51 (1 September 1941), Ch. III, Section 23; War Diary of 2nd Armoured Irish Guards, 2 January 1942, WO 166/8576.

45. War Diary of 2nd Armoured Irish Guards, 16 June 1942, WO 166/8576.

46. '5TH GUARDS ARMOURED BRIGADE TRAINING INSTRUCTION NO. 2 of 1943', 26 May 1943, at Appendix A to War Diary of Brigade HQ, June 1943, WO 166/10733.

47. *MTP* No. 41, *The Armoured Regiment* (draft, 1942), The Tank Museum, Bovington, 355.31(41)REGIMENTS/11, pp. 95–102.

48. See *NTW* No. 1, *Cyrenaica, November 1941* (19 February 1942), Part I, Sections 1 and 2, Part II Sections 11–13, and *NTW* No. 2, *Cyrenaica November/December 1941* (7 March 1942), Part I.

49. *NTW* No. 4, *Cyrenaica, November 1941/January 1942* (May 1942), Part I, Section 1.

50. 'Gds Armd Div Collective Training Instruction No. 1', 3 April 1942, at Appendix A to divisional G Branch War Diary, April 1942, WO 166/6474.

51. War Diary of 2nd Armoured Irish Guards, 16 and 19 October 1942, WO 166/8576.

52. 'Training Directive No. 3, The Armd Bn Group', 9 November 1942, at Appendix K to War Diary of 1st Armoured Coldstream Guards, November 1942, WO 166/8564.

53. Ibid.

54. War Diary of 2nd Fife and Forfar Yeomanry, 22–23 November 1942, WO 166/6904.

55. For criticisms of Hobart, see G.LeQ. Martel, *Our Armoured Forces* (London: Faber & Faber, 1945), p. 122, and *An Outspoken Soldier: His Views and Memoirs* (London: Sifton Praed, 1949), pp. 175–6, and Harris, *Men, Ideas and Tanks*, pp. 259–60. For the biographer's changing views see Macksey, *Armoured Crusader*, p. 198, and *A History of the Royal Armoured Corps and its Predecessors, 1914–1975* (Beaminster, Dorset: Newtown, 1983), p. 85.

56. '11 ARMOURED DIVISION TRAINING INSTRUCTION NO. 3 (Troop Training)', at Appendix L to divisional G Branch War Diary, May 1941, WO 166/860.

57. 'GUARDS ARMOURED DIVISION TRAINING DIRECTIVE NO. 1. DETAILED NOTES ON INDIVIDUAL AND CREW TRAINING', 21 August 1941, at Appendix C to divisional G Branch War Diary, July–October 1941, WO 166/879.

58. War Diary of 2nd Armoured Irish Guards, 16 June 1942, WO 166/8576.

59. *MTP* No. 34, *Royal Armoured Corps: Weapon Training*, Part 4, *Fire Tactics for Tank Commanders and Troop Leaders* (May 1940), Section 3.

60. *MTP* No. 34, Part 6, Section 5, 15 November 1942.

61. Ibid. (practice 8); *ATM* No. 47 (15 January 1944), Part II, para. 22; S. Bidwell, *Gunners at War: A Tactical Study of the Royal Artillery in the Twentieth Century* (London: Arms & Armour Press, 1970), p. 234. See also G. MacLeod Ross, *The Business of Tanks, 1933–1945* (Ilfracombe, Devon: Arthur H. Stockwell, 1976), pp. 171–6; M. Hastings, *Overlord: D-Day and the Battle for Normandy* (London: Pan, 1985), pp. 224–7; I.S.O. Playfair, *The Mediterranean and the Middle East*, Vol. 3 (London: HMSO, 1960), Appendix 8.

62. Liddell Hart, *The Tanks*, Vol. 2, p. 95, and D. Fletcher, *The Great Tank Scandal: British Armour in the Second World War, Part 1* (London: HMSO, 1989), p. 7. See also diagrams at Appendix B to *MTP* No. 41, Part 2 (February 1943).

63. War Diary of 2nd Armoured Irish Guards, 19 October 1942, WO 166/8576; 'Report on RA Combined Trng Camp, Butterworth, 26th July to Aug 11th', 13 August 1943, at Appendix A to War Diary of 2nd Fife and Forfar Yeomanry, July 1943, and War Diary entries for 28 April and 14–16 August, WO 166/11080; War Diary of 8th Rifle Brigade, 6 May 1943, WO 166/12687; *NTW* No. 14 (June 1943), Part III, Section 15, para. 12, and *NTW* No. 16, *North Africa, November 1942–May 1943* (October 1943), Part III, Section 11, para. 6. See also Rowland Ryder, *Oliver Leese* (London: Hamish Hamilton, 1987), pp. 114–15.

64. 'Narrative and Orders for the Stanford Battle Friday 7 May 1943', nd, issued by BM 29th Armoured Brigade, at Appendix A to War Diary of 2nd Fife and Forfar Yeomanry, April 1943, WO 166/11080; see, for example, War Diary of 1st Motor Grenadier Guards, 25–26 April 1943, WO 166/12464.

65. *NTW* No. 10, *Cyrenaica and Western Desert, January/June 1942* (October 1942), Section 3, para. 2.
66. *ATI* No. 3 (19 May 1941), Part I, Section 3.
67. *NTW* No. 10 (October 1942), Section 3, para. 2.
68. 'Notes on Armoured Divisional Tactics', text of address to officers of 11th Armoured Division by Maj.-Gen. G.P.B. Roberts, 13 December 1943, at Appendix C to divisional G Branch War Diary, December 1943, WO 166/10521.
69. See, for example, War Diary of 1st Motor Grenadier Guards, 15–16 July 1943, WO 166/12464; War Diary of 2nd Fife and Forfar Yeomanry, 1–3 June and 14–16 August 1943, WO 166/11080; exercise papers at Appendix C to War Diary of G Branch, 11th Armoured Division, August 1943, WO 166/10521; War Diary of 2nd Armoured Irish Guards, 4 February 1944, WO 171/1256.
70. See, for example, description of exercise MOON in War Diary of 1st Motor Grenadier Guards, 25 November 1943, WO 166/12464.
71. *MTP* No. 41, Part 3 (June 1943), Ch. 1, Section 4.
72. Roberts, 'Notes on Armoured Divisional Tactics', at Appendix C to War Diary of G Branch, 11th Armoured Division, December 1943, WO 166/10521.
73. War Diary of 1st Motor Grenadier Guards, 22 and 24 February 1944, WO 171/1253; War Diary of 8th Rifle Brigade, 13–25 February 1944, WO 171/1359.
74. *MTP* No. 41, Part 2 (February 1943), Ch. V, Section 29 and Appendix B.
75. 'Training Instruction No. 14. To cover the Interim Period 1 May–15 June 43', 27 April 1943, Appendix B 'Corps Commander's Special Points for Study', at Appendix D to War Diary of G Branch, 11th Armoured Division, April 1943, WO 166/10521.
76. 'BLACKBULL 29 ARMD BDE OPERATION ORDER NO. 1', 3 May 1943, and 'Narrative and Orders for the Stanford Battle Friday 7 May 43', both at Appendix A to War Diary of 2nd Fife and Forfar Yeomanry, April 1943, WO 166/11080.
77. Roberts, 'Notes on Armoured Divisional Tactics', at Appendix C to War Diary of G Branch, 11th Armoured Division, December 1943, WO 166/10521.
78. War Diary of 2nd Fife and Forfar Yeomanry, 1–3 June 1943, WO 166/11080.
79. Papers for exercise MOON, including one entitled 'Possible Sequence of Events', at Appendix D to War Diary of 1st Armoured Coldstream Guards, November 1943, WO 166/12460.
80. See, for example, War Diary of HQ 5th Guards Armoured Brigade, 17 July 1943, WO 166/10733.
81. '1 Armd Coldm Gds, Trg Instruction No. 15', 29 February 1944, at Appendix G2 to the battalion's War Diary, February 1944, WO 166/1250.
82. Roberts, 'Notes on Armoured Divisional Tactics', at Appendix C to War Diary of G Branch, 11th Armoured Division, December 1943, WO 166/10521; Army Operational Research Group Report No. 122, 'Lethal Effect of Artillery Fire. Trials at School of Artillery on 22nd June 1943', WO 291/113.
83. Letter signed by Maj.-Gen. E. Fanshawe (Maj.-Gen., Armoured Training) for the DMT, 20 August 1943, WO 32/10525.
84. 'A Statement of Modern AFV Weapons and the Instruments Necessary for their Control (As at 9th October 1943)', signed by R. Briggs, DRAC, WO 32/10525.
85. Letter to Fanshawe from GHQ Middle East Forces, 1 December 1943, WO 32/10390.
86. Whitaker, undated minute on GHQ MEF letter, 1 December 1943, WO 32/10390. See also 'Report on Visit to Mediterranean Theatres by DMT', 24 November 1943, WO 260/50.
87. 'Field Firing – Sept 43', at Appendix B to War Diary of 2nd Fife and Forfar Yeomanry, September 1943, WO 166/11080.
88. *ATM* No. 47 (15 January 1944), Appendix B.
89. Briggs minute dated 11 December 1943, WO 32/10390.

90. 'Minutes of Gunnery Conference, North Africa and CMF held at RAC School North Africa 17/20 January 1944 – Appendix – Record of written views and final conclusions and recommendations of the conference', WO 32/10390.
91. Letter from DMT to AFV School, Bovington, 2 March 1944, WO 32/10390.
92. *ATM* No. 49 (June 1944), Appendix B.
93. Letter to Fanshawe from GHQ Middle East Forces, 1 December 1943, WO 32/10390.
94. *MTP* No. 41, Part 2 (February 1943), Ch. V, Section 29, and Appendix B.
95. *ATM* No. 48 (May 1944), Part I, para. 2.
96. See *NTW* No. 16 (October 1943), Part IV, Section 17, para. 8, and *ATM* No. 47 (15 January 1944), Appendix B.
97. *NTW* No. 16 (October 1943), Part IV, Section 17, para. 8; Roberts, 'Notes on Armoured Divisional Tactics', at Appendix C to War Diary of G Branch, 11th Armoured Division, December 1943, WO 166/10521.
98. J. Baynes, *The Forgotten Victor: General Sir Richard O'Connor, KT, GCB, DSO, MC* (London: Brassey's, 1989), p. 186. For Montgomery's perception of this affair see Adair, *A Guards' General*, p. 150.
99. Carlo D'Este, *Decision in Normandy: The Unwritten Story of Montgomery and the Allied Campaign* (London: Pan, 1984), pp. 372–3.

8: Tank co-operation with infantry

1. B.H. Liddell Hart, *The Tanks: The History of the Royal Tank Regiment and its Predecessors Heavy Branch Machine Gun Corps and Royal Tank Corps* (London: Cassell, 1959) , Vol. 2, pp. 84–5.
2. L.F. Ellis, *Victory in the West*, Vol. 1, *The Battle of Normandy* (London: HMSO, 1962), p. 252.
3. Ibid., p. 261; Immediate Report No. 6, 'Capture of CRISTOT (8770) by one bn supported by one sqn tanks on 16 June 44', 17 June 1944, CAB 106/963; and *CRO* No. 45 (8 July 1944), Section 2.
4. *MTP* No. 22, *Tactical Handling of Army Tank Battalions*, Part III, *Employment* (September 1939), Section 5, paras 5, 6, 8, 9.
5. Staff College, Quetta, 1941, 'Co-operation of Army Tank Units with other arms in the deliberate Attack. To illustrate the principles of Military Training Pamphlet No. 22 Part III', Pyman Papers, Ref. 2/10, LHCMA.
6. *MTP* No. 22, Part III (September 1939), Section 5, para. 8.
7. Bryan Perrett, *Through Mud and Blood: Infantry/Tank Operations in World War II* (London: Robert Hale, 1975), pp. 28–38; and Kenneth Macksey, *The Tank Pioneers* (London: Jane's, 1981), pp. 161–2.
8. Liddell Hart, *The Tanks*, Vol. 2, pp. 40–1.
9. *ATM* No. 39 (17 April 1941), Part II, para. 2.
10. *ATI* No. 2, *The Employment of Army Tanks in Co-operation with Infantry* (March 1941), para. 5 and diagram V.
11. Ibid.
12. *ATM* No. 32 (20 May 1940), Part I, para 1.
13. Tom Wintringham, *New Ways of War* (Harmondsworth: Penguin, 1940), p. 58.
14. Ibid., pp. 55–61.
15. J. Weeks, *Men Against Tanks: A History of Anti-Tank Warfare* (Newton Abbot, Devon: David & Charles, 1975), pp. 40–50.
16. Personal memorandum by Schreiber to his divisional commanders, 2 May 1941, at annexure A to War Diary of G Branch, V Corps, May 1941, WO 166/249/5. See also '5 Corps Intelligence Summary No. 24', 4 January 1941, Appendix B, at annexure A to War Diary, January 1941, WO 166/249/4.
17. Frederick Myatt, *The British Infantry 1660–1945: The Evolution of a Fighting Force*

(Poole, Dorset: Blandford Press, 1983), p. 200.

18. Michael Carver, *Tobruk* (London: Batsford, 1964), p. 28.

19. *NTW* No. 2 (7 March 1942), *Cyrenaica, November/December 1941*, Part 2, Section 4.

20. *NTW* No. 4 (May 1942), *Cyrenaica, November 1941/January 1942*, Part I, Section 1.

21. See War Diary of HQ 25th Tank Brigade, 24 and 25 November 1941, WO 166/1135, and War Diary of 4th Somerset Light Infantry, 26 November 1941, WO 166/4655.

22. *The Times*, 3 February 1942, p. 2.

23. 'TRAINING EXERCISE NO. 1 (WOOLF), EXERCISE INSTRUCTION NO. 1', undated, appended to War Diary of 4th Somerset Light Infantry, April 1942, WO 166/8964.

24. See War Diaries of HQ 34th Tank Brigade and 147th RAC for June–August 1942, WO 166/6674 and WO 166/6941 respectively.

25. War Diary of G Branch, 43rd Division, 19 August 1942, WO 166/6249.

26. 'Confirmatory Notes on Conference Held on Exercise ADVENT I & II', 30 November 1942, at Appendix 68 to War Diary of HQ 34th Tank Brigade, November 1942, WO 166/6674.

27. 'Umpire Instructions – Points to be Watched by Umpires', among papers for exercise ADVENT III at Appendix 69 to War Diary of HQ 34th Tank Brigade, December 1942, WO 166/6674.

28. *ATI* No. 2 (March 1941), para. 5.

29. See '34 Tk Bde Training Directive Tk/Inf Co-op (Sep 43)', 6 September 1943, at Appendix 156 to War Diary of HQ 34th Tank Brigade, September 1943, WO 166/10747.

30. Stephen Dyson, *Twins in Tanks: East End Brothers-in-Arms, 1943–45* (London: Leo Cooper, 1994), p. 57. (The 107th RAC replaced 151st RAC in 34th Tank Brigade at the end of December 1943, at which time 151st RAC was disbanded and its personnel transferred to 107th RAC.)

31. Ken Tout, *Tanks Advance! Normandy to the Netherlands, 1944* (London: Robert Hale, 1987), p. 120.

32. See 'Lessons of the Tunisian Campaign, 1942–3 (British Forces)', Ch. 3, Section 3, WO 231/10; 'Infantry and Tank Co-operation: Training Memorandum and Notes on Recent Fighting', produced by Main HQ Eighth Army June 1944, WO 204/7957; *CRO* No. 14 (4 September 1943), Section 5; an address by Lt-Gen. C.W. Allfrey, GOC V Corps in Italy, on inter-arm co-operation, approx. 1944, Allfrey Papers, 2.5, LHCMA.

33. 'Operations by First Army in North Africa, November 1942–May 1943. Despatch by Lieut.-General K.A.N. Anderson, CB, MC, 7th June 1943', PREM 3/440/2.

34. 'Lessons of the Tunisian Campaign, 1942–3 (British Forces)', prepared under the instructions of GOC 18 Army Group and the GOC-in-C Allied Forces in North Africa, Appendix C, 'Co-operation of Churchills with Infantry', stated in the main body of the report to be the joint views of the commanders of 21st and 25th Tank Brigades. Undated but appears to have reached the War Office in July 1943, WO 231/10.

35. Ibid.

36. Ibid.

37. *CRO* No. 17 (25 September 1943), Section 2, para. 31. The source was not identified but must have been either 21st or 25th Tank Brigade.

38. Response by First Army to British Military Training Directorate (North Africa) BNAF, General Questionnaire, question 7, WO 231/10.

39. *CRO* No. 17 (25 September 1943), Section 2, para. 25.

40. Response by 1st Division to British Military Training Directorate (North Africa) BNAF, General and Infantry Questionnaires questions 7 and 4 respectively, WO 231/10.

41. *ATI* No. 2 (May 1943) *The Co-operation of Infantry and Tanks*, Foreword.

42. Ibid., Sections 1–5 .

43. Ibid., Sections 11–13.

44. Ibid., Sections 12 and 14.

45. Ibid., Section 14.
46. Ibid., Section 15.
47. *CRO* No. 8 (24 July 1943), Section 2.
48. *NTW* No. 16 (October 1943), *North Africa, November 1942–May 1943*, Part III, Section 11, para. 4.
49. See *MTP* No. 63, *The Co-operation of Tanks with Infantry Divisions* (May 1944), Sections 17 and 18.
50. D. Fletcher, *The Universal Tank: British Armour in the Second World War, Part 2* (London: HMSO, 1993), p. 25.
51. *CRO* No. 17 (25 September 1943), Section 2, para. 31.
52. 'Exercise CATTERICK 31 Jul/1 Aug', 31 July 1943, at Appendix B to War Diary of HQ 6th Guards Tank Brigade, July 1943, WO 166/10741.
53. 'CENTAUR II Exercise BOLTON 15–16 June 1943', 14 June 1943, among papers for exercise CENTAUR II appended to War Diary of 3rd Tank Scots Guards, June 1943, WO 166/12470.
54. 'CENTAUR III Exercise HEATHER 16/17 Aug 43', 12 August 1943, among papers for Exercise CENTAUR III appended to War Diary of 3rd Tank Scots Guards, August 1943, WO 166/12470.
55. See 'EXERCISE "TOREADOR" 27 ARMD BDE OPERATION ORDER NO. 1', 1 July 1943, appended to War Diary of HQ 27th Armoured Brigade, August 1943, WO 166/10735; and War Diary of 4th/7th Royal Dragoon Guards 13 and 14 August 1943, WO 166/11070.
56. AORG Memorandum No. 45, 'Casualties to Churchill Tanks in 25 Pdr HE Concentrations', dated 9 July 1943, WO 291/399.
57. *NTW* No. 16 (October 1943), Part III, Section 11, para. 4, footnote.
58. *The Instructors' Handbook on Fieldcraft and Battle Drill* (October 1942), Ch. II, Section 35, paras. 2 and 3.
59. Interview with Brig. P.J. Jeffreys, Department of Sound Records, IWM 11940/12, reel 11. Jeffreys commanded 70th Durham Light Infantry (the demonstration battalion of the School of Infantry from July 1942 to July 1943) until 14 November 1942. See the battalion's War Diary, 1942, WO 166/8669.
60. 'Minutes of a Sub-committee of the Training Committee of the School of Infantry held on Friday 16th July 1943', Brind Papers, WMWTC.
61. 'Notes on Divisional Exercise. Co-operation of Tanks and Inf'. Among documents sent by Bullen-Smith to Brig. G.L. Verney, OC 6th Guards Tank Brigade, and sent by him to Maj.-Gen. G.H.A. MacMillan, GOC 15th Division, in the file entitled 'Div Comd's Discussion. Tk and Inf Co-op 8 Dec 43', papers of Brig. H.D.K. Money, IWM 72/14/1.
62. 'TRAINING NOTES', 4 November 1943, at Appendix C to War Diary of 151st RAC, November 1943, WO 166/11115.
63. '34 Tk Bde Training Directive. Tk/Inf Co-op (Sep 43)', 6 September 1943, at Appendix 156 to War Diary of HQ 34th Tank Brigade, September 1943, WO 166/10747.
64. Ibid., and 'Directions for Trg in 12 Corps with 59 Div in Oct 43', 6 September 1943, at Appendix 156 to War Diary of HQ 34th Tank Brigade, September 1943, WO 166/10747.
65. '34 Tk Bde Training Directive. Tk/Inf Co-op (Sep 43)', 6 September 1943, at Appendix 156 to War Diary of HQ 34th Tank Brigade, September 1943, WO 166/10747.
66. '34 Tk Bde Trg Instr No. 18', 17 November 1943, at Appendix 181 to War Diary of HQ 34th Tank Brigade, November 1943, WO 166/10747.
67. '11 Armd Div Trg Instr No. 22. Period 15 Oct 43 – 1 Jan 44', 14 October 1943, at Appendix 13 to War Diary of G Branch, 11th Armoured Division, October 1943, WO 166/10521. The article concerned was *CRO* No. 17, Section 2.
68. '34 Tk Bde Trg Instr No. 16', 24 October 1943, at Appendix 169 to War Diary of HQ 34th Tank Brigade, October 1943, WO 166/10747.

69. See letter from Roper-Caldbeck, School of Infantry, to House, War Office, 28 October 1943, WO 232/38; and DMT's minute to VCIGS, 17 December 1943, Stephen Brooks (ed.), *Montgomery and the Eighth Army* (London: Bodley Head/Army Records Society, 1991), pp. 343–6.

70. 21 Army Group pamphlet, *The Co-operation of Tanks with Infantry Divisions in Offensive Operations* (November 1943), Part II, paras 59 and 60 and diagram 1.

71. Ibid., Part III, Ch. VI, Section 20.

72. *ATM* No. 47 (15 January 1944), Part II, para. 21.

73. Norrie memoranda, 29 October and 4 November 1943, and Morgan memorandum, 6 November 1943, WO 205/57.

74. H.E. Pyman, *Call to Arms* (London: Leo Cooper, 1971), p. 62, and War Diary of HQ 21 Army Group, 30 December 1943, WO 171/1.

75. *NTW* No. 14 (June 1943), *Western Desert and Cyrenaica, August/December 1942*, Part III, Section 15, para. 4.

76. 'Report on Visit to Mediterranean Theatres by DMT', 24 November 1943, Section 46, WO 260/50.

77. *EIGHTH ARMY Notes on the Employment of Tanks in Support of Infantry in Battle* (November 1943), para. 8 and Appendix A, IWM, Montgomery Papers, BLM 52/17.

78. 'Mins of Bde Comd's Conference at Bde HQ 1630 hrs, 8 Jan 44', 9 January 1944, at Appendix 191 to War Diary of HQ 34th Tank Brigade, January 1944, WO 171/643.

79. 'Notes on the Attached Pamphlet', IWM, Montgomery Papers, BLM 52/18.

80. Montgomery letter to Nye, 7 December 1943 and Nye's reply, 21 December 1943, Brooks (ed.), *Montgomery*, pp. 342 and 346–7. See also Whitaker's minute to Nye on the intervening pages.

81. Copy in the de Guingand Papers, LHCMA.

82. Compare 'Programme for exercise GRAMPIAN', appended to War Diary of 3rd Tank Scots Guards, January 1944, WO 171/1258, with 'EXERCISE CLOCKWORK PROGRAMME – CO-OPERATION OF TKS WITH INF 5–9 OCT 43', at Appendix A to War Diary of 2nd Fife and Forfar Yeomanry, October 1943, WO 166/11080. The 3rd Tank Scots Guards assisted in the latter.

83. 'Bde Comd's Conference 28 Feb 44', at Appendix 204 to War Diary of HQ 34th Tank Brigade, February 1944, WO 171/643.

84. '34th Tank Brigade Standing Operation Instructions 1944', at Appendix E to War Diary of HQ 34th Tank Brigade, May 1944, ibid.

85. 'Infantry and Tank Co-operation: Training Memorandum and Notes on Recent Fighting', issued by AFV Branch, Main HQ, Eighth Army, June 1944, as amended by letter from Chief of Staff Eighth Army, 10 July 1944, WO 204/7957.

86. Pyman, *Call to Arms*, pp. 55–6, 60, 65–6 and 78.

87. 'Notes on the Attached Pamphlet', Montgomery Papers, IWM, BLM 52/18. Montgomery wrote that the pamphlet's length 'condemns it for issue in the field'.

9: Armour in north-west europe

1. For 11th Armoured Division, see War Diaries of HQ 29th Armoured Brigade, HQ 159th Brigade for October and November 1943, WO 166/10737 and WO 166/10792 respectively. See also papers for exercise STANFORD, at Appendix A to War Diary of G Branch, 11th Armoured Division, February 1944, WO 171/456 and War Diary of HQ 29th Armoured Brigade, 3–5 May 1944, WO 171/627. For Guards Armoured Division see War Diaries of 2nd Armoured Irish Guards 21–28 October 1943, WO 166/12468, 1st Armoured Coldstream Guards, October 1943 (Appendix D 'Tank and Infantry Co-ordination Exercise 31/10–1/11, Exercise Instructions'), WO 166/12460, and HQ 5th Guards Armoured Brigade, 13 November 1943, WO 166/10733.

2. 'BATTLE NOTES on recent actions up to D + 10', report by Brig. James Hargest, CAB 106/1060. The relevant passages of Hargest's report are reproduced in Carlo D'Este, *Decision in Normandy: The Unwritten Story of Montgomery and the Allied Campaign* (London: Pan Books, 1984), p. 295.
3. Immediate Report No. 3, 'CO-OPERATION OF ARMOUR AND INFANTRY', by GSO1(L), 7th Armoured Division, 12 June 1944, CAB 106/963. The report was later published in *CRO* No. 44 (1 July 1944), Section 3.
4. L.F. Ellis, *Victory in the West*, Vol. 1, *The Battle of Normandy* (London: HMSO, 1962), pp. 252–5.
5. *CRO* No. 24 (20 November 1943), Sections 1 and, especially, 2.
6. Immediate Report IN20, 17 June 1944, WO 205/422.
7. Immediate Report No. 12, 'Impressions on Fighting in Normandy', 17 June 1944, CAB 106/963; *CRO* No. 48 (29 July 1944), Section 2.
8. 'Operational Research in North-West Europe: The Work of No. 2 Operational Research Section with 21 Army Group, June 1944–July 1945', Report No. 33, pp. 240–7, WO 205/1164.
9. *CRO* No. 41 (10 June 1944), Section 1.
10. Ellis, *Victory in the West*, Vol. 1, pp. 275–86.
11. G.P.B. Roberts, *From the Desert to the Baltic* (London: William Kimber, 1987), p. 168.
12. War Diary of 3rd Irish Guards, 13 July 1944, WO 171/1257. See also War Diaries of: 2nd Armoured Irish Guards, 10–12 July 1944, WO 171/1256; 1st Motor Grenadier Guards, 7–8 July 1944, WO 171/1253; HQ 32nd Guards Brigade, 13 July 1944, WO 171/638; and 5th Coldstream Guards, 13–14 July 1944, WO 171/1252.
13. D'Este, *Decision in Normandy*, p. 372.
14. 'Operational Research in North-West Europe: The Work of No. 2 Operational Research Section with 21 Army Group, June 1944 – July 1945', Report No. 6, Appendix A, pp. 8–9, WO 205/1164.
15. Ellis, *Victory in the West*, Vol. 1, p. 340.
16. D'Este, *Decision in Normandy*, p. 376.
17. Ibid., p. 386.
18. Ibid., p. 362–4.
19. Ibid., p. 367.
20. Max Hastings, *OVERLORD: D-Day and the Battle for Normandy* (London: Pan, 1985), p. 279.
21. Richard Lamb, *Montgomery in Europe 1943–1945: Success or Failure?* (London: Buchan & Enwright, 1983), p. 132.
22. Roberts, *From the Desert to the Baltic*, p. 184; D.J.L. Fitzgerald, *History of the Irish Guards in the Second World War* (Aldershot: Gale & Polden, 1952), pp. 394–5; A.H.S. Adair, *A Guards' General: The Memoirs of Major-General Sir Allan Adair* (London: Hamish Hamilton, 1986), p. 147.
23. Roberts, *Desert*, p. 196. Guards Armoured Division took no part in this advance.
24. M. Carver, *Out of Step: Memoirs of a Field Marshal* (London: Hutchinson, 1989), p. 180.
25. Roberts, *From the Desert to the Baltic*, pp. 201–2 and 214.
26. Adair, *A Guards' General*, p. 152. See also p. 147.
27. Roberts, *From the Desert to the Baltic*, pp. 159 and 240.
28. Ibid., p. 154.
29. 'Notes on Armoured Divisional Tactics', text of address to officers of 11th Armoured Division by Maj.-Gen. G.P.B. Roberts, 13 December 1943, at Appendix C to divisional G Branch War Diary, December 1943, WO 166/10521.
30. 'Operational Research in North-West Europe: The Work of No. 2 Operational Research Section with 21 Army Group, June 1944–July 1945', Report No. 33, pp. 240–7, WO 205/1164.

31. '21 Army Group. Memorandum on British Armour No. 2', signed by Montgomery, 21 February 1945, Montgomery Papers, IWM, BLM 117/20, para. 29.
32. Diary of Maj. B.E.L. Burton, IWM 94/8/1, 6–16 July 1944.
33. Progress Bulletin (Infantry) No. 16, 18 November 1944, Part I, Section II, WO 165/94.
34. Burton, diary, IWM 94/8/1, 12 June 1944.
35. '3rd Tank Battalion Scots Guards 20th July 1944–8th May 1945', account compiled by Captain H.W. Llewellyn Smith, pp. 3–5, CAB 106/1029; W. Whitelaw, *The Whitelaw Memoirs* (London: Headline, 1990), pp. 17–21; and Ellis, *Victory in the West*, Vol. 1, pp. 390–1.
36. *CRO* No. 58 (7 October 1944), Section 3.
37. '3rd Tank Battalion Scots Guards 20th July 1944–8th May 1945', by Llewellyn Smith, pp. 6–8, CAB 106/1029; and Ellis, *Victory in the West*, Vol. 1, pp. 410, 425.
38. War Diary of 1st East Riding Yeomanry, 7, 9 and 28 June 1944, WO 171/862.
39. Ibid., 8 July 1944.
40. War Diary of 13th/18th Hussars, 8 July 1944, and operation order No. 1, 6 July 1944, appended to the July War Diary, WO 171/845.
41. 'Notes from a Battalion Commander's Point of View', circulated by BGS(Ops), 21 Army Group, 4 September 1944, WO 205/405. Unfortunately, the identity of the author was not revealed.
42. RAC Branch minute to Operations Branch, 6 September 1944, and Lewthwaite's minute thereon, 9 September 1944, ibid.
43. 'The Encounter Battle', at Appendix A to War Diary of 1st Herefordshire Regiment, 23 Augus–26 September 1944, WO 171/1307; *CRO* No. 68 (20 December 1944), Section 1.

10: Conclusion

1. See Brooke diary, 8 September 1942, Alanbrooke Papers, 5/6A, LHCMA. Documentary evidence of Liddell's activities seems to be confined to two files in the PRO, WO 216/62 and WO 216/66, neither of which is relevant in this context.
2. See Montgomery's 'Some General Notes on What to Look for When Visiting a Unit', J.A. English, *The Canadian Army and the Normandy Campaign: A Study of Failure in High Command* (New York: Praeger, 1991), pp. 314–19.
3. S.A. Hart, 'Field Marshal Montgomery, 21st Army Group, and North-West Europe, 1944–45' (PhD thesis, University of London, 1995), *passim*.
4. See D. French, '"Tommy is No Soldier": The Morale of the Second British Army in Normandy, June–August 1944', *Journal of Strategic Studies*, 19, 4 (December 1996), pp. 169–70 and note 91.
5. Williamson Murray, 'The German Response to Victory in Poland: A Case Study in Professionalism', *Armed Forces and Society*, 7, 2 (Winter 1981), pp. 285–98; R.M. Ogorkiewicz, *Armoured Forces: A History of Armoured Forces and their Vehicles* (London: Arms & Armour Press, 1970), pp. 72–6.
6. T. Harrison Place, 'British Perceptions of the Tactics of the German Army, 1938–40', *Intelligence and National Security*, 9, 3 (July 1994), pp. 495–519.
7. Kenneth Macksey, *The Tank Pioneers* (London: Jane's, 1981), pp. 161–2.
8. Report of the Bartholomew Committee, WO 32/9581.
9. Hart, 'Montgomery', *passim*, especially p. 280.
10. Shelford Bidwell, *Gunners at War: A Tactical Study of the Royal Artillery in the Twentieth Century* (London: Arms & Armour Press, 1970), p. 32.
11. Max Hastings, *OVERLORD: D-Day and the Battle for Normandy* (London: Pan, 1985), p. 249.

Bibliography

ARCHIVE OF THE GLOUCESTERSHIRE REGIMENT, THE REGIMENTS OF
GLOUCESTERSHIRE MUSEUM, GLOUCESTER

Black File No. 14   Various memoir pieces by individuals who served in the
Gloucestershire Regiment during the Second World War

IMPERIAL WAR MUSEUM, LONDON

Documents

87/23/1   Captain J.F. Amsden, 'A Brief Account of the Military Service of
John Amsden from January 1943 to September 1947' (unpublished
memoir, *c.* 1987)

87/23/1   Cecil George Beech, 'Bury Me in a Shallow Grave – Dig Me Up
Later' (unpublished memoir, *c.* 1987)

92/11/2   Lieutenant H.J. Belsey, letters

PP/MCR/178   Leslie Blackie, letters

87/31/1   Lieutenant H.T. Bone, journal and letters

81/10/1   H. Buckle, 'Recollections from Yesteryear' (unpublished memoir,
n.d.)

94/8/1   Major B.E.L. Burton, diary

88/4/1   Eric A. Codling, unpublished and untitled memoir, n.d.

85/6/1   Squadron Leader J.E. Edney, 'One Three One Over Eight' (unpublished memoir, *c.* 1985)

87/19/1   Captain T.H. Flanagan, 'Tom's War' (unpublished memoir, 1987)

85/18/1   C.T. Framp, 'The Littlest Victory' (unpublished memoir, 1980s)

88/58/1   N.L. Francis, 'We Regret to Inform You . . .' (unpublished
memoir, December 1983)

73/14/1   Papers of Lt-Gen. Sir James A.H. Gammell

90/26/1   Colonel H.S. Gillies, unpublished and untitled memoir

92/1/1   R. Gladman, 'Citizen Soldier' (unpublished memoir, *c.* 1990)

81/44/1   Captain A.G. Gurr, papers

86/49/1   R.I. Higgins, 'A Few Memories' (unpublished memoir, *c.* 1979) and letters

81/16/1   Lieutenant H.P. Hunt, papers

92/15/1   Lieutenant-Colonel A.D. Melville, diary

72/14/1   Brigadier H.D.K. Money, papers

BLM   Field Marshal the Viscount Montgomery of Alamein, papers

88/60/1   Captain David Sheldon, letters

71/5/1   Lieutenant-General Sir William H. Stratton, papers

82/15/1   Major-General G.W. Symes, diary

87/42/1   Len Waller, 'However Did We Win? A Common Soldier's Account of World War Two' (unpublished memoir, n.d.)

91/43/1   Major R.H.D. Young, 'Two Churchill Squadrons: A Scrapbook of the 1944–1945 Campaign in North-West Europe and the part Played by B Sqn 153 RAC and C Sqn 9th Bn RTR' (unpublished scrapbook)

Misc./152 (2344)   Instructions for 1st London Infantry Brigade in Kent 1940

Films

SKC 4 (May 1951) *Tank Troop Tactics Part 2: Tank–Infantry Co-operation*

SKC 22 (June 1943) *Camouflage and Fieldcraft: Fieldcraft*

SKC 23 (June 1943) *Camouflage and Fieldcraft: Movement*

SKC 67 (February 1943) *Use of Fire*

WOY 67 (November 1942) *Close-Quarter Fighting*

WOY 68 (February 1943) *Carriers Close Support*

WOY 102 (August 1943) *Encounter Battle*

WOY 103 (November 1943) *Battalion Battle Technique No. 2*

WOY 110 (1943) *Exercise SPARTAN*

WOY 145 (April 1943) *Frontal Attack (Lane Method)*

WOY 182 (February 1946) *Infantry/Tank Co-operation (Platoon/Troop Level)*

WOY 266 (June 1943) *Camouflage and Fieldcraft: Prepare for Battle*

WOY 299 (November 1942) *Platoon Flanking Attack*

Sound Records (interviews)

15609/4   William John Cron

10385/4   N. Habetin

11940/12   Brigadier Peter John Jeffreys

13137/2A   Robert Henry Walker

BIBLIOGRAPHY

LIDDELL HART CENTRE FOR MILITARY ARCHIVES,
KING'S COLLEGE LONDON

Field Marshal Viscount Alanbrooke, papers
Lieutenant-General Sir Charles Walter Allfrey, papers
Major-General J.B. Churcher, 'A Soldier's Story', unpublished memoir, c. 1984
Colonel Ronald Duncan Cribb, papers
Major-General Sir Francis Wilfred de Guingand, papers
Sir Basil Henry Liddell Hart, papers
Major John North, papers
General Sir Harold English Pyman, papers

NATIONAL ARCHIVE OF CANADA, OTTAWA

RG 24 9764 Minutes of 1st Battle School Conference, 17–18 June 1942

NATIONAL ARMY MUSEUM, LONDON

Oxfordshire and Buckinghamshire Light Infantry, World War II History Notes

PUBLIC RECORD OFFICE (PRO), KEW, SURREY

Cabinet Office documents (CAB)

CAB 106, Cabinet Office historical section papers

Prime Minister's Office documents (Prem)

Prem 3, operations papers

War Office documents (WO)

WO 32, General Series
WO 163, Army Council Records
WO 165, War Diaries or Progress Reports of War Office Directorates
WO 166, War Diaries of Units and Formations in Home Forces
WO 167, War Diaries of Units and Formations in the British Expeditionary
    Force (BEF),1939–40
WO 171, War Diaries of Units and Formations in 21 Army Group
WO 193, Directorate of Military Operations Records
WO 199, Military Headquarters Papers, Home Forces

WO 204, Military Headquarters Papers, Allied Forces HQ
WO 205, Military Headquarters Papers, 21 Army Group
WO 214, Papers of Field Marshal Earl Alexander of Tunis
WO 216, Papers of the Chief of the Imperial General Staff
WO 231, Directorate of Military Training Records
WO 232, Directorate of Tactical Investigation Records
WO 260, Directorate of Staff Duties Papers
WO 277, Historical Monographs
WO 282, Papers of Field Marshal Sir John Dill
WO 291, Operational Research Papers

PRIVATE ARCHIVES

Professor Terry Copp Operational Research Documents from the papers of
    Major M.M. Swann.
David Rooney Transcripts from his diary, October–November 1944 (at 164
    OCTU Barmouth), and June 1945 (at battle school, Dereham, Norfolk).
Anthony Wigram Papers of his father, Lieutenant-Colonel Lionel Wigram,
    including letters to and from his wife and the draft of *Battle School* (then
    entitled 'Two Wasted Years'), plus newspaper cuttings.

TANK MUSEUM LIBRARY, BOVINGTON, DORSET

RH.88.RAC (Box 16) Half-Yearly Progress Reports of the War Office
    Directorate of Armoured Fighting Vehicles, 1941
RH.88.RAC (Box 17) Half-Yearly Reports on the Progress of the Royal
    Armoured Corps, 1942
RH.88.RAC: 5358   'Inter-Allied and RAC Schools Armoured Training
    Conference', July 1944
355.31(41) Regiments/11   Draft of *MTP* No. 41, *The Armoured Regiment*
    (1942). (Apparently a draft of *MTP* No. 41, Part 2, February 1943.)

WEAPONS MUSEUM, WARMINSTER TRAINING CENTRE,
WARMINSTER, WILTSHIRE

Brigadier James L. Brind, DSO, papers
Major J.P. Vivian, 'A History of the School of Infantry', unpublished memoir

BIBLIOGRAPHY

UNPUBLISHED MEMOIRS PRIVATELY SUPPLIED BY THEIR AUTHORS

Brind, Brigadier J.L., 'The Sword and a Piano: The Recollections of a Retired Officer'
St Lawrence, Major Raleigh, 'A Note on the Battle School Movement'
Wallace, Dr Alan S., two untitled pieces: one on his wartime medical training, the other on his attendance at the 3rd Division Battle School in 1942 as a Home Guardsman
Hargreaves, Major Richard, 'Some recollections on the Battle School Movement'

INTERVIEWS CONDUCTED BY THE AUTHOR

Brigadier J.L. Brind, DSO (25 January 1995)
Major R.M.T. Kerr (22 March 1995)
Captain P. Stobart (10 April 1996)
Major J.P. Vivian (9 August 1995)
Mrs Olga Wigram (5 April 1995)

PRINTED OFFICIAL AND SEMI-OFFICIAL MANUALS AND PAMPHLETS

(Note: except where indicated, these are in the keeping of the Department of Printed Books at the Imperial War Museum.)

War Office: *Army Training Instruction (ATI)*

ATI No. 1 (21 January 1941) *Notes on Tactics as Affected by the Reorganisation of the Infantry Division*
ATI No. 2 (March 1941) *The Employment of Army Tanks in Co-operation with Infantry*
ATI No. 2 (May 1943) *The Co-operation of Infantry and Tanks*
ATI No. 3 (19 May 1941) *Handling of an Armoured Division*

War Office: *Army Training Memorandum (ATM)* series, 1939–45

War Office: *Current Reports from Overseas (CRO)* series, 1942–45

War Office: *Infantry Training Memorandum (ITM)* series, 1944–45

War Office: *Military Training Pamphlet (MTP)*

MTP No. 2 (June 1943) *The Offensive*
MTP No. 3 (April 1938) *Notes on the Tactical Handling of the New (1938) Battalion* (private collection)

MTP No. 22 (August 1939) *Tactical Handling of Army Tank Battalions,* Part II, *Battle Drill and Manoeuvre*

MTP No. 22 (September 1939) *Tactical Handling of Army Tank Battalions,* Part III, *Employment*

MTP No. 23 (September 1939) *Operations,* Part I, *General Principles, Fighting Troops and their Characteristics*

MTP No. 23 (6 March 1942) *Operations,* Part I, *General Principles, Fighting Troops and their Characteristics*

MTP No. 23 (21 July 1941) *Operations,* Part IX, *The Infantry Division in the Attack*

MTP No. 31 (February 1940) *Notes on the Organisation and Tactical Handling of Medium Machine Guns*

MTP No. 33 (March 1940) *Training in Fieldcraft and Elementary Tactics*

MTP No. 34 (May 1940) *Royal Armoured Corps: Weapon Training,* Part 4, *Fire Tactics for Tank Commanders and Troop Leaders*

MTP No. 34 (April 1944) *Royal Armoured Corps: Weapon Training,* Part 4, *Tank Fire Tactics*

MTP No. 34 (15 November 1942) *Royal Armoured Corps Weapon Training,* Part 6, *Open Range Practices*

MTP No. 37 (June 1940) *The Training of an Infantry Battalion*

MTP No. 41 (July 1940) *The Armoured Regiment*

MTP No. 41 (July 1943) *The Tactical Handling of the Armoured Division and its Components,* Part 1, *The Tactical Handling of Armoured Divisions*

MTP No. 41 (February 1943) *The Tactical Handling of the Armoured Division and its Components,* Part 2, *The Armoured Regiment*

MTP No. 41 (June 1943) *The Tactical Handling of the Armoured Division and its Components,* Part 3, *The Motor Battalion*

MTP No. 51 (1 September 1941) *Troop Training for Cruiser Tank Troops*

MTP No. 61 (February 1944) *Umpiring*

MTP No. 63 (May 1944) *The Co-operation of Tanks with Infantry Divisions*

War Office: *Notes from Theatres of War (NTW)*

NTW No. 1 (19 February 1942) *Cyrenaica, November 1941*

NTW No. 2 (7 March 1942) *Cyrenaica, November/December 1942*

NTW No. 3 (7 March 1942) *Russia, January 1942*

NTW No. 4 (May 1942) *Cyrenaica, November 1941/January 1942*

NTW No. 5 (May 1942) *Far East, December 1941/February 1942*

NTW No. 6 (July 1942) *Cyrenaica, November 1941/January 1942*

NTW No. 7 (July 1942) *Russia, March/April 1942*

NTW No. 8 (October 1942) *Far East, December 1941/May 1942*

NTW No. 9 (October 1942) *Madagascar, May 1942*

NTW No. 10 (October 1942) *Cyrenaica and Western Desert, January/June 1942*

NTW No. 11 (February 1943) *Destruction of a German Battery by No. 4 Commando during the Dieppe Raid*

NTW No. 12 (May 1943) *South West Pacific, August/December 1942*

NTW No. 13 (May 1943) *North Africa – Algeria and Tunisia, November 1942 –March 1943*

NTW No. 14 (June 1943) *Western Desert and Cyrenaica, August/December 1942*

NTW No. 15 (August 1943) *South West Pacific, January–March 1943*

NTW No. 16 (October 1943) *North Africa, November 1942–May 1943*

NTW No. 17 (May 1944) *Far East, April–November 1943*

NTW No. 18 (December 1944) *Pacific, 1943/1944*

NTW No. 19 (May 1945) *Burma, 1943/1944*

NTW No. 20 (May 1945) *Italy, 1943/1944*

NTW No. 21 (June 1945) *Partisans*

Other War Office publications

Infantry Section Leading, 1938, December 1938

Infantry Training, Vol. I, *Training,* March 1922 (LHCMA LH7/1920/54)

Infantry Training, Vol. II, *War,* November 1921 (LHCMA LH7/1920/53)

Infantry Training, Training and War, 1937, August 1937

Infantry Training, 1937, Supplement No. 1, *Tactical Notes for Platoon Commanders* 3, October 1941

Infantry Training, Part VIII, *Fieldcraft, Battle Drill, Section and Platoon Tactics,* 4 March 1944

Notes for Instructors on the Principles of Instruction, 30 June 1939 (LHCMA, Cribb Papers, Box 4)

Notes from France No. 1, January 1940 (private collection)

Right or Wrong? Elements of Training and Leadership Illustrated 1937, December 1937 (private collection)

The Distribution of General Staff Publications (January) 1942, January 1942

GHQ Home Forces

A Drill for the Assault on a Highly Defended Locality (Provisional), June 1943 (PRO, WO 231/15)

GHQ Home Forces Standing Orders and Instructions for Exercises (3rd edn), 1943

The Instructors' Handbook on Fieldcraft and Battle Drill, October 1942 (LHCMA 15/8/168)

Eighth Army

EIGHTH ARMY Notes on the Employment of Tanks in Support of Infantry in Battle, November 1943 (IWM, BLM 52/17)

21 Army Group

The Co-operation of Tanks with Infantry Divisions in Offensive Operations, November 1943 (PRO, WO 171/1)
Notes on the Employment of Tanks in Support of Infantry in Battle, February 1944 (LHCMA, de Guingand Papers, IV/2/7)
The Armoured Division in Battle, December 1944 (Tactical Doctrine Retrieval Cell, Upavon, Wiltshire)

I Corps

I Corps Tactical Notes, October 1940 (private collection)

Northern Command/Lionel Wigram

Battle School, July 1942 (WMWTC, Brind Papers)

BOOKS

Adair, Allan H.S., *A Guards' General: The Memoirs of Major-General Sir Allan Adair, BT, GCVO, CB, DSO, MC, JP, DL* (London: Hamish Hamilton, 1986).
Ahrenfeldt, R.H., *Psychiatry in the British Army in the Second World War* (London: Routledge & Kegan Paul, 1958).
Anderson, Dudley, *Three Cheers for the Next Man to Die* (London: Robert Hale, 1983).
Anon., *History of the 4th Bn. The Somerset Light Infantry (Prince Albert's) in the Campaign in North-West Europe June 1944–May 1945* (privately published, n.d.).
——, *Street Fighting for Junior Officers* (Aldershot: Gale & Polden, 1941).
——, *A History of 11th Armoured Division* (privately published, c. 1945).
——, *The Story of 34 Armoured Brigade* (privately published, c. 1945).
Barnett, Correlli, *The Desert Generals* (2nd edn; London: George Allen & Unwin, 1983).
Baynes, John, *The Forgotten Victor: General Sir Richard O'Connor, KT, GCB, DSO, MC* (London: Brassey's, 1989).
Beauman, Brigadier-General A.B., *A Short Outline of Modern Tactics* (London: Hugh Rees, 1939).
Beckett, I.F.W. and D.G. Chandler (eds), *The Oxford Illustrated History of the British Army* (Oxford: Oxford University Press, 1994).
Bellamy, Christopher, *The Evolution of Modern Land Warfare: Theory and Practice* (London: Routledge, 1990).
Bidwell, S., *Gunners at War: A Tactical Study of the Royal Artillery in the Twentieth Century* (London: Arms & Armour Press, 1970).
——, *Artillery Tactics 1939–1945* (New Malden, Surrey: Almark, 1976).

Bidwell, S., and D. Graham, *Fire-Power: British Army Weapons and Theories of War, 1904–45* (Boston, MA: Allen & Unwin, 1985).

Bond, Brian, *Liddell Hart: A Study of his Military Thought* (London: Cassell, 1977).

——, *British Military Policy between the Two World Wars* (Oxford: Oxford University Press, 1980).

—— (ed.), *Chief of Staff: The Diaries of Lieutenant-General Sir Henry Pownall*, Vol. 1, *1933–1940* (London: Leo Cooper, 1972).

—— (ed.), *Chief of Staff: The Diaries of Lieutenant-General Sir Henry Pownall*, Vol. 2, (London: Leo Cooper, 1974).

—— (ed.), *Fallen Stars: Eleven Studies of Twentieth-Century Military Disasters* (London: Brassey's, 1991).

Brooks, S. (ed.), *Montgomery and the Eighth Army* (London: Bodley Head, 1991).

Bruce, Colin John, *War on the Ground* (London: Constable, 1995).

Brutton, Philip, *Ensign in Italy* (London: Leo Cooper, 1992).

Bryant, Arthur, *The Turn of the Tide: 1939–1943: A Study Based on the Diaries and Autobiographical Notes of Field Marshal The Viscount Alanbrooke, KG, OM* (London: Reprint Society, 1958).

——, Arthur, *Triumph in the West: 1943–1946: Based on the Diaries and Autobiographical Notes of Field Marshal The Viscount Alanbrooke, KG, OM* (London: Reprint Society, 1960).

Cantwell, John D., *The Second World War: A Guide to the Documents in the Public Record Office* (London: HMSO, 1993).

Captain "X" (pseudonym of William G.C. Shebbeare), *A Soldier Looks Ahead* (London: George Routledge, 1944).

Carver, Michael, *El Alamein* (London: Batsford, 1962).

——, *Tobruk* (London: Batsford, 1964).

——, *The Apostles of Mobility: The Theory and Practice of Armoured Warfare* (London: Weidenfeld & Nicolson, 1979).

——, *Dilemmas of the Desert War: A New Look at the Libyan Campaign 1940–1942* (London: Batsford with IWM, 1986).

——, *Out of Step: Memoirs of a Field Marshal* (London: Hutchinson, 1989).

Chalfont, Alun, *Montgomery of Alamein* (London: Methuen, 1977).

Charters, David A., Marc Milner and J. Brent Wilson (eds), *Military History and the Military Profession* (Westport, CT: Praeger, 1992).

Churchill, W.S., *The Second World War*, 6 vols (London: Cassell, 1950–56).

Citino, Robert M., *Armored Forces: History and Sourcebook* (Westport, CT: Greenwood Press, 1994).

Clausewitz, Carl von, *On War* (Harmondsworth: Penguin, 1982).

Cloake, John, *Templer, Tiger of Malaya: The Life of Field Marshal Sir Gerald Templer* (London: Harrap, 1985).

Connell, John, *Wavell: Soldier and Scholar: To June 1941* (London: Collins, 1964).

Cooper, Matthew, *The German Army, 1933–1945: Its Political and Military Failure* (London: Macdonald & Jane's, 1978).

Cotterel, Anthony, *What! No Morning Tea* (London: Victor Gollancz, 1941).

Craig, Norman, *The Broken Plume: A Platoon Commander's Story, 1940–45* (London: IWM, 1982).

D'Este, Carlo, *Decision in Normandy: The Unwritten Story of Montgomery and the Allied Campaign* (London: Pan, 1984).

Davies, W.J.K., *German Army Handbook 1939–1945* (London: Ian Allan, 1973).

Delaforce, Patrick, *Monty's Iron Sides: From the Normandy Beaches to Bremen with 3rd Division* (Stroud, Gloucestershire: Alan Sutton, 1995).

Denis, Peter, *Decision by Default: Peacetime Conscription and British Defence 1919–39* (London: Routledge & Kegan Paul, 1972).

——, *The Territorial Army 1906–40* (Woodbridge, Suffolk: Royal Historical Society/Boydell Press, 1987).

Dietz, Peter, *The Last of the Regiments: Their Rise and Fall* (London: Brassey's, 1990).

Doubler, Michael D., *Closing with the Enemy: How GIs Fought the War in Europe 1944–1945* (Kansas: University Press of Kansas, 1994).

Dupuy, Trevor N., *The Evolution of Weapons and Warfare* (New York: Bobbs-Merrill, 1980).

Dyson, Stephen W., *Twins in Tanks: East End Brothers-in-Arms, 1943–1945* (London: Leo Cooper, 1994).

Ellis, C. and P. Chamberlain (eds), *Handbook on the British Army 1943* (Military Book Society, 1975).

Ellis, John, *The Social History of the Machine Gun* (New York: Pantheon, 1975)

——, *The Sharp End of War: The Fighting Man in World War II* (Newton Abbot, Devon: David & Charles, 1980).

——, *Brute Force: Allied Strategy and Tactics in the Second World War* (London: André Deutsch, 1990).

Ellis, L.F., *Victory in the West*, Vol. 1, *The Battle of Normandy* (London: HMSO, 1962).

——, *Victory in the West*, Vol. 2, *The Defeat of Germany* (London, HMSO, 1968).

English, John A., *The Canadian Army and the Normandy Campaign: A Study of Failure of High Command* (New York: Praeger, 1991).

English, John A. and B.I. Gudmundsson, *On Infantry* (Westport, CT: Praeger, 1994).

Farran, Roy, *The History of the Calgary Highlanders, 1921–1954* (Canada: Bryant Press, 1954).

Farrar-Hockley, A.R., *Infantry Tactics 1939–1945* (New Malden, Surrey: Almark, 1976).

Fitzgerald, D.J.L., *History of the Irish Guards in the Second World War* (Aldershot: Gale & Polden, 1952).

Fletcher, David, *The Great Tank Scandal: British Armour in the Second World War, Part 1* (London: HMSO, 1989).

——, *The Universal Tank: British Armour in the Second World War, Part 2* (London: HMSO, 1993).

Forbes, Patrick, *6th Guards Tank Brigade: The Story of Guardsmen in Churchill Tanks* (London: Sampson, Low, Marston, n.d.).

Forman, Denis, *To Reason Why* (London: André Deutsch, 1991).

Fraser, D., *Alanbrooke* (London: Collins, 1982).

——, *And We Shall Shock Them* (London: Hodder & Stoughton, 1983).

French, David, *The British Way in Warfare 1688–2000* (London: Unwin Hyman, 1990).

Gamble, Lieutenant-Colonel G.M., *Simplified Tactical Instruction* (Aldershot: Gale & Polden, 1941).

Gooch, J., *Armies in Europe* (London: Routledge & Kegan Paul, 1980).

Gorman, J.T., *The Army of Today* (rev. edn; London: Blackie, 1941).

Griffith, Paddy, *Forward into Battle: Fighting Tactics from Waterloo to Vietnam* (Chichester, Sussex: Antony Bird, 1981).

——, *Battle Tactics of the Western Front: The British Army's Art of Attack 1916–1918* (New Haven, CT, and London: Yale University Press, 1994).

Grove, E., *World War II Tanks* (London: Orbis, 1976).

Gudmundsson, B.I., *On Artillery* (Westport, CT: Praeger, 1993).

Halle, Armin and Carlo Demand *Tanks: An Illustrated History of Fighting Vehicles* (London: Patrick Stephens, 1971).

Hamilton, Nigel, *Monty: Master of the Battlefield 1942–1944* (London: Hamish Hamilton, 1983).

——, *Monty: The Making of a General, 1887–1942* (London: Coronet, 1984).

——, *Monty: The Field Marshal* (London: Hamish Hamilton, 1986).

Harris, J.P., *Men, Ideas and Tanks: British Military Thought and Armoured Forces, 1903–1939* (Manchester and New York: Manchester University Press, 1995).

Harris, J.P. and F.H. Toase (eds), *Armoured Warfare* (London: Batsford, 1990).

Hastings, Max, *OVERLORD: D-Day and the Battle for Normandy* (London: Pan, 1985).

Hay, Ian, *Arms and the Men* (London: HMSO, 1950 and 1977).

Higham, Robin, *Armed Forces in Peacetime: Britain, 1918–40: A Case Study* (London: G.T. Foulis, 1962).

Holmes, Richard, *Firing Line* (London: Pimlico, 1994).

Horne, Alistair, with David Montgomery, *The Lonely Leader: Monty 1944–1945* (London: Macmillan, 1994).

Horrocks, Brian G., *A Full Life* (London: Collins, 1960).

Howlett, Peter, *Fighting with Figures: A Statistical Digest of the Second World War* (London: Central Statistical Office, 1995).

Jackson, W., *The Mediterranean and the Middle East,* Vol. VI, Parts II and III (London: HMSO, 1987 and 1988).

Jary, Sydney, *18 Platoon* (Carshalton Beeeches, Surrey: Sydney Jary, 1987).

Joseph, Michael, *The Sword in the Scabbard* (London: Michael Joseph, 1942).

Joslen, H.F., *Orders of Battle: Second World War, 1939–1945* (London: HMSO, 1960).

Keegan, John, *Six Armies in Normandy: From D-Day to the Liberation of Paris* (Harmondsworth: Penguin, 1983).

—— (ed.), *Churchill's Generals* (New York: Grove Weidenfeld, 1991).

——, *The Face of Battle* (London: Pimlico, 1991).

Kennedy, John, *The Business of War* (London: Hutchinson, 1957).

Lamb, Richard, *Montgomery in Europe 1943–1945: Success or Failure?* (London: Buchan & Enright, 1983).

Lang, Kurt, *Military Institutions and the Sociology of War: A Review of the Literature with Annotated Bibliography* (London: Sage, 1972).

Larson, R.H., *The British Army and the Theory of Armoured Warfare, 1918–40* (London: Associated University Press, 1984).

Lewin, Ronald, *Montgomery as Military Commander* (London: Batsford, 1971)

Liddell Hart, B.H., *New Methods in Infantry Training* (Cambridge: Cambridge University Press, 1918).

——, *The Remaking of Modern Armies* (London: John Murray, 1927).

——, *The Tanks: The History of the Royal Tank Regiment and its Predecessors Heavy Branch Machine Gun Corps and Royal Tank Corps* (2 vols) (London: Cassell, 1959).

——, *The Memoirs of Captain Liddell Hart* (2 vols) (London: Cassell, 1965).

—— (ed.), *The Rommel Papers* (London: Collins, 1953).

Longmate, Norman, *Island Fortress: The Defence of Great Britain 1603–1945* (London: HarperCollins, 1993).

Luvaas, Jay, *The Education of an Army: British Military Thought, 1815–1940* (London: Cassell, 1965).

Mackenzie, J.J.G. and Brian Holden Reid (eds), *The British Army and the Operational Level of War* (London: Tri-Service Press, 1989).

Mackenzie, S.P., *Politics and Military Morale: Current Affairs and Citizenship Education in the British Army 1914–1950* (Oxford: Clarendon Press, 1992).

Macksey, Kenneth, *Armoured Crusader: A Biography of Major-General Sir Percy Hobart* (London: Hutchinson, 1967).

——, *Tank Tactics, 1939–1945* (New Malden, Surrey: Almark, 1976).

——, *The Tank Pioneers* (London: Jane's, 1981).

——, *A History of the Royal Armoured Corps and its Predecessors, 1914–1975* (Beaminster, Dorset: Newtown, 1983).

Macleod, R. and D. Kelly (eds), *The Ironside Diaries 1937–1940* (London: Constable, 1962).

Macleod Ross, G., *The Business of Tanks, 1933–1945* (Ilfracombe, Devon: Arthur H. Stockwell, 1976).

Martel, Giffard Le Quesne, *Our Armoured Forces* (London: Faber & Faber, 1945).

——, *An Outspoken Soldier: His Views and Memoirs* (London: Sifton Praed, 1949).

McInnes, Colin and Gary D. Sheffield (eds), *Warfare in the Twentieth Century: Theory and Practice* (London: Unwin Hyman, 1988).

McKee, Alexander, *Caen: Anvil of Victory* (London: Papermac, 1985).

Mearsheimer, John J., *Liddell Hart and the Weight of History* (Ithaca and London: Cornell University Press, 1988).

Mercer, John, *Mike Target* (Lewes, Sussex: The Book Guild, 1990).

Millet, A.R. and W. Murray (eds), *Military Effectiveness*, Vol. III, *The Second World War* (London: Unwin Hyman, 1988).

Molony, C.J.C. *et al.*, *The Mediterranean and the Middle East*, Vols. V and VI, part I (London: HMSO, 1973 and 1984).

Montgomery, B.L., *The Memoirs of Field Marshal the Viscount Montgomery of Alamein K.G.* (London: Collins, 1958).

Moorehead, Alan, *Montgomery: A Biography* (London: Hamish Hamilton, 1946).

Myatt, F., *The British Infantry, 1660–1945: The Evolution of a Fighting Force* (Poole, Dorset: Blandford Press, 1983).

Nicolson, Nigel, *Alex: The Life of Field Marshal Earl Alexander of Tunis* (London: Weidenfeld & Nicolson, 1973).

Niven, David, *Niven* (London: Hamish Hamilton, 1984).

Ogorkiewicz, R.M., *Armoured Forces: A History of Armoured Forces and their Vehicles* (London: Arms & Armour Press, 1970).

Overy, Richard, *Why the Allies Won* (London: Jonathan Cape, 1995).

Parkinson, C. Northcote, *Always a Fusilier: The War History of the Royal Fusiliers (City of London Regiment) 1939–1945* (London: Sampson Low, 1949).

Pawle, Brigadier Hanbury, *Notes on the Framing of Tactical Exercises for Officers of the Territorial Army* (Aldershot: Gale & Polden, 1939).

Pearton, Maurice, *The Knowledgeable State: Diplomacy, War and Technology since 1830* (London: Burnett Books, 1982).

Perrett, Bryan, *The Churchill* (London: Ian Allan, 1974).

——, *Through Mud and Blood: Infantry/Tank Operations in World War II* (London: Robert Hale, 1975).

Picot, Geoffrey, *Accidental Warrior* (Harmondsworth: Penguin, 1994).

Playfair, I.S.O, *The Mediterranean and the Middle East*, Vols I, II, III and IV (London: HMSO, 1954–66).

Pyman, Harold English, *Call to Arms* (London: Leo Cooper, 1971).

Reid, Brian Holden, *J.F.C. Fuller: Military Thinker* (London: Macmillan, 1987).

——, *Studies in British Military Thought: Debates with Fuller and Liddell Hart* (Lincoln: University of Nebraska Press, 1998).

Richardson, F.M., *Fighting Spirit: A Study of Psychological Factors in War* (London: Leo Cooper, 1978).

Roberts, G.P.B., *From the Desert to the Baltic* (London: William Kimber, 1987).

Rosse, Captain The Earl of, and Colonel E.R.H. Hill *The Story of the Guards Armoured Division* (London: Geoffrey Bles, 1956).

Rowan-Robinson, Major-General H., *The Infantry Experiment* (London: William Clowes, 1934).

Ryan, Cornelius, *A Bridge Too Far* (London: Book Club edn, 1974).

Ryder, Rowland, *Oliver Leese* (London: Hamish Hamilton, 1987).

Samuels, Martin, *Command or Control? Command, Training and Tactics in the British and German Armies, 1888–1918* (London: Frank Cass, 1995).

Sheffield, G.D. (ed.), *Leadership and Command: The Anglo-American Military Experience Since 1861* (London: Brassey's, 1997).

Sixsmith, E.K.G., *British Generalship in the Twentieth Century* (London: Arms & Armour Press, 1970).

Spender, Richard, *Laughing Blood* (London: Sidgwick & Jackson, 1942).

——, *The Collected Poems* (London: Sidgwick & Jackson, 1944).

Taylor, George, *Infantry Colonel* (Upton-on-Severn, Worcestershire: Self-Publishing Association, 1990).

Thompson, R.W., *Montgomery the Field Marshal: A Critical Study of the Generalship of Field Marshal The Viscount Montgomery of Alamein, KG, and of the Campaign in North-West Europe, 1944/45* (London: Allen & Unwin, 1969).

Thornburn, Ned, *The 4th KSLI in Normandy: The Part played by 4th Bn King's Shropshire Light Infantry in the Battle of Normandy, June to August, 1944* (Shrewsbury: 4th Bn KSLI Museum Trust, 1990).

Tout, Ken, *Tanks, Advance! Normandy to the Netherlands, 1944* (London: Robert Hale, 1987).

Travers, T., *The Killing Ground: The British Army, the Western Front and the Emergence of Modern Warfare 1900–1918* (London: Allen & Unwin, 1987).

Tuker, Francis, *Approach to Battle: A Commentary: Eighth Army, November 1941 to May 1943* (London: Cassell, 1963).

Valentine, Major A.W., *More Sand Table Exercises* (Aldershot: Gale & Polden, 1941).

Van Creveld, Martin, *Fighting Power: German and US Army Performance, 1939–1945* (London: Arms & Armour Press, 1983).

——, *Command in War* (Cambridge, MA: Harvard University Press, 1985).

——, *The Training of Officers: From Military Professionalism to Irrelevance* (New York: Free Press; London: Collier Macmillan, 1990).

——, *The Transformation of War* (New York: Free Press, 1991).

Vanderveen, Bart H., *The Observer's Fighting Vehicles Directory, World War II* (London and New York: Frederick Warne, 1972).

Verney, G.L., *The Guards Armoured Division: A Short History* (London: Hutchinson, 1955).

Ward, C.R., *Section Training Exercises* (Aldershot: Gale & Polden, 1942).

Weeks, John, *Men Against Tanks: A History of Anti-Tank Warfare* (Newton Abbot, Devon: David & Charles, 1975).

——, *World War II Small Arms* (New York: Galahad Books, 1979).

Weeks, R.M., *Organisation and Equipment for War* (Cambridge: Cambridge University Press, 1950).

Weller, J., *Weapons and Tactics: Hastings to Berlin* (London: Nicholas Vane, 1966).

White, B.T., *Tanks and other Armoured Fighting Vehicles of World War II* (London: Peerage Books, n.d.).

Whitelaw, W., *The Whitelaw Memoirs* (London: Headline, 1990).

Whiting, Charles, *The Poor Bloody Infantry 1939–1945* (London: Stanley Paul, 1987).

Wilmot, Chester, *The Struggle for Europe* (London: Collins, 1952).

Wilson, Theodore A. (ed.), *D-Day, 1944* (Lawrence, KS: University Press of Kansas, 1994).

Winton, H.R., *To Change an Army: General Sir John Burnett-Stuart and British Armoured Doctrine, 1927–38* (Lawrence, KS: University Press of Kansas, 1988).

Wintringham, Tom, *New Ways of War* (Harmondsworth: Penguin, 1940)

——, and J.N. Blashford-Snell, *Weapons and Tactics* (Harmondsworth: Penguin, 1973).

ARTICLES

Barclay, Brigadier C.N., 'The Training of National Armies in War: A Comparison of British and American Methods', *Army Quarterly*, April 1949.

Bernays, Captain R., 'Reflections on a Tour of OCTUs', *Army Quarterly*, April 1944.

Boucher, Major-General C.H., 'Infantry Tactics', *Army Quarterly*, July 1948.

Cartwright, Captain J.A.D., 'The Film in Military Training', *Army Quarterly*, April 1944.

Ferris, John, '"Worthy of Some Better Enemy?": The British Estimate of the Imperial Japanese Army 1919–41, and the Fall of Singapore', *Canadian Journal of History*, XXVIII (August 1993).

French, David, '"Tommy is No Soldier": The Morale of the Second British Army in Normandy, June–August 1944', *Journal of Strategic Studies*, 19, 4 (December 1996).

——, 'Colonel Blimp and the British Army: British Divisional Commanders in the War against Germany, 1939–1945', *English Historical Review*, CXI (November 1996).

Fuller, Major-General J.F.C., 'Training for Armoured Warfare', *Harper's Magazine*, March 1943.

Gat, Azar, 'Liddell Hart's Theory of Armoured Warfare: Revising the Revisionists', *Journal of Strategic Studies*, 19, 1 (March 1996).

'Gee' (pseudonym of Major-General J.L.I. Hawkesworth), 'A Good Gallop', *Blackwood's Magazine*, 254 (September 1943).

Gooderson, Ian, 'Heavy and Medium Bombers: How Successful Were They in the Close Air Support Role During World War II?', *Journal of Strategic Studies*, 15, 3 (September 1992).

Harrison Place, T., 'British Perceptions of the Tactics of the German Army, 1938–40', *Intelligence and National Security*, 9, 3 (July 1994).

Hart, Russell A., 'Feeding Mars: The Role of Logistics in the German Defeat in Normandy, 1944', *War in History*, 3, 4 (November 1996).

Hart, Stephen, 'Montgomery, Morale, Casualty Conservation and "Colossal Cracks": 21st Army Group's Operational Technique in North-West Europe, 1944–1945', *Journal of Strategic Studies*, 19, 4 (December 1996).

Hickson, J.G.E., 'Battle School', *Blackwood's Magazine*, 253 (March 1943).

Kaulback, Lieutenant-Colonel R.J.A., 'Army Training after the War', *Journal of the Royal United Service Institution*, February 1945.

Kiszely, John, 'The British Army and Approaches to Warfare since 1945', *Journal of Strategic Studies*, 19, 4 (December 1996).

Kohn, Richard H. (ed.), 'The Scholarship on World War II: Its Present Condition and Future Possibilities', *Journal of Military History*, 55, 3 (July 1991).

Martel, Lieutenant-General G.LeQ., 'Gun versus Armour', *Army Quarterly*, October 1944.

McAndrew, William J., 'Fire or Movement? Canadian Tactical Doctrine, Sicily – 1943', *Military Affairs*, 51, 3 (July 1987).

Morgan, General Sir William, 'The Revival of Battle Drill in World War 2', *Army Quarterly and Defence Journal*, 104, 1 (October 1973).

Mowrer, Paul Scott, 'The New Tactics', *Harper's Magazine*, February 1943.

Murray, Williamson, 'The German Response to Victory in Poland: A Case Study in Professionalism', *Armed Forces and Society*, 7, 2 (winter 1981).

Naumann, Anthony, 'Into the Battle', *Blackwood's Magazine*, 254 (July 1943).

Peaty, John, 'Myth, Reality and Carlo D'Este', *War Studies Journal*, 1, 2 (spring 1996).

Powers, Stephen T., 'The Battle of Normandy: The Lingering Controversy', *Journal of Military History*, 56, 3 (July 1992).

'Sarkie', 'Anti-Tank Artillery – Has it a Future?', *Journal of Royal Artillery*, July 1944.

Tuker, Major-General F.S, 'The Preparation of Infantry for Battle', *Army Quarterly*, October 1944.

Wilson, Major-General T.N.F., 'The Role of Infantry', *Journal of the Royal United Service Institution*, 89, 553 (February 1944).

Young, Captain W.R., 'Artillery Support for Tanks', *Army Quarterly*, (November 1942).

CONTEMPORARY NEWSPAPERS AND PERIODICALS

Battle Training in Word and Picture (1, 2, 3), 1939–40
The Glen (Regimental Journal of the Calgary Highlanders), III, 13 (November 1941)
The Times, 1940–44

STANDARD WORKS OF REFERENCE

Army List
War Office List

DISSERTATIONS

Crang, J.A., 'A Social History of the British Army, 1939–45' (University of Edinburgh, PhD thesis, 1992).
Drewienkiewicz, K.J., 'Examine the Build-Up, Early Training and Employment of the Territorial Army in the Lead-Up to, and the Early Days of, the Second World War' (Royal College of Defence Studies, thesis 1992).
Hart, Stephen A., 'Field Marshal Montgomery, 21st Army Group, and North-West Europe, 1944–45' (University of London: PhD thesis, 1995).
House, Jonathan M., 'Towards Combined Arms Warfare: A Survey of Tactics, Doctrine and Organisation in the 20th Century' (US Army Command and General Staff College, Fort Leavenworth, Kansas, master's thesis, 1984).
Newbold, D.J., 'British Planning and Preparations to Resist Invasion on Land, September 1939–September 1940' (University of London: PhD thesis, 1988).

Index

12804694R00137

Printed in Poland
by Amazon Fulfillment
Poland Sp. z o.o., Wrocław